Learn Android Studio 4

Efficient Java-Based Android Apps Development

Second Edition

Ted Hagos

Apress®

Learn Android Studio 4: Efficient Java-Based Android Apps Development

Ted Hagos
Manila, National Capital Region, Philippines

ISBN-13 (pbk): 978-1-4842-5936-8   ISBN-13 (electronic): 978-1-4842-5937-5
https://doi.org/10.1007/978-1-4842-5937-5

Copyright © 2020 by Ted Hagos

Managing Director, Apress Media LLC: Welmoed Spahr
Acquisitions Editor: Steve Anglin
Development Editor: Matthew Moodie
Coordinating Editor: Mark Powers

Cover designed by eStudioCalamar

Distributed to the book trade worldwide by Apress Media, LLC, 1 New York Plaza, New York, NY 10004, U.S.A. Phone 1-800-SPRINGER, fax (201) 348-4505, e-mail orders-ny@springer-sbm.com, or visit www. springeronline.com. Apress Media, LLC is a California LLC and the sole member (owner) is Springer Science + Business Media Finance Inc (SSBM Finance Inc). SSBM Finance Inc is a Delaware corporation.

For information on translations, please e-mail booktranslations@springernature.com; for reprint, paperback, or audio rights, please e-mail bookpermissions@springernature.com.

Apress titles may be purchased in bulk for academic, corporate, or promotional use. eBook versions and licenses are also available for most titles. For more information, reference our Print and eBook Bulk Sales web page at http://www.apress.com/bulk-sales.

Any source code or other supplementary material referenced by the author in this book is available to readers on GitHub via the book's product page, located at www.apress.com/9781484259368. For more detailed information, please visit http://www.apress.com/source-code.

Printed on acid-free paper

For Adrianne and Stephanie.

Table of Contents

About the Author xi

About the Technical Reviewer xiii

Acknowledgments xv

Introduction xvii

Chapter 1: Android Overview 1

   History 1

   The Operating System 3

   Summary 5

Chapter 2: Android Studio 7

   Setup 7

   Configuring Android Studio 10

   Hardware Acceleration 14

   Summary 15

Chapter 3: Project Basics 17

   Create a Project 17

   Create an AVD 22

   Summary 29

Chapter 4: Android Studio IDE 31

   The IDE 31

   Main Editor 34

   Editing Layout Files 35

   TODO Items 38

How to Get More Screen Space for Codes 39

Project Tool Window 41

Preferences/Settings 43

Summary 45

Chapter 5: Android Application Overview 47

What Makes Up an Android Project 47

Application Entry Point 50

Activities 51

Intents 53

Summary 54

Chapter 6: Activities and Layouts 55

Activity 55

    Layout File 55

    Activity Class 60

Hello World 61

Modifying Hello World 64

Summary 74

Chapter 7: Event Handling 75

Intro to Event Handling 75

Handling Long Clicks 81

Summary 87

Chapter 8: Intents 89

What Intents Are 89

Implicit Intents 94

Summary 99

Chapter 9: Fragments 101

Introduction to Fragments 101

Summary 110

Chapter 10: Navigation 111

Navigation Before Architecture Components 111

Navigation Components 114

Working with Jetpack Navigation 116

Summary 129

Chapter 11: Running in the Background 131

Basic Concepts 131

The UI Thread 132

Threads and Runnables 136

Summary 146

Chapter 12: Debugging 147

Types of Errors 147

    Syntax Errors 147

    Runtime Errors 148

    Logic Errors 150

Debugger 153

    Single Stepping 154

Summary 156

Chapter 13: Testing 157

Types of Testing 157

Unit Testing 159

    JVM Test vs. Instrumented Test 160

    A Simple Demo 161

    Implementing the Test 165

    Running a Unit Test 167

Instrumented Testing 170

    Setting Up a Simple Test 171

    Recording Espresso Tests 175

    More on Espresso Matchers 178

    Espresso Actions 179

Summary 180

Chapter 14: Working with Files 181

Internal and External Storage 181

Cache Directory.. 182

How to Work with Internal Storage 183

Summary.. 191

Chapter 15: BroadcastReceivers 193

Introduction to BroadcastReceivers... 193

System Broadcast vs. Custom Broadcast................................ 194

Two Ways to Register for Broadcast.. 194

Summary.. 202

Chapter 16: Jetpack, LiveData, ViewModel, and Room 203

Lifecycle Aware Components... 203

ViewModel 207

LiveData 212

Room... 217

Summary.. 224

Chapter 17: Distributing Apps 225

Prepare the App for Release 225

Prepare Material and Assets for Release 226

Configure the App for Release.. 226

Build a Release-Ready Application 227

Releasing the App 232

Summary.. 237

Chapter 18: Short Takes 239

Productivity Features 239

Importing Samples 239

Refactoring... 241

Generate 243

Coding Styles.. 248

Live Templates 250

Important Keyboard Shortcuts 251

Summary 252

Appendix A: Java Refresher 253

A Brief History 253

Editions 254

Setup 255

Writing, Compiling, and Running 256

Syntax 257

    A Typical Java Program 258

    Compilation Unit 260

    Comments 260

    Statements 261

    Keywords 261

    Identifiers 262

    Methods 263

    Packages and Imports 265

    Program Entry Point 266

Data Types 267

    Overflow 271

    Casting 271

    Strongly and Statically Typed 272

    Reference Types 273

    Stack and Heap 274

    Constants 275

Operators 276

    Assignment 276

    Arithmetic 276

    Unary 278

    Equality and Relational 279

    Logical Operators 281

Loops and Branches...282

    If and Switch Statements 282

    Switch Statement 284

    While Loop...287

    For-Loop 288

    Simple Application of Control Structures......................................289

Arrays..291

    Array Creation...292

    Managing Arrays...293

    Using the Enhanced for-loop 295

    More on Arrays 297

Reference Types..299

Classes..301

    Inheritance 301

    Constructors 303

    Overloading 305

    Overriding..306

Strings...308

    String Creation..308

    Strings Are Immutable..309

    Why Can't We Modify Strings 311

    Comparing Strings..312

    Common Usage 314

Exceptions...316

Index..319

About the Author

Ted Hagos is a software developer by trade. At the moment, he's Chief Technology Officer and Data Protection Officer of RenditionDigital International, a software development company based out of Dublin. He wore many hats in his 20+ years in software development, for example, team lead, project manager, architect, and director for development. He also spent time as a trainer for IBM Advanced Career Education, Ateneo ITI, and Asia Pacific College.

About the Technical Reviewer

Jeff Friesen is a freelance teacher and software developer with an emphasis on Java. In addition to authoring *Java I/O, NIO and NIO.2* (Apress) and *Java Threads and the Concurrency Utilities* (Apress), Jeff has written numerous articles on Java and other technologies (such as Android) for JavaWorld (www.javaworld.com), InformIT (www.informit.com), Java.net, SitePoint (www.sitepoint.com), and other websites. Jeff can be contacted via his website at JavaJeff.ca or via his LinkedIn profile (www.linkedin.com/in/javajeff).

Acknowledgments

To Stephanie and Adrianne, my thanks and my love.

To Mark Powers and Steve Anglin, and to all who made this book possible. Many, many thanks.

Introduction

Welcome to *Learn Android Studio 4*. This book will help you get started in your programming journey with the little green robot. You already bought the book (many thanks to you), so you don't need to be convinced that programming for the mobile platform offers many opportunities for software developers.

The book is aimed at beginning Android programmers but not wholly new to programming. The book assumes that you have prior programming experience with any of the CFOL (C family of languages, e.g., C, C++, Java, C#, JavaScript). Ideally, you are already a Java programmer trying to get your feet wet in Android; if you're not, don't worry. Basic Java programming is covered in the Appendix, and you can refer to that as you try to feel your way into the language.

The book covers two fronts: the fundamentals of Android programming and the use of Android Studio 4. Android programming concepts and the use of the IDE are explained using a combination of graphics and code walk-throughs: there's plenty of those in the book.

Chapter Overview

Chapter 1: Android Overview—This chapter introduces Android. It deals with a bit of Android's history and the technical makeup of its OS.

Chapter 2: Android Studio—If you haven't set up your Android environment yet, don't skip this chapter; it walks you through the setup of Android Studio, whether you're on macOS, Windows, or Linux. It also introduces the essential parts of the IDE.

Chapter 3: Project Basics—This chapter introduces the concept and mechanics of an Android project. It walks through creating a project and running a project in an AVD (Android Virtual Device).

Chapter 4: Android Studio IDE—Android Studio is a full-fledged IDE; it has lots of features and parts. This chapter introduces you to the most common tools and windows of Android Studio.

Chapter 5: Android Application Overview—What makes up an Android project? What are components? What are Intents? These are some of the questions this chapter addresses. You'll discover how different an Android app is from a desktop app.

Chapter 6: Activities and Layouts—We get into the basics of UI building. Activities are the primary means by which the user sees your app. We get to learn how to build these and other UI elements that are in common use.

Chapter 7: Event Handling—Handling user actions is a very common task in Android programming. This chapter walks you through the basics of listener objects, how to create them, and how to bind them to View elements (like Buttons).

Chapter 8: Intents—Intents are uniquely Android's. See how this message-passing mechanism works in Android and how it glues all the other Android components.

Chapter 9: Fragments—Fragments are a granular way to compose a screen. This chapter walks through the fundamental concepts of Fragments.

Chapter 10: Navigation—Navigation components are quite new. They are a part of Jetpack. This chapter introduces you to the more modern ways on how to build multiscreen apps.

Chapter 11: Running in the Background—When you start building nontrivial apps, you will need to read or write from I/O sources, fetch data from the network, and so on. These activities take time, and they need to be run in the background. This chapter is all about that.

Chapter 12: Debugging—You will often make coding mistakes. This chapter introduces you to the types of errors you may encounter and how to use Android Studio's debugging features to solve them.

Chapter 13: Testing—At some point, you have to test your code before you release them. This chapter introduces you to the many kinds of testing you can do to an app. More importantly, it introduces you to unit testing and Espresso testing.

Chapter 14: Working with Files—You'll need to save to a text file or read from it; this chapter walks through the basics of file input and output in Android.

Chapter 15: BroadcastReceivers—One of Android's foundational components is the BroadcastReceiver; this component lets you build decoupled apps by adopting the publish-subscribe pattern.

Chapter 16: Jetpack, LiveData, ViewModel, and Room—More goodies from Architecture components. This chapter walks through the basics of how to build components that have lifecycle awareness of other components and how to use Room.

Chapter 17: Distributing Apps—When you're ready to distribute your app, you'll need to sign it and list it in a marketplace like Google Play. This chapter walks you through the steps on how to do it.

Chapter 18: Short Takes—More Android Studio goodness.

Appendix—The Appendix breezes through the Java language. It deals with some of the basic language concepts you will need to get started in Android programming.

CHAPTER 1

Android Overview

What the chapter covers:

- Brief history of Android

- The Android operating system

It's been quite a while since the little green robot made waves and disrupted the mobile computing world. It started as an operating system for phones, but it has, since, made its way into all sorts of places like TVs, car systems, watches, e-readers, netbooks, and game consoles, among other things.

Android, to many people, may seem like an OS only, which for the most part it is; but apart from the OS, Android also includes a software development kit, libraries, application frameworks, and reference design.

History

2003. Andy Rubin founded Android Inc.; Google backed the company but didn't own yet.

2005. Google bought Android Inc

2007. Android was officially given to open source; Google turned over the ownership to the Open Handset Alliance (OHA).

2008. Android v1.0 was released. The Google Play Store was called by a different name then; it was called the "Market."

2009. Versions 1.1, 1.5 (Cupcake), 1.6 (Donut), and 2.0 (Eclair) were released. Cupcake was the first version to get the sugary treats naming scheme. This was a significant release because it featured an on-screen keyboard. Donut is remembered as the first version to include the "search box." Eclair is remembered as the first to include Google maps, which started the death of built-in car navigation, because Google offered Maps for free.

© Ted Hagos 2020
T. Hagos, *Learn Android Studio 4*, https://doi.org/10.1007/978-1-4842-5937-5_1

2010. Versions 2.2 (Froyo) and 2.3 through 2.3.7 (Gingerbread) were released. Froyo improved the Android experience; it featured five home screens instead of three during the previous versions. Gingerbread coincided with the release of Nexus S (the one from Samsung). Gingerbread may also be remembered as the version that introduced support for a front-facing camera; and the selfie avalanche began.

2011. Versions 3.0 (Honeycomb) and 4.0 through 4.0.4 (Ice Cream Sandwich) were released. The previous versions of Android were all (exclusively) for the phones; Android 3.0 changed that because Honeycomb was meant for tablets. It hinted at design cues for future versions of Android. It removed physical buttons; the home, back, and menu buttons were part of the software. Google and Samsung partnered once again for the release of Galaxy Nexus (successor for the Nexus S), which used Ice Cream Sandwich as the OS.

2012. Versions 4.1 through 4.3.1 (Jelly Bean) were released. Jelly Bean introduced "Google Now" which could be accessed via a quick swipe from the home screen; this allowed access to Calendar, Events, Emails, and weather reports all in a single screen. It was an early version of Google Assistant. It was also with this version where Project Butter was implemented which allowed for a smoother Android experience.

2013. Versions 4.4 through 4.4.4 (KitKat) were released. KitKat was a big aesthetic upgrade; the blue accents of the previous versions were replaced with a more refined white accent, and many stock apps were redesigned with lighter color schemes. This version also brought us the "Ok Google" search command

2014. Versions 5.0–5.1/5.1.1 (Lollipop) were released; Android became 64-bit. Lollipop featured the first use of Google's material design philosophy. The changes were not just cosmetics; under the hood, Android 5 moved away from the Dalvik VM and used the Android Runtime (ART) instead. Android TV was also released during this time.

2015. Versions 6.0 and 6.01 (Marshmallow) were released. The app menu changed dramatically, and Google added search bar so users can find apps quickly. The memory managers were introduced in this version so users can check the memory usage of apps. The permission system was revamped as well; apps can no longer request for permissions on a wholesale basis; permissions were requested (and granted) on a per-permission basis and as they were required.

2016. Versions 7.0–7.1.2 (Nougat) were released. "Google Now" was replaced with "Google Assistant." The improved multitasking system allowed for split-screen mode.

2017. Versions 8.0 and 8.1 (Oreo) were released; and with it were more multitasking features. Picture-in-picture and native split-screen was introduced with this version.

2018. Android 9.0 (Pie) was released—exactly 10 years after v1.0. This release brought with it quite a number of visual changes which made it the most significant update in recent years. The three-button setup was replaced with a single-pill shaped button and gestures to control things like multitasking.

2019. Android 10 was released; this is a shift for Google in terms of naming the versions. Google did away with the dessert names and simply named the version according to its number. The green robot is being rebranded. This version also marks the end of the Android navigation buttons. While Android 9 kept the "back" button, v10 has completely removed it and will use gestures instead.

The Operating System

The most visible part of Android, at least for developers, is its operating system. Android OS may appear complex, but its purpose is simple; it stands between the user and the hardware. That may be an oversimplification, but it will suffice for our purposes. By "user," I don't literally mean an end user or a person; by "user" I mean an application, a piece of code that a programmer creates, like a word processor or an email client.

Take the email app, for example; as you type each character, the app needs to communicate to the hardware for the message to make its way to your screen and hard drive and eventually send it to the cloud via your network. It's a more involved process than I describe it here, but that is the basic idea. At its simplest, an OS does three things:

- Manages hardware on behalf of applications.

- Provides services to applications like networking, security, memory management, and so forth.

- Manages execution of applications; this is the part that allows us to run multiple applications (seemingly) almost at the same time.

Figure 1-1 shows a logical diagram of Android's system architecture; it is far from complete, since it doesn't show all the apps, components, and libraries in the Android platform, but it should give you an idea on how things are organized.

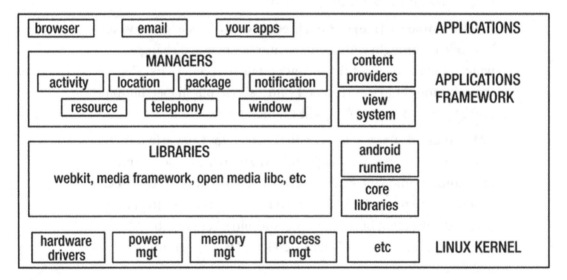

Figure 1-1. *Platform architecture*

The lowest level in the diagram is the one responsible for interfacing with the hardware, various services like memory management, and executions of processes. This part of the Android OS is Linux. Linux is a very stable OS and is quite ubiquitous itself. You can find it in many places like server hardware on data centers, appliances, medical devices, and so forth. Android uses Linux which handles hardware interfacing and some other kernel functions.

On top of the Linux kernel are low-level libraries like SQLite, OpenGL, and so on. These are not part of the Linux kernel but are still low level and as such are written mostly in C/C++. On the same level, you will find the Android Runtime which is where Android applications are run.

Next up is the application framework layer. It sits on top of both the low-level libraries and the Android Runtime because it needs both. This is the layer that we will interact with as an application developer because it contains all the libraries we need to write apps.

Finally, on top is the application layer. This is where all our apps reside, both the ones we write and the ones that come prebuilt with the OS. It should be pointed out that prebuilt applications which come with the device do not have any special privileges over the ones we will write. If you don't like the email app of the phone, you can write your own and replace it. Android is democratic like that.

Summary

- Android has gone a long way, from the clunky Cupcake version to Android 10, which is very advanced and provides a buttery smooth user experience. Android's release cadence was frenetic during the early years, but it has since subsided and settled on a more uniform 12-month cycle.

- Android isn't just an OS, it also includes an application framework, software development kit, prebuilt applications, and a reference design.

- Android uses the Linux OS for interfacing with hardware, memory management, and executions of processes.

CHAPTER 2

Android Studio

What the chapter covers:

- Getting Android Studio

- Configuring the IDE

- Basic parts of the IDE

Developing Android applications wasn't always done in Android Studio (AS). In the early days of Android, developers built apps using just the bare SDK, a bunch of command-line tools, and Ant build scripts (Apache Ant)—it was quite the old school; soon after, the Android Developer Tools (ADT) for Eclipse was released. Eclipse became the dominant tool for Android development until Android Studio came along.

Android Studio came in 2013. To be sure, it was still on beta, but the writing on the wall was clear; it was going to be the official development tool for Android development. Android Studio is based on JetBrains' IntelliJ; it's a commercial Java IDE, which also has a nonpaid or community version. It was the community version of IntelliJ that served as the basis for Android Studio.

Setup

At the time of writing, Android Studio 4 was on preview release; the version I used for this book was Canary 9. Android Studio 4 might be on stable release by the time you're reading this book; hopefully, the diagrams and screenshots won't be too different by then. To download Android Studio 4 (preview release), you can go to `https://developer.android.com/studio/preview`.

The installer is available for Windows (both 32- and 64-bit), macOS, and Linux. I ran the installation instructions on macOS (Catalina), Windows 10 64-bit, and Ubuntu 18. I work primarily in a macOS environment, which explains why most of the screen grabs for this book look like macOS. Android Studio looks, runs, and feels (mostly) the same in

© Ted Hagos 2020
T. Hagos, *Learn Android Studio 4*, https://doi.org/10.1007/978-1-4842-5937-5_2

all three platforms, with very minor differences like key bindings and the main menu bar in macOS.

Before we go further, let's look at the system requirements for Android Studio; at a minimum, you'll need either of the following:

- Microsoft Windows 7, 8, or 10 (32- or 64-bit)

- macOS 10.10 (Yosemite or higher)

- Linux (Gnome or KDE Desktop), Ubuntu 14.04 or higher; 64-bit capable of running 32-bit applications

- GNU C Library (glibc 2.19 or later) if you're on Linux

For the hardware, your workstation needs to be at least

- 4GB RAM minimum (8GB or more recommended)

- 2GB of available HDD space (4GB is recommended)

- 1280 x 800 minimum screen resolution

The preceding list came from the official Android website (`https://developer.android.com/studio`); of course, more is better.

There are no prerequisite software for Android Studio. It used to be that you needed to install a Java Development Kit prior to installing Android Studio; starting from Android Studio 2.2, the installer includes an embedded OpenJDK—you no longer need to bother with installing a separate JDK.

Download the installer from `https://developer.android.com/studio/`, and get the proper binary file for your platform.

If you're on macOS, do the following:

1. Unpack the installer zipped file.

2. Drag the application file into the Applications folder.

3. Launch Android Studio.

Android Studio will prompt you to import some settings if you have a previous installation. You can import that—it's the default option.

Note   If you have an existing installation of Android Studio, you can keep using that version and still install the preview edition. Android Studio 4 can coexist with your existing version of Android Studio; its settings will be kept in a different directory.

If you're on Windows, do the following:

1. Unzip the installer file.

2. Move the unzipped directory to a location of your choice, for example, `C:\Users\myname\AndroidStudio`.

3. Drill down to the "AndroidStudio" folder; inside it, you'll find "studio64.exe". This is the file you need to launch. It's a good idea to create a shortcut for this file—if you right-click studio64.exe and choose "Pin to Start Menu," you can make Android Studio available from the Windows Start menu; alternatively, you can also pin it to the Taskbar.

The Linux installation requires a bit more work than simply double-clicking and following the installer prompts. In future releases of Ubuntu (and its derivatives), this might change and become as simple and frictionless as its Windows and macOS counterparts, but for now, we need to do some tweaking. The extra activities on Linux are mostly because AS needs some 32-bit libraries and hardware acceleration.

Note   The installation instructions in this section are meant for Ubuntu 64-bit and other Ubuntu derivatives, for example, Linux Mint, Lubuntu, Xubuntu, Ubuntu MATE, and so on. I chose this distribution because I assumed that it is a very common Linux flavor; hence, the readers of this book will be using that distribution. If you are running a 64-bit version of Ubuntu, you will need to pull some 32-bit libraries in order for AS to function well.

To start pulling the 32-bit libraries for Linux, run the following commands on a terminal window:

```
sudo apt-get update && sudo apt-get upgrade -y
sudo dpkg --add-architecture i386
sudo apt-get install libncurses5:i386 libstdc++6:i386 zlib1g:i386
```

When all the prep work is done, you need to do the following:

1. Unpack the downloaded installer file. You can unpack the file using command-line tools or using the GUI tools—you can, for example, right-click the file and select the "Unpack here" option, if your file manager has that.

2. After unzipping the file, rename the folder to "AndroidStudio".

3. Move the folder to a location where you have read, write, and execute privileges. Alternatively, you can also move it to /usr/local/AndroidStudio.

4. Open a terminal window and go to the AndroidStudio/bin folder, then run ./studio.sh.

5. At first launch, Android Studio will ask you if you want to import some settings; if you have installed a previous version of Android Studio, you may want to import those settings.

Configuring Android Studio

Let's configure a couple of things first before we go to coding. Let's do the following:

1. Get some more software that we need so we can build programs that target specific versions of Android.

2. Make sure we have all the tools we need.

3. (optionally) change the way we get updates.

Launch Android Studio and click "Configure" (as shown in Figure 2-1), then choose "Preferences" from the drop-down list.

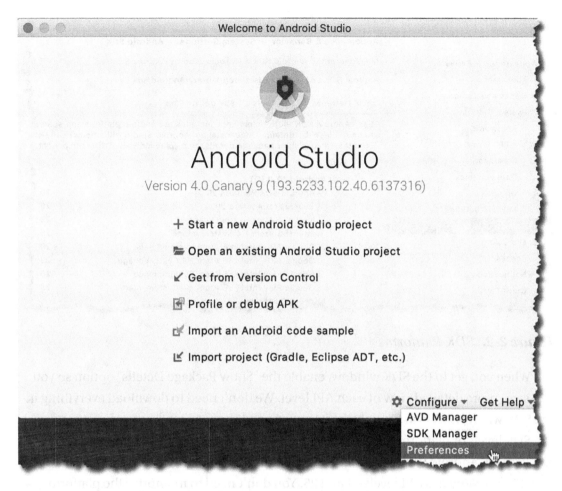

Figure 2-1. *Go to "Preferences" from Android Studio's opening dialog*

The "Preferences" option opens the *Preferences* dialog. On the left-hand side, go to **Appearance & Behavior ➤ System Settings ➤ Android SDK**, as shown in Figure 2-2.

11

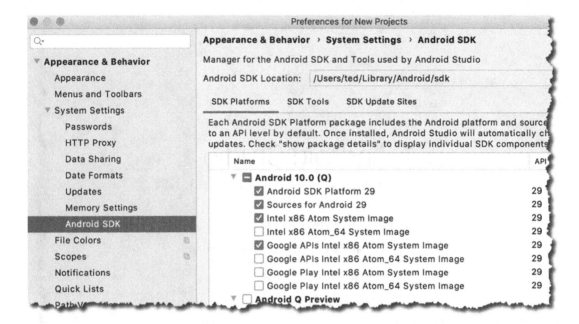

Figure 2-2. *SDK Platforms*

When you get to the SDK window, enable the "Show Package Details" option so you can see a more detailed view of each API level. We don't need to download everything in the SDK window. We will get only the items we need.

SDK levels or platform numbers are specific versions of Android. Android 10 is API level 29, Android 9 or "Pie" is API level 28, Android 8 or "Oreo" is API levels 26 and 27, and Nougat is API levels 24 and 25. You don't need to memorize the platform numbers, at least not anymore because the IDE shows the platform number with the corresponding Android nickname.

Download the API levels you want to target for your applications, but for the purpose of this book, please download API level 29 (Android 10). That's what we will use for the sample projects. Make sure that together with the platforms, you will also download "Google APIs Intel x86 Atom_64 System Image." We will need those when we get to the part where we test run our applications.

Choosing an API level may not be a big deal right now because at this point, we're simply working with practice apps. When you plan to release your application to the public, you may not be able to take this choice lightly. Choosing a minimum SDK or API level for your app will determine how many people will be able to use your application. At the time of writing, 17% of all Android devices are using "Marshmallow," 19% for "Nougat," 29% for "Oreo," and only 10% for "Pie"; the stats for Android 10 were not out yet. These stats are from the dashboard page of the official Android website. It's a good idea to check these statistics from time to time; you can find it here: `http://bit.ly/droiddashboard`.

We go next to the "SDK Tools" section, as shown in Figure 2-3.

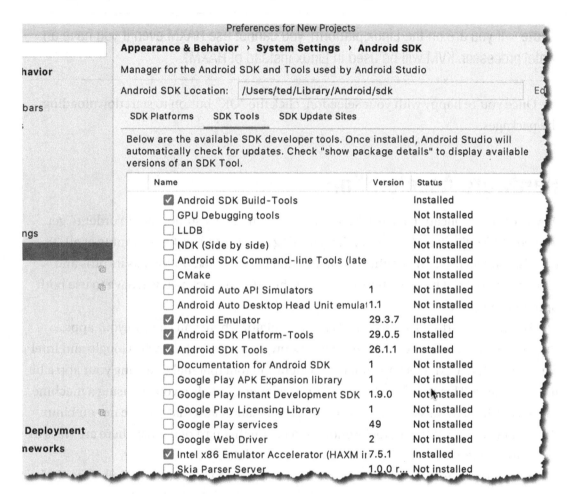

Figure 2-3. *SDK Tools*

You don't generally have to change anything on this window, but it wouldn't hurt to check if you have the tools, as shown in the following list, marked as "Installed":

- Android SDK Build Tools

- Android SDK Platform Tools

- Android SDK Tools

- Android Emulator

- Support Repository

- HAXM Installer

Note   If you are on the Linux platform, you cannot use HAXM even if you have an Intel processor. KVM will be used in Linux instead of HAXM.

Once you're happy with your selection, click the "OK" button to start downloading the packages.

Hardware Acceleration

As you create applications, it will be useful to test and run it sometimes in order to get immediate feedback and find out if it is running as expected or if it is running at all. To do this, you will use either a physical or a virtual device. Each option has its pros and cons, and you don't have to choose one over the other; in fact, you will have to use both options eventually.

An Android Virtual Device or AVD is an emulator where you can run your apps. Running on an emulator can sometimes be slow; this is the reason why Google and Intel came up with HAXM. It is an emulator acceleration tool that makes testing your app a bit more bearable. This is definitely a boon to developers. That is if you are using a machine that has an Intel processor which supports virtualization and that you are not on Linux. But don't worry if you're not lucky enough to fall on that part of the pie, there are ways to achieve emulator acceleration in Linux, as we'll see later.

macOS users probably have it the easiest because HAXM is automatically installed with Android Studio. They don't have to do anything to get it; the installer took care of that for them.

Windows users can get HAXM either by

- Downloading it from `https://software.intel.com/en-us/android`. Install it like you would any other Windows software, double-click, and follow the prompts.

- Alternatively, you can get HAXM via the SDK manager; this is the recommended method.

For Linux users, the recommended software is KVM instead. KVM (Kernel-based Virtual Machine) is a virtualization solution for Linux. It contains virtualization extensions (Intel VT or AMD-V).

To get KVM, we need to pull some software from the repos; but even before you can do that, you need to do the following first:

1. Make sure that virtualization is enabled on your BIOS or UEFI settings. Consult your hardware manual on how to get to these settings. It usually involves shutting down the PC, restarting it, and pressing an interrupt key like F2 or DEL as soon as you hear the chime of your system speaker, but like I said, consult your hardware manual.

2. Once you made your changes, and rebooted to Linux, find out if your system can run virtualization. This can be accomplished by running the following command from a terminal: `egrep -c '(vmx|svm)' /proc/cpuinfo`. If the result is a number higher than zero, that means you can go ahead with the installation.

To install KVM, type the commands, as shown in Listing 2-1, on a terminal window.

Listing 2-1. Commands to install KVM

```
sudo apt-get install qemu-kvm libvirt-bin ubuntu-vm-builder bridge-utils
sudo adduser your_user_name kvm
sudo adduser your_user_name libvirtd
```

You may have to reboot the system to complete the installation.

Hopefully, everything went well, and you now have a proper development environment. In the next chapter, we will familiarize ourselves with the various parts of Android Studio IDE.

Summary

- Android Studio is based on the community edition of IntelliJ. If you have used IntelliJ before, all the techniques and keyboard shortcuts you've learned can be used in Android Studio.

- You can use different versions of Android Studio side by side; you don't have to uninstall previous editions of Android Studio in order to try out the Preview edition.

- Install the hardware accelerator (HAXM) if you can; it will make your testing activities a lot more pleasant. If you're on Linux, use the Kernel-based Virtual Machine (KVM) instead of HAXM.

CHAPTER 3

Project Basics

What the chapter covers:

- Create a simple project in Android Studio
- Create an emulator (an AVD or Android Virtual Device)
- Run a test project in the emulator

You can build many things in Android Studio, a business app, an ebook, a casual game (even triple AAA titles, why not?), and so on, but before you can do all that, you need to know the basics of creating, building, and testing an app in Android Studio. This chapter is all about that.

Create a Project

Launch Android Studio. Click "Start a new Android Studio Project," as shown in Figure 3-1. You have to be online when you do this because Android Studio's Gradle (a project build tool) pulls quite a few files from online repositories when you start a new project.

© Ted Hagos 2020
T. Hagos, *Learn Android Studio 4*, https://doi.org/10.1007/978-1-4842-5937-5_3

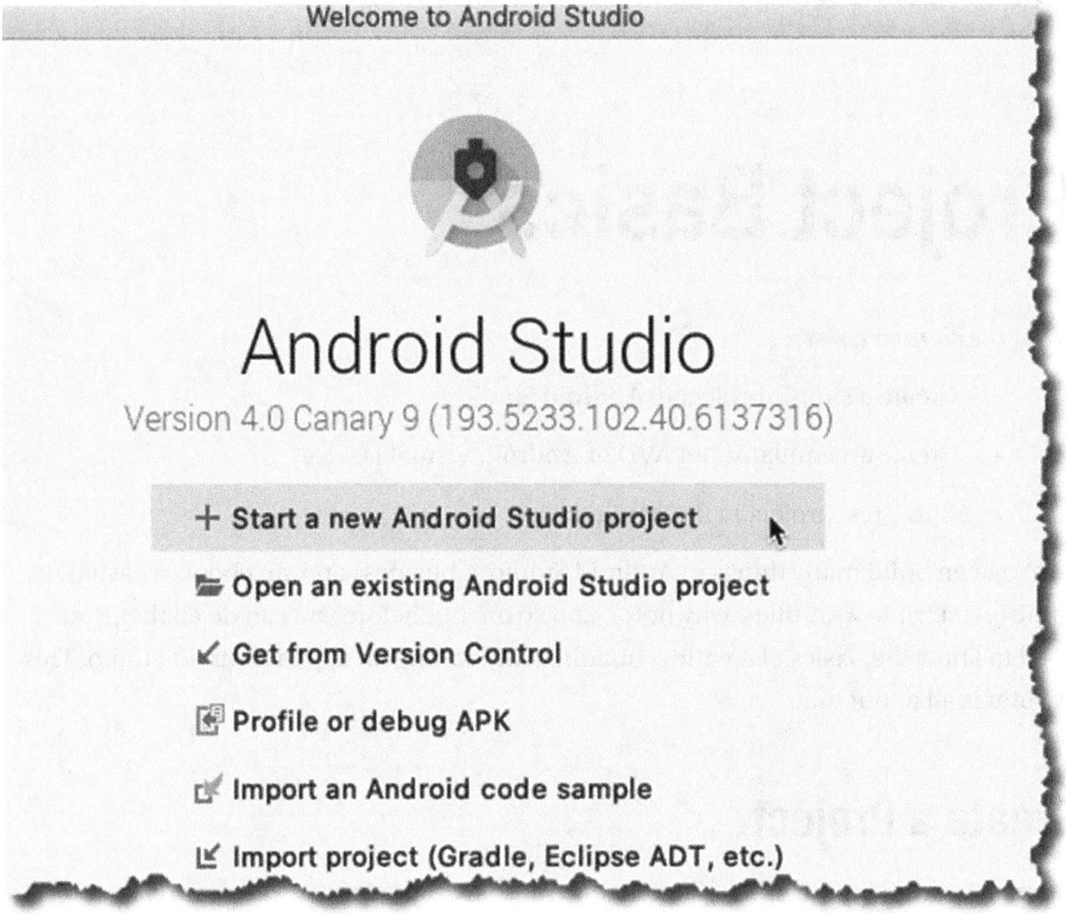

Welcome to Android Studio

Android Studio

Version 4.0 Canary 9 (193.5233.102.40.6137316)

+ **Start a new Android Studio project**

🗁 **Open an existing Android Studio project**

✔ **Get from Version Control**

▣ **Profile or debug APK**

▣ **Import an Android code sample**

⬏ **Import project (Gradle, Eclipse ADT, etc.)**

Figure 3-1. *Opening screen*

During the creation process, Android prompts for what kind of project you want to build; choose **Phone and Tablet ➤ Empty Activity**, as shown in Figure 3-2—we'll discuss Activities in the coming chapters, but for now, think of an Activity as a screen or a form; it's something that the user sees and interacts with.

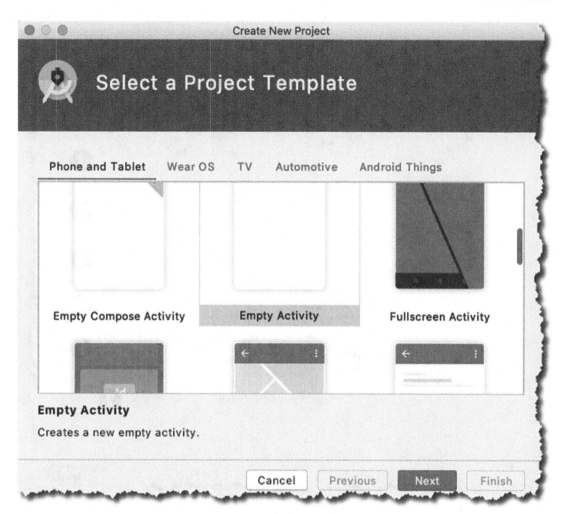

Figure 3-2. *Create a new project; choose an Activity type*

In the next screen, we get to configure the project. We set the app's name, package name (domain), and the target Android version. Figure 3-3 shows the annotated picture of the "Create New Project" screen.

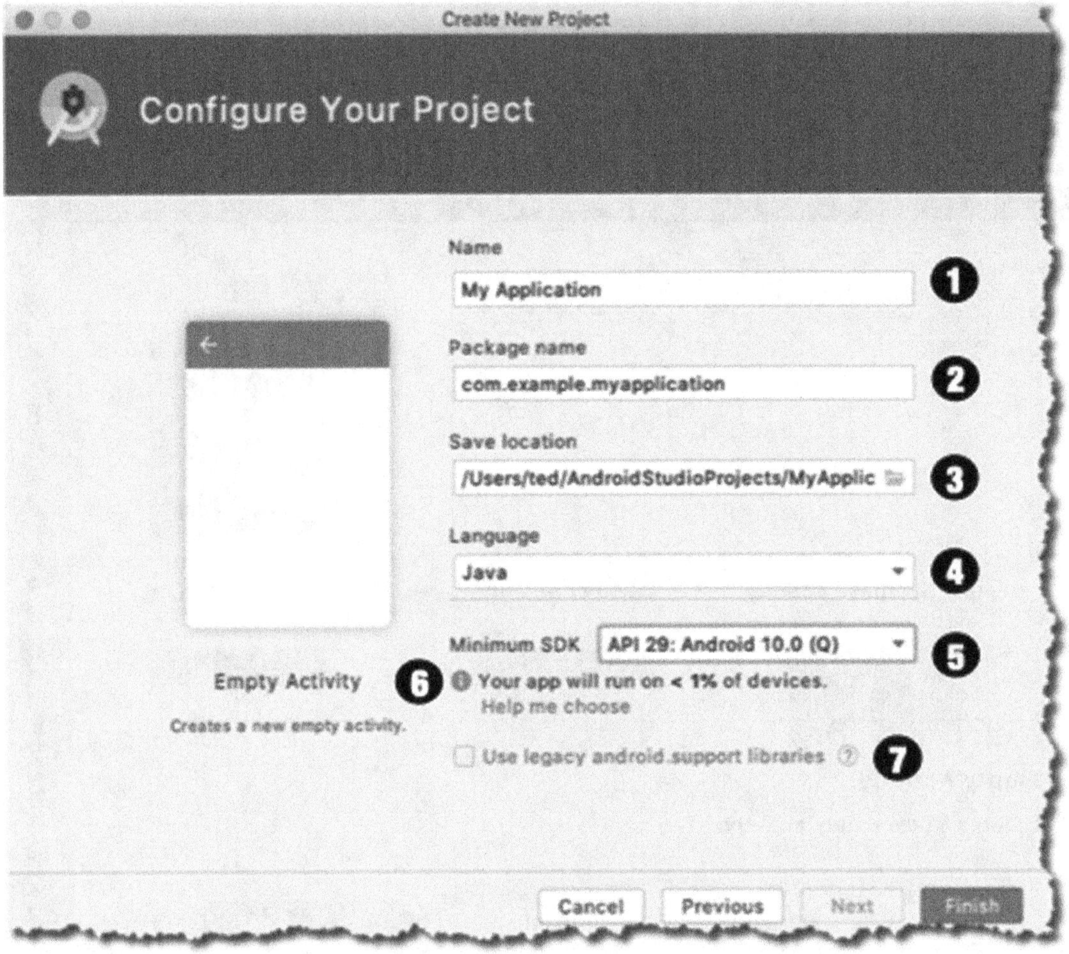

Figure 3-3. *Configure your project*

---

❶ **Name**. This is also known as the project name; this also becomes the name of the top-level folder, which will contain all of the project's files. This name also becomes part of the application's identity, should you release it in the Play Store.

❷ **Package name**. This is your organization or company's domain name in reverse DNS notation. If you don't have a company name, you can use anything that resembles a web domain. At the moment, it won't matter if we use a real company name or not, since we won't release this to the Play Store.

❸ **Save location**. This is a location in your local directory where the project files will be kept.

❹ **Language**. You can use either Kotlin or Java; for this project, we will use Java.

❺   **Minimum API level**. The min API level will determine the lowest version of Android, which your application can run on. You need to choose wisely and prudently because it can severely limit the potential audience for your app.

❻   **Help me choose**. This shows the percentage of Android devices that your app can run on. If you click the "Help me choose" link, it will open a window that shows the distribution of Android devices, per Android version.

❼   **Legacy Android support libraries**. These are support libraries. They're included so that you can use modern Android libraries (like the ones included in Android 9) but still allow your app to be run on devices with lower Android versions.

When you're all done, click "Finish" to begin the project creation. Android Studio scaffolds the project and creates startup files like the main Activity file, Android manifest, and other files to get the project propped up. The build tool (Gradle) will pull quite a few files from online repos; it can take some time.

After all that, hopefully, the project is created, and you get to see Android Studio's main editor window, as shown in Figure 3-4.

Figure 3-4. Main editor window

Android Studio's screen is composed of several sections that can collapse and expand, depending on your needs. The section on the left (Figure 3-4) is the Project panel. It's a tree-like structure that shows all the (relevant) files in the project. If you want to edit a particular file, simply select it in the Project panel and double-click; at that point, it will be opened for editing in the main editor window. In Figure 3-4, you can see the *MainActivity.java* file available for editing. Over time, we will spend a lot of hours doodling in the main editor window, but for now, we simply want to go through the basic process of application development. We won't add or modify anything in the Java files or any other files in the project. We'll leave them as is.

Create an AVD

The next step is to build and test the app. We can do that either by running it in an emulator or plugging in a physical Android device to your workstation. This section covers setting up an emulator.

From Android Studio's main menu bar, go to **Tools ➤ AVD Manager**, as shown in Figure 3-5.

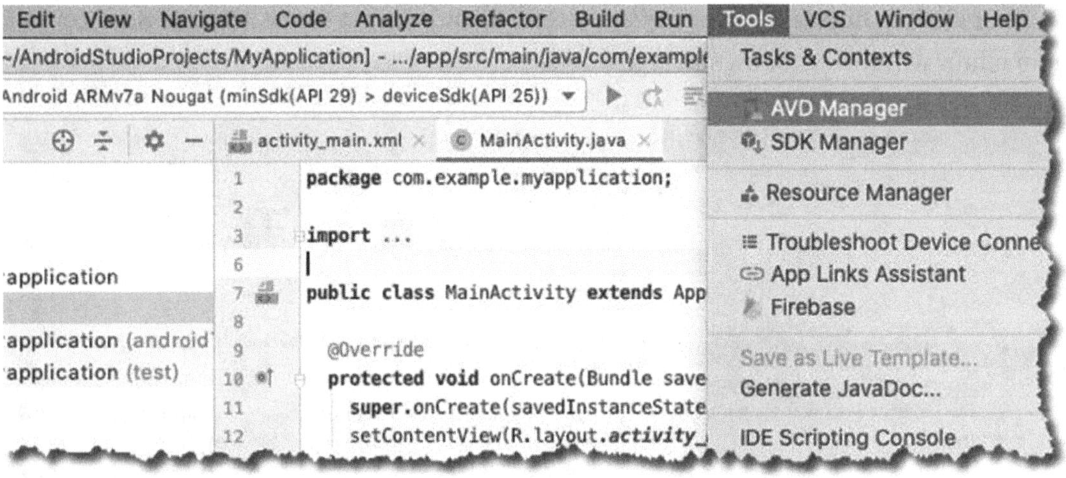

Figure 3-5. *Menu bar, Tools, AVD Manager*

The AVD manager window launches; AVD stands for Android Virtual Device. It's an emulator that runs a specific version of the Android OS, which we can use for testing the app. The AVD manager (shown in Figure 3-6) shows all the defined emulators in the local development environment.

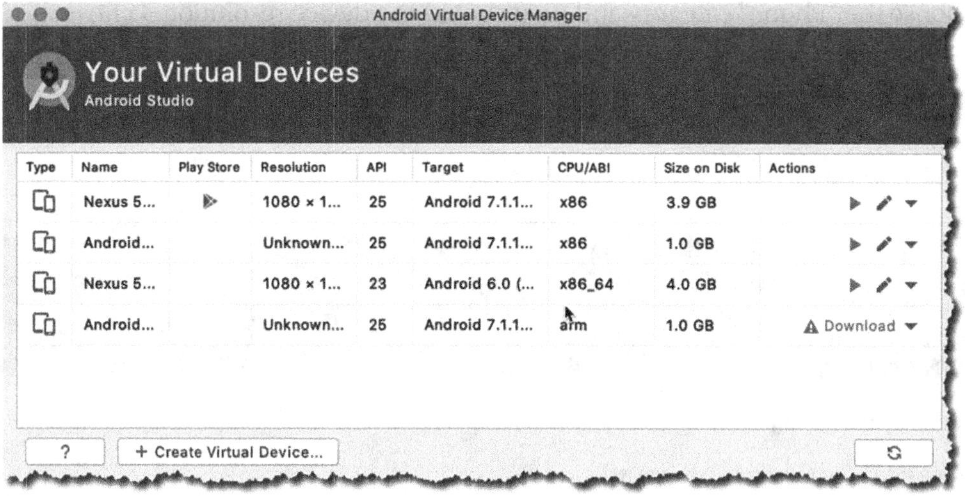

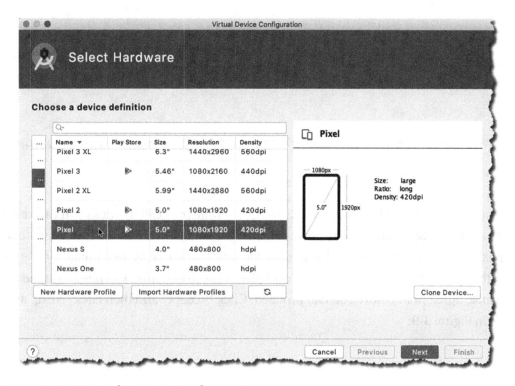

Figure 3-6. *AVD manager*

As you can see, I've already created a couple of emulators, but let's create another one; to do that, click the "+ Create Virtual Device" button, as shown in Figure 3-6. That action launches the "Virtual Device Configuration" screen, as shown in Figure 3-7.

Figure 3-7. *Virtual Device Configuration*

Choose the "Phone" category and then choose the device resolution. I chose the Pixel 5.0" 420dpi screen. Click the "Next" button, and we get to choose the Android version for the emulator; we can do this on the "System Image" screen, shown in Figure 3-8.

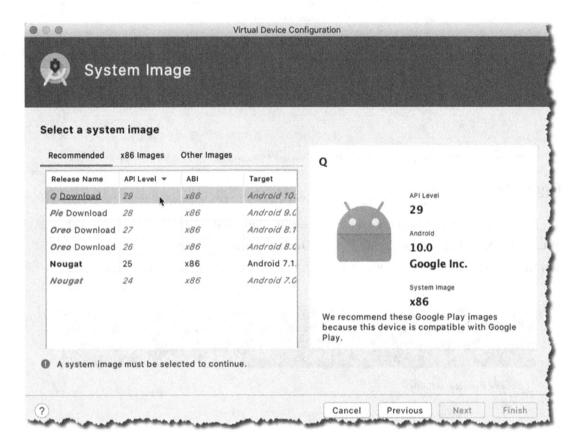

Figure 3-8. *System Image*

I want to use Android 10 (API level 29) or Q, as some may call it; but as you can see, I don't have that system image in my machine just yet—when you can see the "Download" link next to the Android version, that means you don't have that system image locally yet. To get the system image for Android 10, click the "Download" link. You need to agree to the license agreement before you can proceed. Click "Accept" and then click "Next," as shown in Figure 3-9.

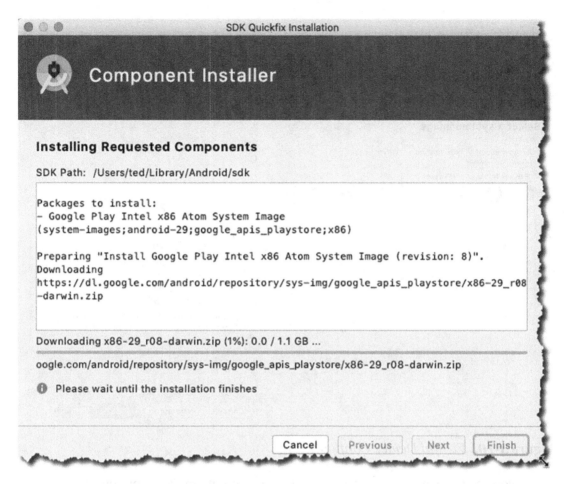

Figure 3-9. *SDK Quickfix Installation*

The download process can take some time, depending on your Internet speed; when it's done, you'll get back to the "System Image" selection screen, as shown in Figure 3-10.

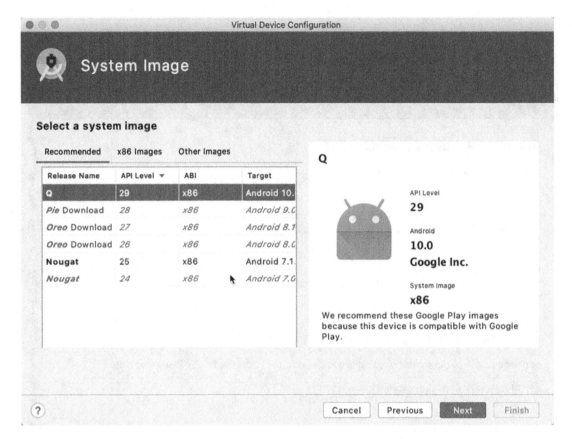

Figure 3-10. *Virtual Device Configuration*

As you can see, we can now use Android 10 as a system image for our emulator. Select it, then click "Next." The next screen shows a summary of our past choices for creating the emulator; the "Verify Configuration" screen is displayed next (Figure 3-11).

Figure 3-11. *Verify Configuration*

The "Verify Configuration" screen not only shows the summary of our past choices, you can configure some additional functionalities here. If you click the "Show Advanced Settings" button, you can also configure the following:

- Front and back camera

- Emulated network speed

- Emulated performance

- Size of internal storage

- Keyboard input (whether enabled or disabled)

When you're done, click the "Finish" button. When the AVD gets created, we'll be back in the "Android Virtual Device Manager" screen, as shown in Figure 3-12.

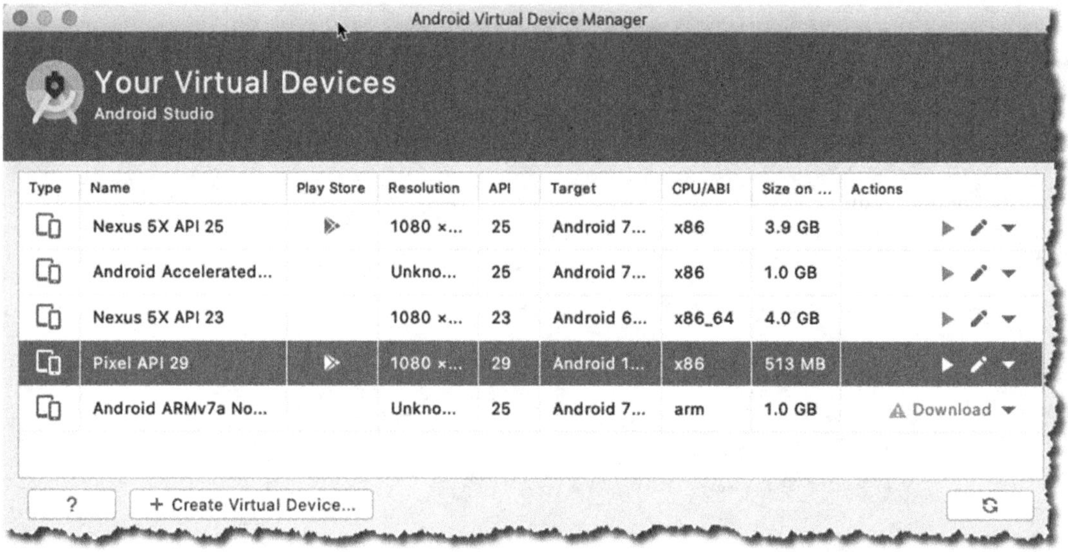

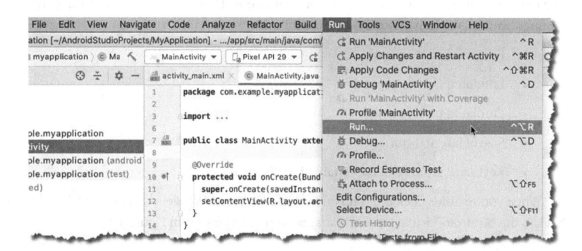

Figure 3-12. *Android Virtual Device Manager*

Now we can see the emulator (Pixel API 29). Click the little green arrow on the "Actions" column to launch the emulator—the pencil icon edits the emulator's configuration, and the green arrow launches it.

When the emulator launches, you'll see an image of the Pixel phone pop up on the desktop; it needs time to boot up completely. Go back to the main editor window of Android Studio to run the app.

From the main menu bar, go to **Run ➤ Run** app, as shown in Figure 3-13.

Figure 3-13. *Main menu bar, Run*

Android Studio compiles the project; then, it looks for either a connected (physical) Android device or a running emulator. We already launched the emulator a while ago, so Android Studio should find it and install the app in that emulator instance.

If all went well, you should see the Hello World app that Android Studio scaffolded for us, as shown in Figure 3-14.

Figure 3-14. *Hello World*

Summary

- An Android project (almost) always has an Activity. You can start with a basic project and choose "Empty Activity," as we did in the examples. Then, build from there.

- Pay some attention to the project package name during creation; if you release the project to Google Play, you won't be able to change the package name; it will be part of your application.

- Choose the minimum SDK carefully; it will limit the number of potential users of your app.

- You can use an emulator to run the app and see how it's shaping up. Testing using an emulator is much better if you have HAXM (emulator accelerator) enabled on your system; if you're on Linux, you can have acceleration using KVM.

CHAPTER 4

Android Studio IDE

What the chapter covers:

- Working with files in Android Studio

- The main editor

- Working with layout files

- The Project tool window

Previously, we built a simple app by creating a project with an empty Activity, opened it in the main editor window (briefly), and ran it in an emulator. In this chapter, we'll spend some time focused on the parts of IDE where you'll spend most of the time.

The IDE

From the opening dialog of Android Studio, you can launch the previous project we created. Links to existing projects appear on the left panel of the opening dialog, as shown in Figure 4-1.

© Ted Hagos 2020
T. Hagos, *Learn Android Studio 4*, https://doi.org/10.1007/978-1-4842-5937-5_4

Figure 4-1. *Welcome to Android Studio*

When you open a project, you'll see the main editor window, the Project panel, and other panels that Android Studio opens by default. An annotated picture of an opened project is shown in Figure 4-2.

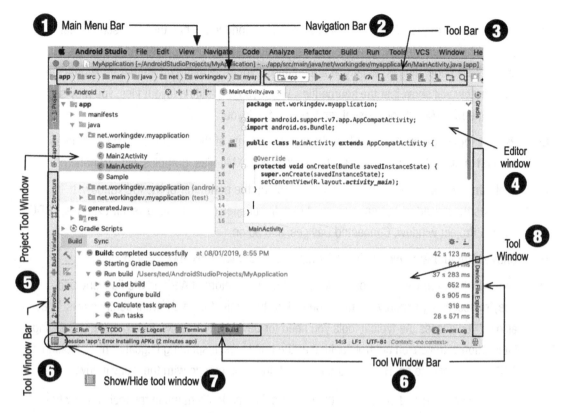

Figure 4-2. *The Android Studio IDE*

❶   **Main menu bar**. You can navigate Android Studio in various ways. Often, there's more than one way to do a task, but the primary navigation is done in the main menu bar. If you're on Linux or Windows, the main menu bar sits directly at the top of the IDE; if you're on macOS, the main menu bar is disconnected from the IDE (which is how all macOS software works).

❷   **Navigation bar**. This bar lets you navigate the project files. It's a horizontally arranged collection of chevrons that resembles some sort of breadcrumb navigation. You can open your project files either through the navigation bar or the Project tool window.

❸   **Toolbar**. This lets you do a wide range of actions (e.g., save files, run the app, open the AVD manager, open the SDK manager, undo, redo actions, etc.).

❹   **Main editor window**. This is the most prominent window and has the most screen real estate. The editor window is where you can create and modify project files. It changes its appearance depending on what you are editing. If you're working on a program source file, this window will show just the source files. When you are editing layout files, you may see either the raw XML file or a visual rendering of the layout.

❺   **Project tool window**. This window shows the contents of the project folders; you'll be able to see and launch all your project assets (source code, XML files, graphics, etc.) from here.

❻   **Tool window bar**. The tool window bar runs along the perimeter of the IDE window. It contains the individual buttons you need to activate specific tool windows, for example, TODO, Logcat, Project window, Connected Devices, and so on.

❼   **Show/hide tool window**. It shows (or hides) the **tool window bar**. It's a toggle.

❽   **Tool window**. You will find tool windows on the side bottom of Android Studio workspace. They're secondary windows that let you look at the project from different perspectives. They also let you access the typical tools you need for development tasks, for example, debugging, integration with version control, looking at the build logs, inspecting Logcat dumps, looking at TODO items, and so on. Here are a couple of things you can do with the tool windows:

- You can expand or collapse them by clicking the tool's name in the tool window bar. You can also drag, pin, unpin, attach, and detach the tool windows.

- You can rearrange the tool windows, but if you feel you need to restore the tool window to the default layout, you can do so from the main menu bar; click **Window ➤ Restore Default Layout**. Also, if you want to customize the "Default Layout," you rearrange the windows to your liking; then, from the main menu bar, click **Window ➤ Store Current Layout as Default**.

Main Editor

Like in most IDEs, you can modify and work with source files in the main editor window. What makes Android Studio stand out is how well it understands Android development files. Android Studio lets you work with a variety of file types, but you'll probably spend most of your time editing these types:

- Java source files
- XML files
- UI layout files

When working with Java programs, you get all the code hinting and completions that we've come to expect from a modern editor. What's more, it gives us plenty of early warnings when something is wrong. Figure 4-3 shows a Java class file opened in the main editor. The class file is an Activity and it's missing a semicolon on one of the statements. You could see Android Studio peppering the IDE with (red) squiggly lines which means that the class won't compile.

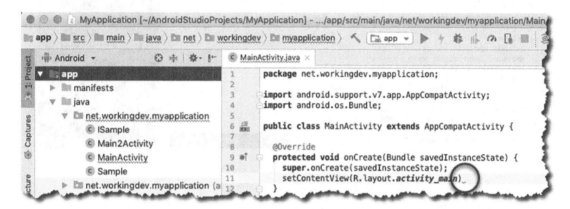

Figure 4-3. *Main editor showing error indicators*

Android Studio puts the squiggly lines very near the offending code. As you can see in Figure 4-3, the squiggly lines are placed at the point where the semicolon is expected.

Editing Layout Files

What the user sees as screens or windows of your app are actually Android Activities. Activities are Android components that are made up of Java source files and XML layout files. Android Studio, undoubtedly, can edit XML files, but what sets it apart is how intuitively it can render the XML files in a WYSIWYG mode (what you see is what you get). Figure 4-4 shows the two ways you can work with layout files.

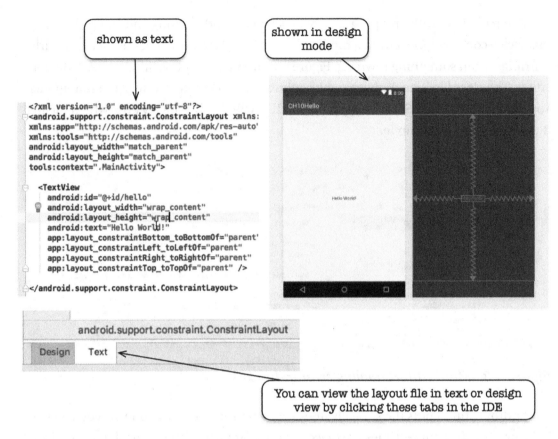

Figure 4-4. *Design mode and text mode editing of layout files*

Figure 4-5 shows the various parts of Android Studio that are relevant when working on a layout file during the design mode.

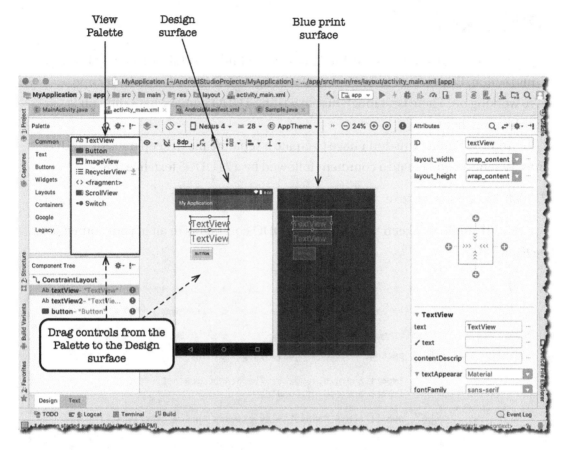

Figure 4-5. *Layout design tools of Android Studio*

- **View palette**—The View palette contains the Views (widgets) that you can drag and drop on either the design surface or blueprint surface.

- **Design surface**—It acts like a real-world preview of your screen.

- **Blueprint surface**—Similar to the design surface, but it only contains the outlines of the UI elements.

- **Attributes window**—You can change the properties of the UI element (View) in here. When you make a change on properties of a View using the Attributes window, that change will be automatically reflected on the layout's XML file. Similarly, when you make a change on the XML file, that will automatically be reflected on the Attributes window.

TODO Items

This may look like a trivial feature, but I hope you'll find it useful—that's why I squeezed in this section. Each one of us has a way of writing TODO items for whatever app we're working on. There isn't much fuss in writing TODO items; what's difficult is consolidating them.

In Android Studio, you don't have to create a separate file to keep track of TODO items. Whenever you create a comment followed by a "TODO" text, like this

```
// TODO This is a sample todo
```

Android Studio will keep track of all the TODO comments in all of your source files. See Figure 4-6.

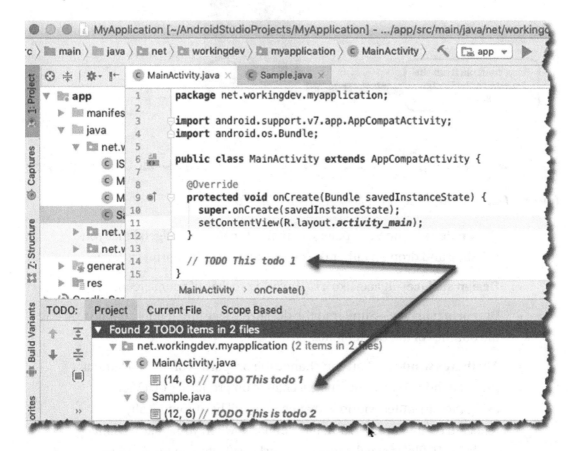

Figure 4-6. *TODO items*

To view all your TODO items, click the "TODO" tab in the tool window bar.

How to Get More Screen Space for Codes

You can have more screen space by closing all tool windows. Figure 4-7 shows a Java program opened in the main editor while all the tool windows are closed. You can collapse any tool window by clicking its name, for example, to collapse the Project tool window, click "Project."

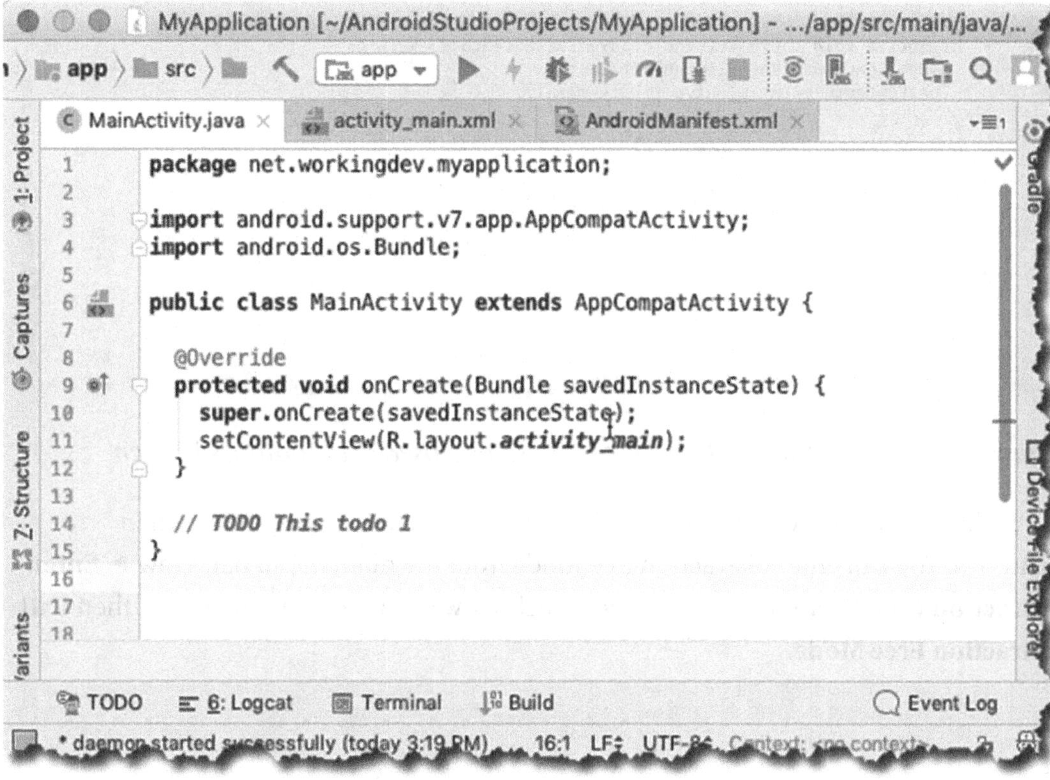

Figure 4-7. *Main editor, with all tool windows closed*

You can even get more screen space by hiding all the tool window bars, as shown in Figure 4-8.

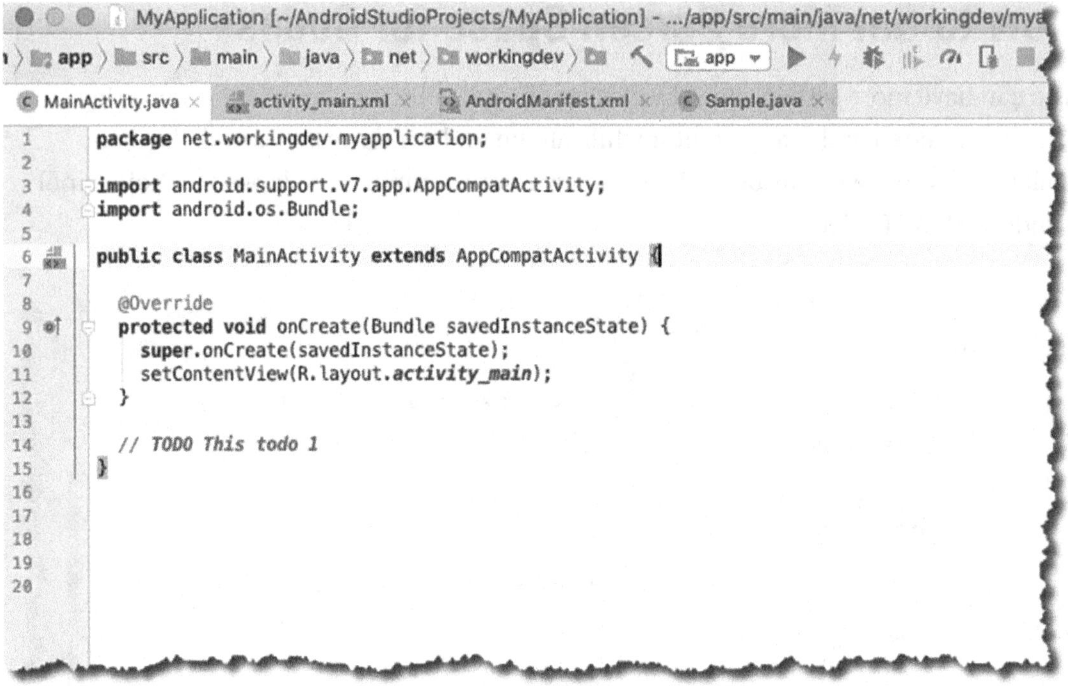

```
● ● ●  ⬡  MyApplication [~/AndroidStudioProjects/MyApplication] - .../app/src/main/java/net/workingdev/mya

) ▦ app ) ▦ src ) ▦ main ) ▦ java ) ▦ net ) ▦ workingdev ) ▦   ⟨  [⬚ app ▾ ]  ▶  ⚡  ⚒  ⬚ ⬚ ⟲ ⬚ ■

  © MainActivity.java ×      activity_main.xml ×      AndroidManifest.xml ×      © Sample.java ×

1        package net.workingdev.myapplication;
2
3        import android.support.v7.app.AppCompatActivity;
4        import android.os.Bundle;
5
6        public class MainActivity extends AppCompatActivity {
7
8            @Override
9            protected void onCreate(Bundle savedInstanceState) {
10               super.onCreate(savedInstanceState);
11               setContentView(R.layout.activity_main);
12           }
13
14           // TODO This todo 1
15       }
16
17
18
19
20
```

Figure 4-8. *Main editor, with all tool windows closed and toolbars hidden*

You'll get even more screen by entering "distraction free mode," as shown in Figure 4-9. You can enter distraction free mode from the main menu bar, **View ➤ Enter Distraction Free Mode**. To exit the mode, click **View** from the main menu bar, then **Exit Distraction Free Mode**.

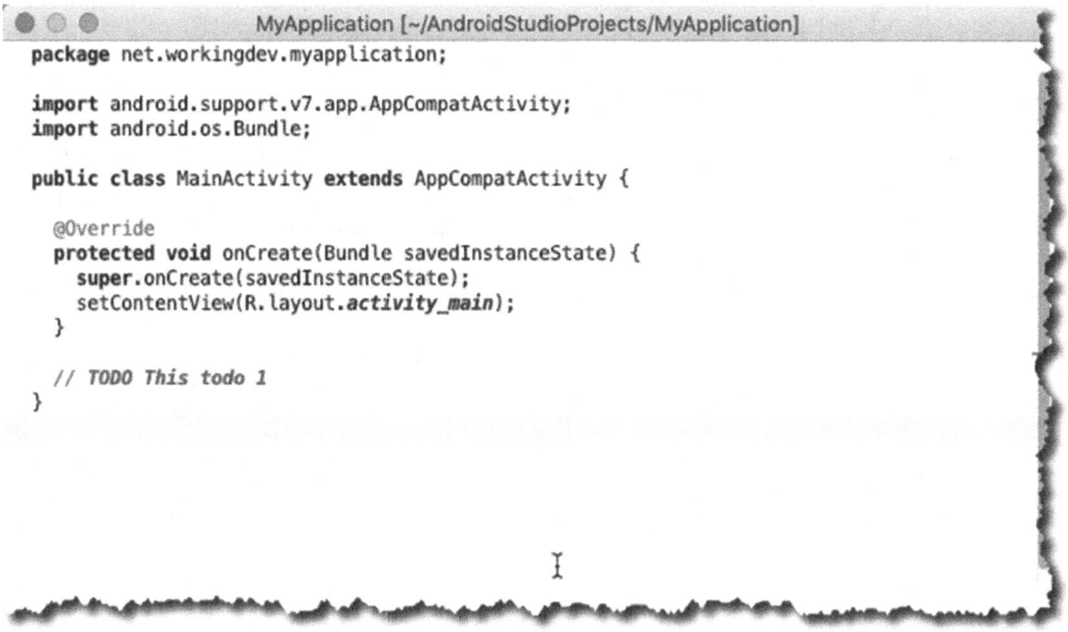

```
● ● ●              MyApplication [~/AndroidStudioProjects/MyApplication]
package net.workingdev.myapplication;

import android.support.v7.app.AppCompatActivity;
import android.os.Bundle;

public class MainActivity extends AppCompatActivity {

  @Override
  protected void onCreate(Bundle savedInstanceState) {
    super.onCreate(savedInstanceState);
    setContentView(R.layout.activity_main);
  }

  // TODO This todo 1
}
```

Figure 4-9. *Distraction free mode*

You may also try two other modes that can increase the screen real estate. They're also found on the View menu from the main menu bar.

- Presentation mode

- Full screen

Project Tool Window

You can work with the project's files and assets via the Project tool window, as shown in Figure 4-10. It has a tree-like structure and the sections are collapsible. You can launch any file from this window. To open a file, just double-click it.

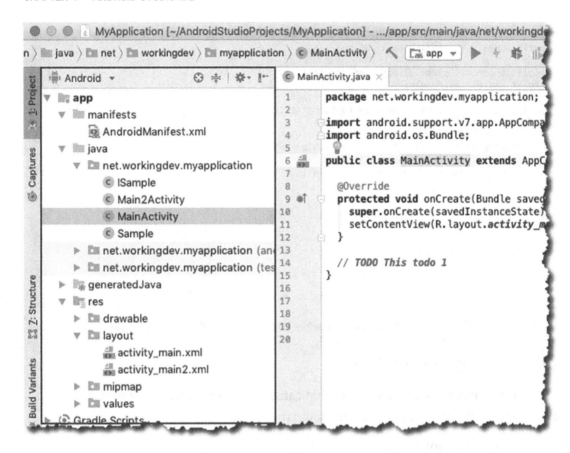

Figure 4-10. *Project tool window*

By default, Android Studio displays the **Project Files** in *Android View*, as shown in Figure 4-10. The "Android View" is organized by modules to provide quick access to the project's most relevant files. You change how you view the project files by clicking the down arrow on top of the Project window, as shown in Figure 4-11.

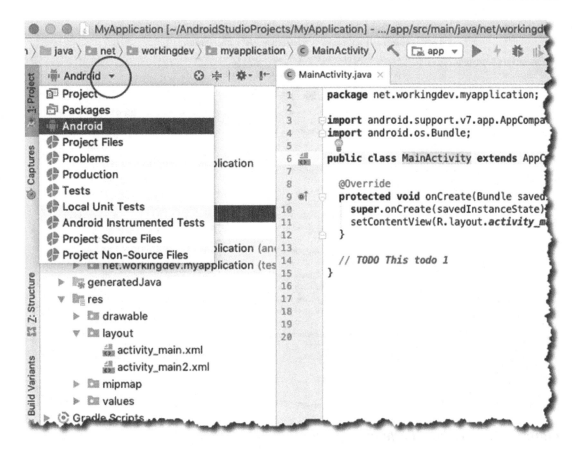

Figure 4-11. *How to change Views in the Project tool window*

Preferences/Settings

You can customize the behavior or look of Android Studio from the Settings or Preferences window; it's called **Settings** if you're on Windows or Linux, and it's called **Preferences** if you're on macOS. Figure 4-12 shows the Preferences (Settings) window.

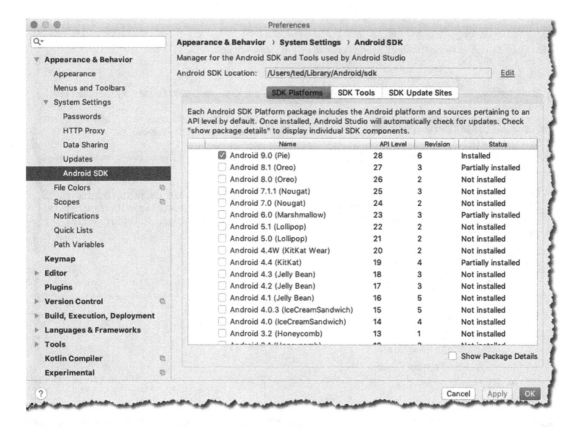

Figure 4-12. *Settings/Preferences window*

On Windows or Linux, you can go to the Settings window in one of two ways:

- From the main menu bar, click **File ➤ Settings**.

- Use the keyboard shortcut **Ctrl + Alt + S**.

On macOS, you can do it this way:

- From the main menu bar, click **Android Studio ➤ Preferences**.

- Use the keyboard shortcut **Command + ,**

There's a lot of things you can customize in here, ranging from how Android Studio looks, whether to use spaces or tabs on the editor, how many spaces to use for tabs, which version control to use, what API to download and what system images to use for AVD, and so on.

Summary

- You can see more of your codes by increasing the screen real estate for the main editor. You can do this by

  - Collapsing all the tool windows

  - Hiding the tool window bars

  - Entering distraction free mode

  - Going to full screen mode

- You can change how you view the project files from switching the view in the **Project tool window**.

- Adding a TODO item is easy in Android Studio; just add a single line comment followed by a TODO text, like this: // TODO This is my todo list.

CHAPTER 5

Android Application Overview

What the chapter covers:

- What makes up an Android project
- Overview of Android components
- The manifest file
- Intents

Now that we know our way around Android Studio, let's look closer at the structure of an Android app.

What Makes Up an Android Project

An Android app may look a lot like a desktop app; some may even think of them as mini desktop apps, but that wouldn't be correct. Android apps are structurally different from their desktop or web counterparts. A desktop app generally contains all the routines and subroutines it needs in order to function; occasionally, it may rely on dynamically loaded libraries, but the executable file is self-contained. An Android app, on the other hand, is made up of loosely coupled components that communicate to each other using a message-passing mechanism. Figure 5-1 shows the logical structure of an app.

© Ted Hagos 2020
T. Hagos, *Learn Android Studio 4*, https://doi.org/10.1007/978-1-4842-5937-5_5

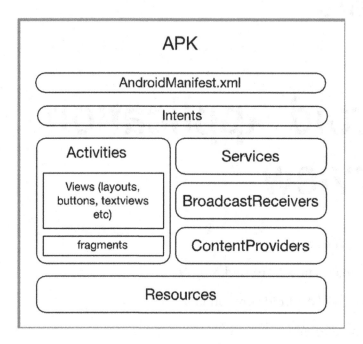

Figure 5-1. *Logical representation of an Android app*

The app in Figure 5-1 is a big one—it's got everything in it. Your app doesn't have to be as big. You don't need to put all kinds of components in your app, just build what you need; but it's worth our while to learn about all of the components (some more than others), especially the basic ones like Activities and Intents.

Note   APK is short for Application Package Kit. It's the package file format that Android uses to distribute and install applications. If Windows apps are packaged either via EXE or MSI and macOS apps use DMG, Android uses APK.

Activities, Services, BroadcastReceivers, and ContentProviders are called *Android components*. They are the key building blocks of an application. They are high-level abstractions of useful things like showing a screen to a user, running a task in the background, and broadcasting an event so that interested applications may respond to them. Components are precoded or prebuilt classes with very specific behavior, and we use them by extending them so we can add the behavior that's unique to our application.

Building an Android app is a lot like building a house. Some people build houses the traditional way—they assemble beams, struts, floor panels, and so on. They build the doors and other fittings from raw materials by hand, like an artisan. If we build

Android applications this way, it might take us a long time, and it also might be quite difficult. The skill necessary to build applications from scratch could be out of reach for some programmers. In Android, applications are built using components. Think of components like prefabricated pieces of a house; the parts are manufactured in advance, and all they require is assembly.

An **Activity** is where we put together things that the user can see. It's a focused thing that a user can do. For example, an Activity can be made so a user can view a single email or maybe fill up a form. In Figure 5-1, inside the Activity, there are *Views* and *Fragments*. Views are classes that draw content to the screen; some examples of View objects are *Buttons* and *TextViews*. A Fragment is similar to an Activity in a way that it's also a composition unit but a smaller one. Like Activities, they also hold View objects. Some apps use Fragments to address the problem of deploying them on multiple form factors—Fragments can be turned on or off depending on the available screen space and/or orientation.

Services. With Services, we can run program logic behind the scenes, without freezing the user interface. Services run in the background; they can be very useful when your app is supposed to download a file from the Web or maybe play music.

BroadcastReceivers. With BroadcastReceivers, our app can listen to messages from other applications or from the Android Runtime itself; a sample use case for this might be if you want to display a warning message when the battery dips to below 10%.

ContentProviders lets you write apps that can share data to other apps without exposing the underbellies of your apps' SQL structure. It manages access to some sort of central data repository. The details of database access are completely hidden from other apps. An example of a prebuilt application that is a ContentProvider is the "Contacts" app in Android.

Your application may need some visual or audio assets; these are the kinds of things we mean by "Resources" in Figure 5-1.

The AndroidManifest is exactly what its name implies; it's a manifest and it's written in XML. It declares quite a few things about the application, like

- The name of the app.

- Which Activity will show up first when the user launches the app.

- What kind of components are in the app. If it has activities, the manifest declares them—names of classes and all. If the app has services, their class names will also be declared in manifest.

- What kinds of things can the app do? What are its permissions? Is it allowed to access the Internet or the camera? Can it record GPS locations and so on?

- Does it use external libraries?

- What version(s) of Android will this app run on?

- Does it support a specific type of input device?

- Are there specific screen densities that this application requires?

As you can see, the manifest is a busy place; there's a lot of things to keep an eye on. But don't worry too much, most of the entries here are automatically taken care of by the creation wizards of Android Studio. One of the few occasions you will interact with it is probably when you need to add permissions to your app.

The manifest is also important for Google Play when it displays your app on the store. Your app won't appear to devices that do not meet the requirements stipulated in your manifest file.

Application Entry Point

An app typically interacts with a user, and it does so using Activity components. These kinds of apps usually have, at least, these three things. They have

1. An Activity class that the user sees first as soon as the app launches

2. A layout file for the Activity class which contains all the UI definitions like text views, buttons, and so on

3. The AndroidManifest file, which ties all the project resources and components together

When an application is launched, the Android Runtime creates an Intent object and inspects the manifest file. It's looking for a specific value of the `intent-filter` node (in the xml file). The runtime is trying to see if the application has a defined entry point, something like a *main function*. Listing 5-1 shows an excerpt from the Android manifest file.

Listing 5-1. Excerpt from AndroidManifest.xml

```
<activity android:name=".MainActivity">
 <intent-filter>
   <action android:name="android.intent.action.MAIN" />
   <category android:name="android.intent.category.LAUNCHER" />
 </intent-filter>
</activity>
```

If the application has more than one Activity, there will be several activity nodes in the manifest file, one node for each Activity. The first line of the definition has an attribute called *android:name*; this points to the class name of an Activity. In this example, the name of the class is "MainActivity."

The second line declares the *intent-filter*, when you see something like `android.intent.action.MAIN`, on the intent-filter node, it means the Activity is the entry point for the application. When the app launches, this is the Activity that the user will see.

Activities

You can think of an Activity as a screen or a window. It's something that a user can interact with. This is the UI of the app. An Activity is a class that inherits from the *android.app.Activity* class (one way or another), but we usually extend the *AppCompatActivity* class (instead of Activity) so we can use modern UI elements but still make the app run on older Android versions; hence, "Compat" in the name AppCompatActivity, which stands for "compatibility."

An Activity component has two parts, a Java class (or Kotlin if that's your language of choice) and a layout file in XML format. The layout file is where you put all the definitions of the UI, for example, the text box, button, labels, and so on. The Java class is where you code all the behavior parts of the UI, for example, what happens when the button is clicked, when text is entered into the field, when the user changes the orientation of the device, when another component sends a message to the Activity, and so on.

An Activity, like any other component in Android, has a lifecycle. Each lifecycle event has an associated method in the Activity's Java class; we can use these methods to customize the behavior of the application. Figure 5-2 shows the Activity lifecycle.

In Figure 5-2, the boxes show the state of an Activity on a particular stage of existence. The name of the method calls are embedded in the directional arrows which connect the stages.

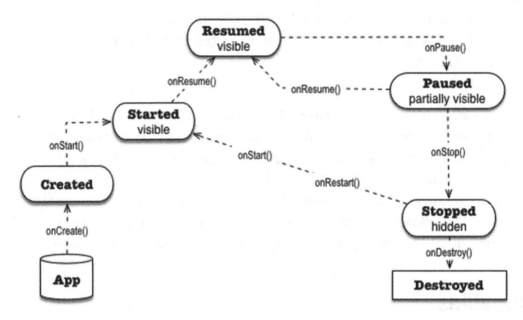

Figure 5-2. *Activity lifecycle*

When the Android Runtime launches the app, it calls the onCreate() method of the main Activity which brings the state of the Activity to "created." You can use this method to perform initialization routines like preparing event handling codes and so on.

The Activity proceeds to the next state which is "started"; the Activity is visible to the user at this point, but it's not yet ready for interaction. The next state is "resumed"; this is the state where the app is interacting with the user.

If the user clicks anything that takes the focus away from the Activity (answering a phone call or launching another app), the runtime pauses the current Activity and it enters the "paused" state. From there, if the user goes back to the Activity, the onResume() function is called, and the Activity *runs* again. On the other hand, if the user decides to open a different application, the Android Runtime may "stop" and eventually "destroy" the application.

Intents

If you have experience with object-oriented programming, you might be used to the idiom of activating an object's behavior by simply creating an instance of the object and calling its methods—that's a straightforward and simple way of making objects communicate to each other; unfortunately, Android's components don't follow that idiom. The code shown in Listing 5-2, while idiomatically object oriented, isn't going to work in Android.

Listing 5-2. Wrong way to activate another Activity

```
public class MainActivity extends AppCompatActivity {

  @Override
  protected void onCreate(Bundle savedInstanceState) {
    super.onCreate(savedInstanceState);
    setContentView(R.layout.activity_main);

    Button b = (Button) findViewById(R.id.button);
    b.setOnClickListener(new View.OnClickListener() {
      @Override
      public void onClick(View v) {
        new SecondActivity(); // WON'T WORK
      }
    });
  }
}
```

Android's architecture is quite unique in the way it builds application. It has this notion of components instead of just plain objects. Android uses *Intents* as a way for its components to communicate; it also uses the same Intents to pass messages across components.

The reason Listing 5-2 won't work is because an Android Activity isn't a simple object, it's a component. You cannot simply instantiate a component in order to activate it. Component activation is done by creating an *Intent* object and then passing it to the component you want to activate, which, in our case now, is another Activity.

There are two kinds of Intents, an explicit Intent and an implicit Intent. Listing 5-3 shows a sample code on how to create an explicit Intent and how to use it to activate another Activity—highlighted in bold.

Listing 5-3. How to activate another Activity

```java
public class MainActivity extends AppCompatActivity {

  @Override
  protected void onCreate(Bundle savedInstanceState) {
    super.onCreate(savedInstanceState);
    setContentView(R.layout.activity_main);

    Button b = (Button) findViewById(R.id.button);
    b.setOnClickListener(new View.OnClickListener() {
      @Override
      public void onClick(View v) {
        Intent i = new Intent(v.getContext(), SecondActivity.class);
        v.getContext().startActivity(i);
      }
    });
  }
}
```

It may look like there's a lot of things to unpack on our sample codes, but don't worry, I'll explain the codes with more context as we move further along in the coming chapters.

Summary

- Android applications are made up of loosely coupled components. These components communicate via Intent objects.

- An app's entry point is usually a launcher Activity. This launcher Activity is designated in the app's AndroidManifest file.

- The manifest file is like a glue that holds together the components of the application; everything the application has, can do, or cannot do is reflected in the manifest.

CHAPTER 6

Activities and Layouts

What we'll cover:

- Overview of Android activities
- Layout files
- View objects

Most of the apps you will build will have a UI. In the previous chapter, we learned that to create a simple app with UI, we need (1) an Activity class, (2) a layout file for that Activity class, and (3) a manifest file. Thankfully, we get these three things from the project creation wizard.

In this chapter, we will examine the Activity component a lot closer. We will learn more about the constituent parts of an Activity, the Java class, and its related layout file.

Activity

The Activity component is responsible for what the user sees on the screen. It's made up of an Activity class and a layout file (an XML file that contains definitions for UI elements like buttons, text fields, etc.).

Layout File

The layout file is an XML file. It contains definitions of UI elements such as buttons, text fields, drop-downs, labels, and so on. Some people may cringe at the thought of composing UI by hand using only an XML editor, but don't worry, Android Studio makes it easy to compose user interfaces. You can work with the layout file either in text mode or in design mode (WYSIWYG), as shown in Figure 6-1.

© Ted Hagos 2020
T. Hagos, *Learn Android Studio 4*, https://doi.org/10.1007/978-1-4842-5937-5_6

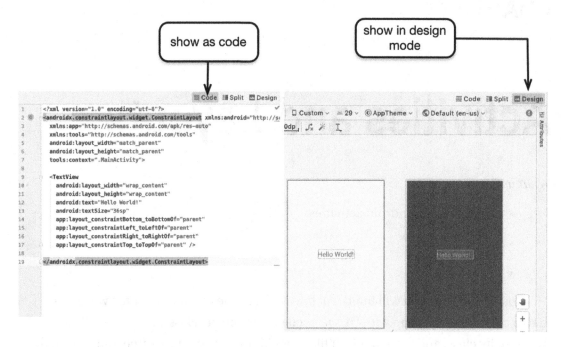

Figure 6-1. *Layout file, shown as text mode and in design mode*

In Figure 6-1, the picture on the left shows the activity_main layout file as in XML mode (or code mode), and the one on the right shows the layout file in design mode. You can work with the layout file visually (click the "Design" button) or as raw XML code (click the "Code" button). When you change an element by editing the XML, Android Studio automatically updates the design view's rendition. Similarly, when you make a change in the design view, the XML file gets updated.

Listing 6-1 shows a typical layout file.

Listing 6-1. /res/layout/activity_main.xml

```
<?xml version="1.0" encoding="utf-8"?>
<androidx.constraintlayout.widget.ConstraintLayout
xmlns:android="http://schemas.android.com/apk/res/android"
  xmlns:app="http://schemas.android.com/apk/res-auto"
  xmlns:tools="http://schemas.android.com/tools"
  android:layout_width="match_parent"
  android:layout_height="match_parent"
  tools:context=".MainActivity">
```

```
<TextView
  android:layout_width="wrap_content"
  android:layout_height="wrap_content"
  android:text="Hello World!"
  android:textSize="36sp"
  app:layout_constraintBottom_toBottomOf="parent"
  app:layout_constraintLeft_toLeftOf="parent"
  app:layout_constraintRight_toRightOf="parent"
  app:layout_constraintTop_toTopOf="parent" />

</androidx.constraintlayout.widget.ConstraintLayout>
```

A layout file generally has two parts: a declaration of a container and the declarations of each UI element inside. In Listing 6-1, the second line, which is also the root of the XML document, is the container's declaration. The TextView element is declared as a child node of the container. This is how containers and UI elements are arranged in a layout file.

View and ViewGroup Objects

A UI is simply a collection of user interface elements such as text input element, text label, buttons, and so on. In the example code shown in Listing 6-1, we have one UI element, the TextView. This is the element that holds the text "Hello World." In Android speak, the TextView is called a View object; some people also refer to these as widgets, and some others with web programming background may refer to these as input elements or form elements—we're in Android world now, so we'll call them View objects or simply Views.

A View object is a composition unit. You build a UI by arranging one or more View objects alongside each other or sometimes embedded in each other. There are two kinds of views as the Android library defines it, a "View" and a "ViewGroup." An example of a View object is a button or a text field. These objects are meant to be composed alongside other views, but they are not meant to contain child views; they are intended to stand alone. A ViewGroup, on the other hand, can contain child views—it's the reason why they're sometimes called containers.

Figure 6-2 shows the class hierarchy of some of the more common UI elements. Every item in a user interface is a child of the **android.view.View** class. We can use prebuilt user interface elements in the Android SDK such as TextView, Button,

ProgressBars, and so on, or, if need be, we can construct custom controls (widgets or views are sometimes called "controls") by either (1) subclassing existing elements like TextViews, (2) subclassing the View class itself and ultimately drawing a custom widget from scratch, or (3) subclassing the ViewGroup and embedding other widgets in it; this is known as a *composite view*—the RadioGroup in Figure 6-2 is an example of such.

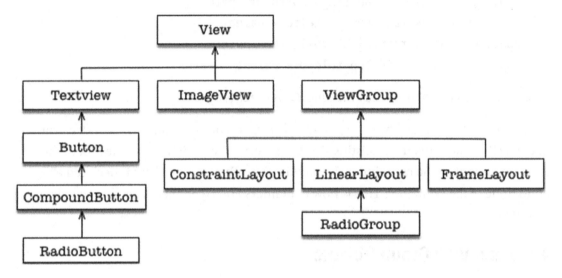

Figure 6-2. *ViewGroup class hierarchy*

Each View object ultimately becomes a Java object at runtime, but we work with them as XML elements during design time. We don't have to worry about how Android inflates the XML into Java objects because that process is invisible to us. It happens behind the scenes; Figure 6-3 shows the logical representation of the Android compilation process.

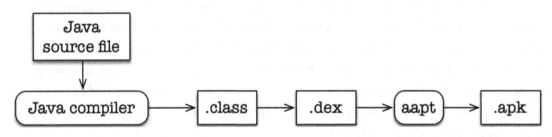

Figure 6-3. *Android compilation process*

The compiler transforms the program source files into Java byte codes. The resulting byte codes are then further converted to a DEX file. A DEX file is a Dalvik Executable; it's the executable format that the Android Runtime (ART) understands. Before the DEX files and other resources get wrapped into an Android package (APK), it also produces as a side effect a special file named "R.class". We use the R.class to get a programmatic reference to the UI elements defined in the layout file.

Containers

Apart from creating composite views, the ViewGroup class has another use. They form the basis for layout managers. A layout manager is a container responsible for controlling how child views are positioned on the screen, relative to the container and each other. Android comes with a couple of prebuilt layout managers; Table 6-1 shows us some of them.

Table 6-1. *Layout managers*

Layout manager	Description
LinearLayout	Positions the widgets in single row or column, depending on the selected orientation. Each widget can be assigned a weight value which determines the amount of space the widget occupies compared to the other widgets
TableLayout	Arranges the widgets in a grid format of rows and columns
FrameLayout	Stacks child views on top of each other. The last entry on the XML layout file is the one on top of the stack
RelativeLayout	Views are positioned relative to other views and the container by specifying alignments and margins on each view
ConstraintLayout	The ConstraintLayout is the newest layout. It positions widgets relative to each other and the container (like RelativeLayout). But it accomplishes the layout management by using more than just alignments and margins. It introduces the idea of a "constraint" object, which anchors a widget to target. This target could be another widget or a container or another anchor point. This is the layout we will use for most of our examples in this book

There is more to learn about Views, containers, and layouts, but we know enough to create some decent projects. Let's move on to the Activity class.

Activity Class

An Activity class must inherit from **android.app.Activity**, either directly or indirectly, but we usually don't inherit from this class directly; instead, we extend the **AppCompatActivity** class to run the app on older versions of Android but still use modern UI elements. The "Compat" in the class name stands for "compatibility."

While the layout file contains the definitions for the Views (buttons, text fields, etc.), the Activity class is responsible for the behavior; this is where we write the codes when we want something to happen in response to a user action, like a button click. When you create an "empty Activity" project, the Activity class you'll get looks like the code in Listing 6-2.

Listing 6-2. MainActivity.java

```
import androidx.appcompat.app.AppCompatActivity;
import android.os.Bundle;

public class MainActivity extends AppCompatActivity { ❶

  @Override  ❷
  protected void onCreate(Bundle savedInstanceState) { ❸
    super.onCreate(savedInstanceState);  ❹
    setContentView(R.layout.activity_main); ❺
  }

}
```

---

❶ We inherit from **AppCompatActivity**, which is a child class of **android.app.Activity** class. All Activity classes must inherit from android.app.Activity one way or another, but as you can see, the project creation wizard gave us AppCompatActivity. This is the recommended superclass for an Activity

❷ The @Override annotation tells the compiler that we intend to override the method immediately following the annotation.

❸ onCreate() is one of the lifecycle methods of the Activity class. The Android Runtime calls this method right after the user launches the app. This is a good place to write initialization codes.

❹ We call the onCreate() method in the superclass (AppCompatActivity). This is necessary, so we don't break the chain of calls within the onCreate methods. If we don't call this method, the codes inside the onCreate of AppCompatActivity (which is our superclass) won't run; that will result in errors.

❺ The setContentView method selects which View resource to display when the Activity becomes visible to the user. This method is overloaded; you can pass an integer (which points to a resource ID) or an instance of a View object. In this case, we passed a resource ID. You may recall that our layout file is named /res/layout/activity_main.xml. You may also recall that during the compilation process, an "R.class" was generated for our convenience so we can reference UI resources programmatically—R.layout.activity_main points to the file /res/layout/activity_main.xml. In this statement, we are associating *MainActivity.java* with *activity_main.xml*.

Hello World

Now that we have some working knowledge about Activities and layouts, let's explore them in a sample project.

Table 6-2. *Project information for the Hello app*

Project detail	Value
Application name	ActivitySample
Company domain	Use your website name
Language	Java
Form factor	Phone and tablet
Minimum SDK	API 29 (Q) Android 10
Type of activity	Empty
Activity name	MainActivity
Layout name	activity_main

When the project is created, you will see a bunch of files in the project window, but we're only interested in three. Figure 6-4 shows the location of (1) the main program file, (2) the manifest file, and (3) the main layout file in the project file window.

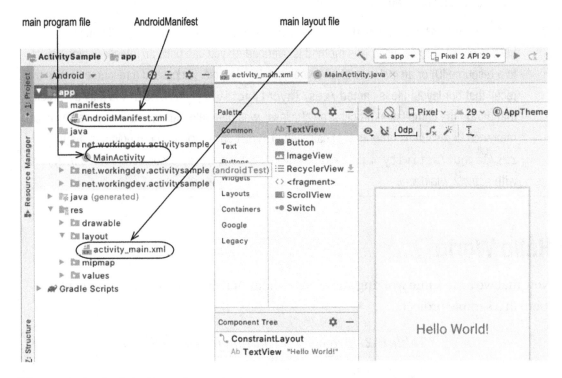

Figure 6-4. *ActivitySample project*

The main layout file, named *activity_main.xml*, is inside the *app* ➤ *res* ➤ *layout* folder. All user interface elements are written in an XML layout file.

The main program file, *MainActivity.java*, is found in *app* ➤ *java* ➤ *package name* folder (your package name will be different from mine). This Java file is the Activity class. If you want to do something as a reaction to a user action, like clicking a button, this is where we write that program logic.

The manifest file describes the app's essential information to the Android build tools, Android OS, and Google Play. Looking at Figure 6-4, it appears as if the manifest file is in *app* ➤ *manifests* ➤ *AndroidManifest.xml*. You need to remember that what we're looking at is the "Android View" of the Project window. It's a logical representation of the project files; it's not the literal arrangements of the files with respect to the root folder of the project. If you want to see the actual location of the project files, switch to "Project view," as shown in Figure 6-5.

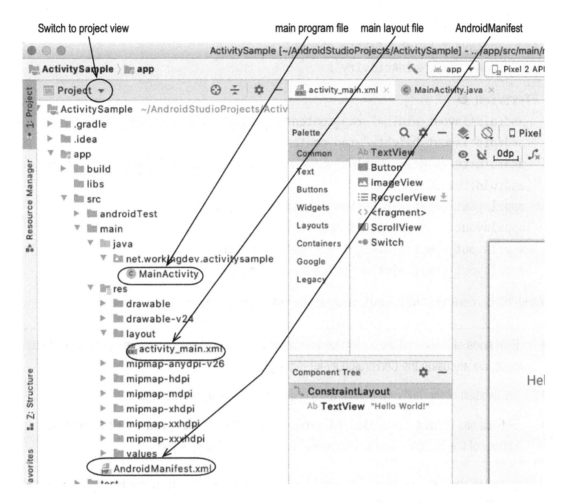

Figure 6-5. *Project view*

We've got a pretty good map of where things are. We know the location of the manifest file, the MainActivity (Java) file, and the activity_main (layout) file. Since we've already examined the contents of the MainActivity file earlier, let's explore the activity_main layout file (shown in Listing 6-3).

Listing 6-3. Annotated activity_main

```xml
<?xml version="1.0" encoding="utf-8"?>
<androidx.constraintlayout.widget.ConstraintLayout  ❶
xmlns:android="http://schemas.android.com/apk/res/android"
  xmlns:app="http://schemas.android.com/apk/res-auto"
  xmlns:tools="http://schemas.android.com/tools"
```

```
    android:layout_width="match_parent"
    android:layout_height="match_parent"
    tools:context=".MainActivity">

    <TextView ❷
      android:layout_width="wrap_content"
      android:layout_height="wrap_content"
      android:text="Hello World!"
      android:textSize="36sp"
      app:layout_constraintBottom_toBottomOf="parent" ❸
      app:layout_constraintLeft_toLeftOf="parent"
      app:layout_constraintRight_toRightOf="parent"
      app:layout_constraintTop_toTopOf="parent" />

</androidx.constraintlayout.widget.ConstraintLayout>
```

---

❶   Root node of the layout file, which also declares what kind of layout manager is in effect. In this case, we are using the ConstraintLayout manager.

❷   Declaration of the TextView object. It's a child node of the layout manager.

❸   Defines one of the constraints of the TextView object. It says, there's an anchor point to the bottom of the TextView, and it anchored to the bottom of the container.

Try to run the project in an emulator just to make sure that nothing is broken, and then we will make some modifications.

Modifying Hello World

We'll make some minor changes to both the layout file and the Activity. We'll do the following:

1. Change the text in the TextView control.

2. Add a Button View to the screen; we'll place it right below the TextView.

3. Add a function to the Activity. The function, when called, will increment the value of the TextView.

4. We will associate the new function to the Button. Every time we click the button, the value of the TextView will change.

Figure 6-6 shows the general layout of the project. Currently, we're looking at activity_main.xml in design mode. While in this mode, we can see the view palette, design surface, and blueprint surface.

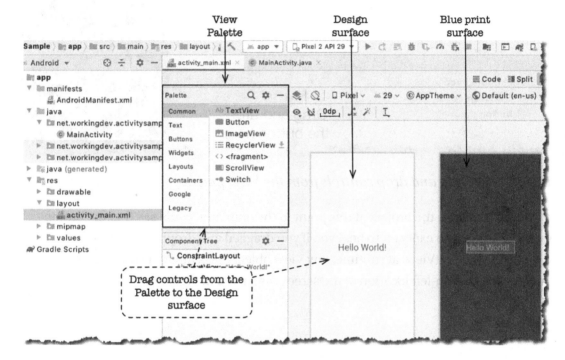

Figure 6-6. *ActivitySample project shown in design view*

To add a Button control, drag and drop the Button from the View palette to the design surface as shown in Figure 6-7—you can also drop it in the blueprint surface, which will work.

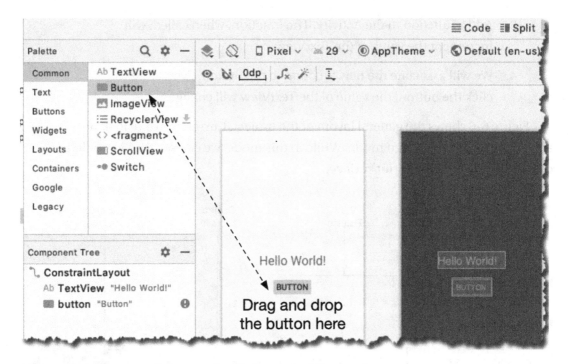

Figure 6-7. *Drag and drop controls from the View palette*

If you try to run the project at this point in the emulator, you'll see that the button won't be where you expect it to be. Even if you dragged and dropped the Button right below the TextView, at runtime, any View object that's not "constrained" will be anchored at the top-left location of the screen, as shown in Figure 6-8.

Figure 6-8. *Button View without constraint*

The Hello TextView is nicely centered in the screen because it has four anchor points (constraints). The Button appears right below the Hello text in design time, but in runtime, it's on position 0,0 (top left) of the screen—this is how controls are positioned at runtime when they don't have constraints.

The Button control doesn't have any constraint yet because we didn't put any. Constraints are not automatically added when you add a control to the design surface. The TextView has constraints because that was generated by the wizard when we created the project.

Let's start fresh. Remove all existing constraints on the design surface. You can do this by selecting all the View objects and clicking "clear constraints" on the design toolbar, as shown in Figure 6-9.

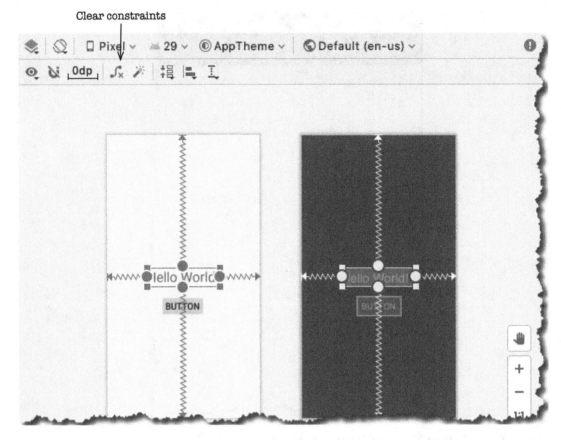

Figure 6-9. *TextView with constraints*

When all the constraints are removed, reposition the controls on the design surface in the way you would like them to appear during runtime. Next, select all the controls again—you can do this by clicking and dragging the mouse around the controls.

To "magically" add all the constraints for our controls, click "infer constraints" as shown in Figure 6-10. Android Studio will try to best guess the needed constraints for the controls that will match your arrangement in the design surface.

Infer constraints

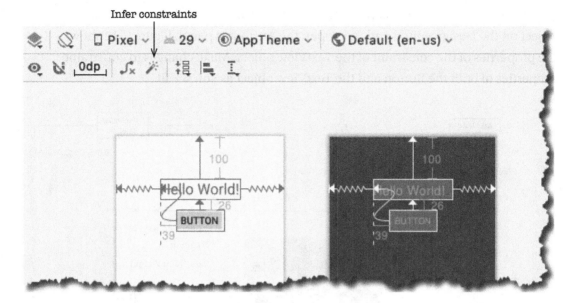

Figure 6-10. *Infer constraints*

The properties of the controls can be set in the "Attributes" window. We need to change some properties of the TextView and the Button controls. An object's properties will appear on the Attributes panel when the object is selected in the design surface. The Attributes panel is collapsed by default. To open the Attributes panel, you need to click the panel to open it, as shown in Figure 6-11.

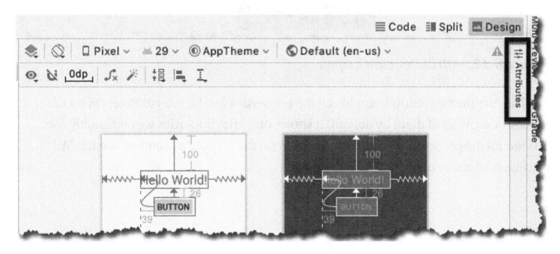

Figure 6-11. *Attributes panel, collapsed*

To inspect the View object properties in the Attributes panel, select the View object on the Design editor, and then open the Attributes panel. Figure 6-12 shows the properties of the constraint of the TextView object. Make changes to constraint properties of both the Button and the TextView object as you see fit.

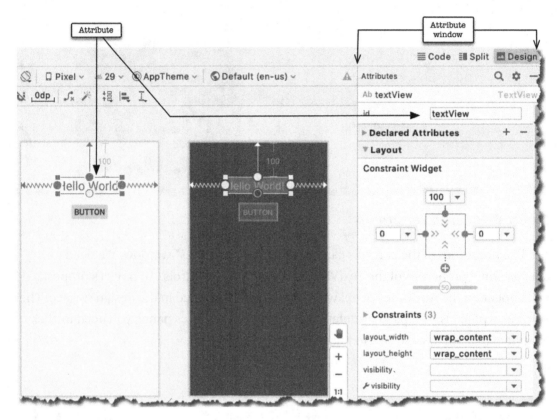

Figure 6-12. *Attributes panel, open*

The Attributes window contains all the properties for the selected View object, but it doesn't show all of them by default. It shows only the properties we commonly use. To view all the properties, scroll further down on the Attributes panel to see the "All Attributes" button, as shown in Figure 6-13.

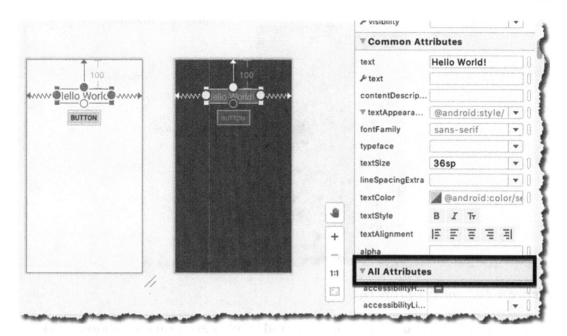

Figure 6-13. *All attributes*

Now that we can move around in the Design editor, we can make some changes. Try to do the following:

1. Change the **id** property of the TextView object from *textView* to *textHello*.

2. Change the textSize property of the TextView object to 36sp.

The View object's id property is very important because we'll refer to it later in our code (in the Activity class).

We will also change the Button's **onClick** property. Select the Button object, then find its **onClick** property, and then turn the value to "addNumber," as shown in Figure 6-14.

Figure 6-14. *onClick property*

Setting the Button's **onClick** property to **addNumber** associates the Button's click event to a method called **addNumber()** in the Activity class. Of course, this method doesn't exist yet; that's why we need to implement it next. Open *MainActivity.java* and make the changes as shown in Listing 6-4.

Listing 6-4. MainActivity.java

```
import androidx.appcompat.app.AppCompatActivity;
import android.os.Bundle;
import android.view.View;
import android.widget.TextView;

public class MainActivity extends AppCompatActivity {

  @Override
  protected void onCreate(Bundle savedInstanceState) {
    super.onCreate(savedInstanceState);
    setContentView(R.layout.activity_main);
    ((TextView) findViewById(R.id.textHello)).setText("1"); ❶
  }
```

```
public void addNumber(View v) { ❷
  TextView tv = ((TextView) findViewById(R.id.textHello)); ❸
  int currVal = Integer.parseInt(tv.getText().toString()); ❹
  tv.setText((++currVal) + ""); ❺
}
}
```

❶   This code sets the TextView's text value to "1". First, we get a reference to the TextView using its **id**. All View objects can be referenced at runtime using the **R.class**, so **R.id.textHello** refers to the instance of the TextView object at runtime. Next, we cast it to a *TextView* object; then, we call the setText() method.

❷   This is the implementation of the **addNumber()** method; it takes a View object as a parameter. When this method is called, the Android Runtime will pass the instance of the Button object as an argument to this method.

❸   This code gets the programmatic reference to the TextView object, the same idea as in ❶, but this time, we assign the object reference to a variable.

❹   **tv.getText()** gets the current value of TextView. This call returns a CharSequence; that's why I needed to call the toString() method on it to make it workable for our purpose. The Integer.parseInt() method converts an alphanumeric digit to an **integer**.

❺   The setText() method sets the value of the TextView. The **++currVal + ""** expression increments the current value of the *currVal* variable and then converts it to a String object; adding an empty String literal to any primitive data type effectively converts it to a String.

When you're done with the edits, run the application on an emulator. Figure 6-15 shows the project running on an emulator.

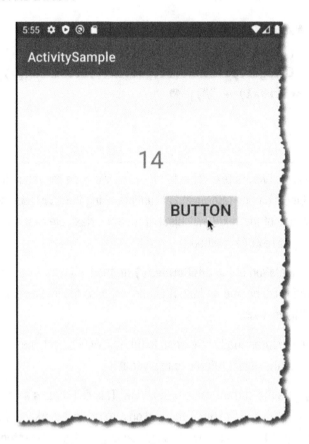

Figure 6-15. *ActivitySample on the emulator*

Summary

- A layout file describes the UI structure in an XML file. You can work with the layout file either in design mode (WYSIWYG) or raw XML mode.

- Each View element in a layout file is described as an XML node, but the XML file is inflated during runtime. The inflation process produces the object representations of the UI elements.

- You can reference UI elements programmatically using the R.class.

- Composite views can be constructed by inheriting from the ViewGroup class.

- Layout managers provide ways to arrange UI elements on a screen. The Android SDK has plenty of prebuilt managers we can use out of the box.

CHAPTER 7

Event Handling

What we'll cover:

- Listener objects

- Anonymous inner classes

In the previous chapter, we already did some event handling. The part of the exercise where we incremented the TextView's value for each button click was an exercise on *declarative event handling*. To bind a method name to a click event, we simply set a View's **android:onClick** attribute to the name of a method in the associated Activity class. This is a low-ceremony and straightforward way to handle events but is limited to the "click" event. When you need to handle events like long clicks or gestures, you need to use event listeners—this is the topic of this chapter.

Intro to Event Handling

The user interacts with your app by touching, clicking, swiping, or typing something. The Android framework captures, stores, processes, and sends these actions to your app as event objects. We respond to these events by writing methods that are specifically designed to handle them. Methods that handle events are written inside *listener objects*—and there's quite a few of them. Figure 7-1 shows a simplified model of how the Android framework and your app handle user actions.

© Ted Hagos 2020
T. Hagos, *Learn Android Studio 4*, https://doi.org/10.1007/978-1-4842-5937-5_7

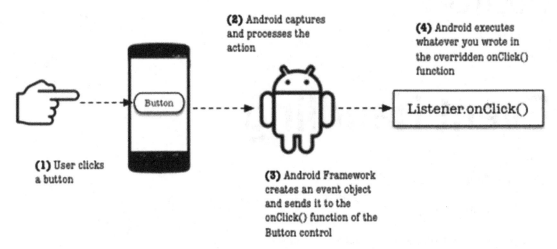

(2) Android captures and processes the action

(4) Android executes whatever you wrote in the overridden onClick() function

Button

Listener.onClick()

(1) User clicks a button

(3) Android Framework creates an event object and sends it to the onClick() function of the Button control

Figure 7-1. *Simplified event handling model*

When a user does something with your app, like clicking a button, the Android framework catches that action and turns it into an event object. An event object contains data about the user's action, for example, which button was clicked, the location of the button when it was clicked, and so on. Android sends this event object to the application, and it calls a specific method that corresponds with the user's action. If the user *clicked* the button, Android would call the **onClick()** method on the Button object; if the user clicks the same button but holds it a bit longer, then the **onLongClick()** method will be called. View objects, like the Button, can respond to a range of events like clicks, keypresses, touch or swipes, and so on. Table 7-1 lists some of the common events and their corresponding event handlers.

Table 7-1. *Common listener objects*

Interface	Method	Description
View.OnClickListener	onClick()	This gets called when the user either touches and holds the control (when in touch mode) or focuses upon the item with the navigation keys and then presses the ENTER key
View.OnLongClickListener	onLongClick()	Almost the same as a click, but only longer

(*continued*)

Table 7-1. (*continued*)

Interface	Method	Description
View.OnFocusChangeListener	onFocusChange()	When the user navigates onto or away from the control
View.OnTouchListener	onTouch()	Almost the same as the click action, but this handler lets you find out if the user swiped up or down. You can use this to respond to gestures
View.OnCreateContext MenuListener	onCreateContext Menu()	Android calls this when a ContextMenu is being built, as a result of a long sustained click

To set up a listener, the View object can set or—more appropriately—register a *listener object*. Registering a listener means you tell the Android framework which method to call when the user interacts with the View object. Figure 7-2 shows an annotated code for registering a listener object.

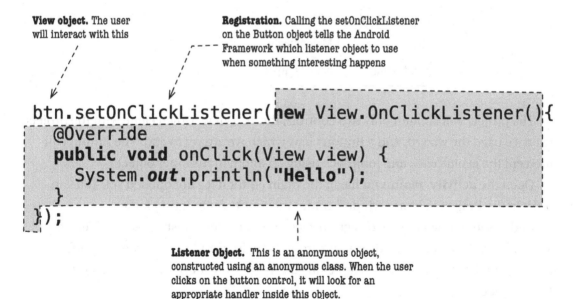

Figure 7-2. *Annotated event registration and handling*

The **setOnClickListener** is a member method of the **android.view.View** class, which means every child class of View has it. The method expects an **OnClickListener** object as an argument—this becomes the listener for the button control. When the button is clicked, the codes inside the **onClick** method will run.

We created the listener object by creating an instance of an anonymous class that inherits from **View.OnClickListener**; this type is declared as a nested interface in the View class.

Now that we know some bits about events, let's put them into practice. Let's create a new project; Table 7-2 shows the details of the project.

Table 7-2. *Project details*

Project detail	Value
Application name	EventHandling
Company domain	Use your website name
Language	Java
Form factor	Phone and tablet only
Minimum SDK	API 29 (Q) Android 10
Type of activity	Empty
Activity name	MainActivity
Layout name	activity_main

The project will contain only two controls, the TextView, which came with the project when we used the wizard, and a Button view, which we are yet to add. The Button will intercept the events click and long click using an anonymous inner object.

Open the **activity_main.xml** file in the main editor if it's not opened yet. You can find it in the Project Explorer window under the *app* ➤ *res* ➤ *layout* folder.

Add a Button object to the design surface and put some constraints on it. You can add a Button to the layout by dragging it from the palette and onto the design surface, just like you did in the previous chapter. Figure 7-3 shows our project with an added Button object.

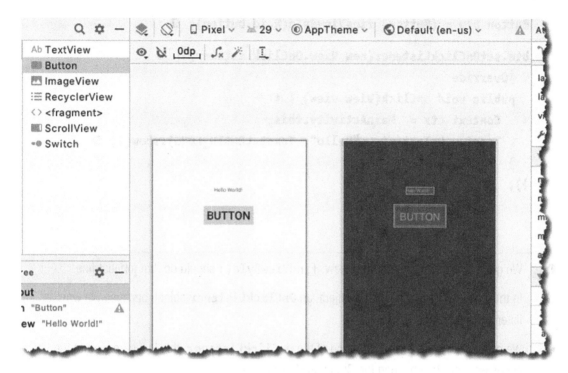

Figure 7-3. *Add a Button View to the project*

We want the Button to respond to the click event, so we'll set up an **OnClickListener** object to do precisely this. Open the MainActivity.java in the main editor and add the event handling code, as shown in Listing 7-1.

Listing 7-1. MainActivity.java

```java
import androidx.appcompat.app.AppCompatActivity;
import android.os.Bundle;
import android.view.View;
import android.widget.Button;
import android.widget.Toast;

public class MainActivity extends AppCompatActivity {

  @Override
  protected void onCreate(Bundle savedInstanceState) {
    super.onCreate(savedInstanceState);
    setContentView(R.layout.activity_main);
```

```java
Button btn = (Button) findViewById(R.id.button); ❶

btn.setOnClickListener(new View.OnClickListener(){ ❷
  @Override
  public void onClick(View view) { ❸
    Context ctx =  MainActivity.this;
    Toast.makeText(ctx, "Hello", Toast.LENGTH_LONG).show(); ❹
  }
});
  }
}
```

❶   We get a reference to the Button View; `findViewById()` should do that job just fine.

❷   In this case, we set up a listener object, an **OnClickListener** object, because we want to listen to click events.

❸   We override the **onClick()** method of the **OnClickListener**; this is where we put the codes we want to run when the Button is clicked.

❹   We display a **Toast** message. A Toast is a small pop-up message that disappears after a couple of seconds. You can use it to send small feedback to the user. Showing a Toast message is a two-step process. The first step is to create a Toast message using the `makeText()` function. It takes three parameters: (1) the context of the application, which in our case is the instance of MainActivity, (2) the message to show, and (3) how long to display it. The second step is to make it visible by calling the **.show()** method.

Figure 7-4 shows the app when the Button is clicked.

Figure 7-4. *Toast message*

Handling Long Clicks

View objects can handle more than one kind of event. We can make our Button respond to both clicks (which we just did) and long clicks (which we're about to do).

We will set up another listener object for the Button object, this time, a listener for long-click events. Like the click listener, we will set up the long-click listener inside the onCreate method of the Activity class, since the Activity doesn't have to be visible before we set up the listeners. If you feel that the **onCreate** method is getting crowded already, feel free to refactor the method and relocate all the event handling codes somewhere else. For our example, I'll keep the event handling codes inside the **onCreate** method. The code for the long-click listener is shown in Listing 7-2.

Listing 7-2. Long-click listener

```
btn.setOnLongClickListener(new View.OnLongClickListener() {
  @Override
  public boolean onLongClick(View view) {

    return true;
  }
});
```

It is very similar to the click handler in construction; we call the **setXXXListener** method and pass an instance of an anonymous *listener* class to it as an argument. We override the method (onLongClick, in this case) of the same listener object and put our codes in it—and that's about it.

We could do another Toast message here, but I thought it might be instructive to use a different feedback mechanism, like Snackbar. Snackbar is like Toast, but instead of floating the text message, Snackbar's message is anchored at the bottom of the screen. You can make it disappear after some timeout (just like Toast) or make the user swipe it away. Snackbar is more capable than Toast because you can include some actions in the message, like a small dialog box.

Before we can proceed, we need to make two changes to the project. We need to

1. Change the value of the layout container's id property. By default, the layout container doesn't have an id, and it's usually okay because we didn't have to refer to it from our Java code. Now, we will have to. The Snackbar's construction requires that we refer to the layout container.

2. Add a dependency in our Gradle file. The Snackbar isn't readily available for use; you will have to include it in the project's dependency file.

Let's deal with the layout file first. Open the *activity_main* layout file, then change the value of the main layout file's id property. By default, the layout container doesn't have a value on its **id** property; we need to give it one right now because we need to reference it in code later.

When activity_main is open in the main editor, switch to design mode; click somewhere in the body of the layout container, as shown in Figure 7-5. In the Attributes panel, edit the **id** property and set the value to **root_layout**.

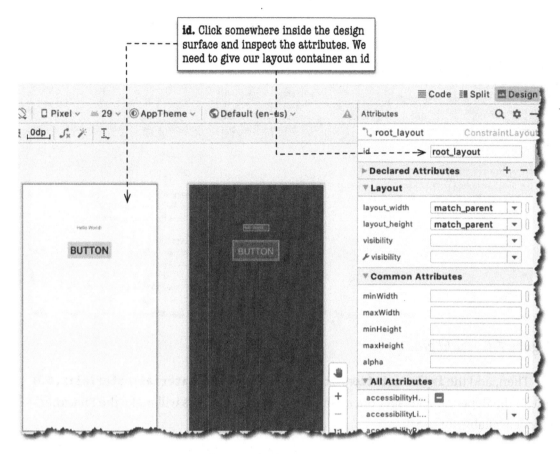

Figure 7-5. Change the id property of the layout container

Next, open the **build.gradle** file. There are two gradle files: one is at the project's root folder, and the other is inside the app folder. It's the latter that we need to update. Open the module-level gradle file by double-clicking the **build.gradle (Module: App)**, as shown in Figure 7-6.

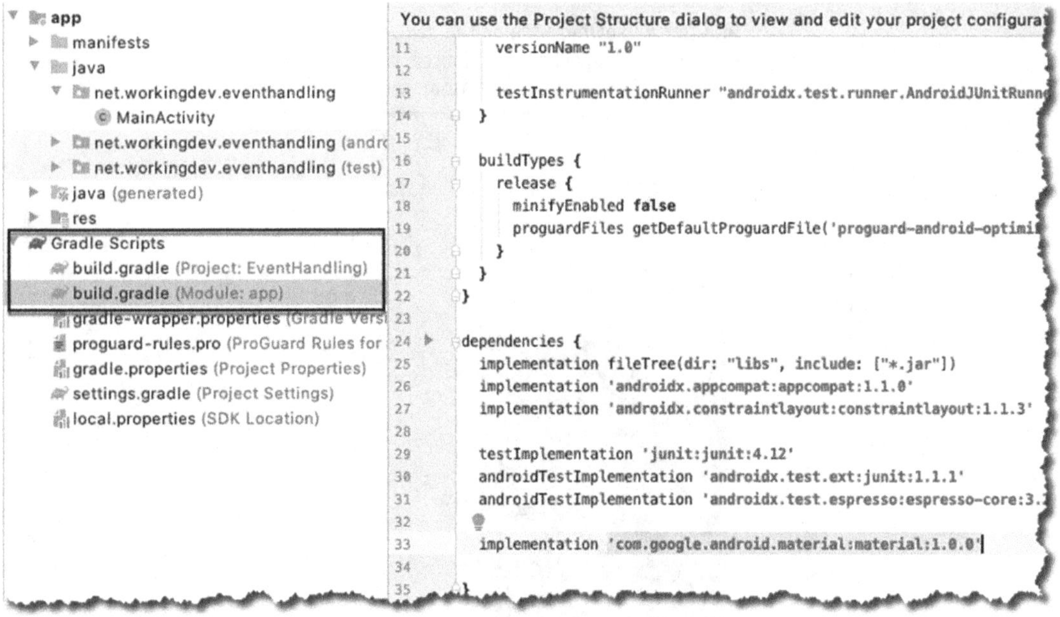

Figure 7-6. *build.gradle file*

Then, add the **implementation 'com.google.android.material:material:1.0.0'** line in the dependencies section, as shown in Listing 7-3. This will make the Snackbar object available for use.

Listing 7-3. The dependencies section of build.gradle

```
dependencies {
  implementation fileTree(dir: "libs", include: ["*.jar"])
  implementation 'androidx.appcompat:appcompat:1.1.0'
  implementation 'androidx.constraintlayout:constraintlayout:1.1.3'

  testImplementation 'junit:junit:4.12'
  androidTestImplementation 'androidx.test.ext:junit:1.1.1'
  androidTestImplementation 'androidx.test.espresso:espresso-core:3.2.0'

  implementation 'com.google.android.material:material:1.0.0'
}
```

Now that we fixed the Gradle file and the layout container id, we can write the Snackbar code; Listing 7-4 shows the code to display a Snackbar.

Listing 7-4. Codes for displaying Snackbar

```
btn.setOnLongClickListener(new View.OnLongClickListener() {
  @Override
  public boolean onLongClick(View view) {
    View vtemp = findViewById(R.id.root_layout);
    Snackbar.make(vtemp,"Long click", Snackbar.LENGTH_LONG).show();
    return true;
  }
});
```

The **onLongClick** method returns a boolean value. We returned *true* from the method to tell the Android Runtime that we have already consumed it; there's no need for other handlers (like **onClick**) to consume it again. Had we returned false, the **onClick** handler would have kicked right in after the onLongClick method returns.

Listing 7-5 shows the full code of MainActivity.java for your reference.

Listing 7-5. Complete code for MainActivity.java

```
import androidx.appcompat.app.AppCompatActivity;
import android.content.Context;
import android.os.Bundle;
import android.view.View;
import android.widget.Button;
import android.widget.Toast;
import com.google.android.material.snackbar.Snackbar;

public class MainActivity extends AppCompatActivity {

  @Override
  protected void onCreate(Bundle savedInstanceState) {
    super.onCreate(savedInstanceState);
    setContentView(R.layout.activity_main);

    Button btn = (Button) findViewById(R.id.button);
```

```
btn.setOnClickListener(new View.OnClickListener(){
  @Override
  public void onClick(View view) {
    Context ctx =  MainActivity.this;
    Toast.makeText(ctx, "Hello", Toast.LENGTH_LONG).show();
  }
});

btn.setOnLongClickListener(new View.OnLongClickListener() {
  @Override
  public boolean onLongClick(View view) {
    View vtemp = findViewById(R.id.root_layout);
    Snackbar.make(vtemp,"Long click", Snackbar.LENGTH_LONG).show();
    return true;
  }
});
  }
}
```

Figure 7-7 shows the app on the emulator after a long click to the Button.

Figure 7-7. *App showing the Snackbar message*

Summary

- You can set the **android:onClick** attribute to a name of a function if you want to handle simple click events.

- Listener objects must be registered to the Android Runtime if you're going to intercept certain events.

- There are many kinds of listener objects, and they are listed as nested interfaces in the View class.

- You can associate multiple listeners to the same View object.

- Make sure to return false on an **onLongClick** method, if you don't want other event handlers to handle it.

CHAPTER 8

Intents

What we'll cover:

- Intent overview

- Explicit and implicit Intents

- Passing data between activities

- Returning results from Intents

Android's architecture is unique in the way it builds applications. It has this notion of components instead of just plain objects. And the way that Android makes these components interact is something that you can only find in the Android platform. Android uses Intents as a way for its components to communicate; it uses it to pass messages across components. In this chapter, we'll look at Intents, what they are, and how we use them.

What Intents Are

An Intent is an abstract description of an operation to be performed. It's a unique Android concept because no other platform uses the same thing as a means of component activation. In the earlier chapters, we looked at what's inside an Android application. You might remember that an app is just a bunch of "components" (see Figure 8-1) that are loosely held together, and each component is declared in the AndroidManifest file.

© Ted Hagos 2020
T. Hagos, *Learn Android Studio 4*, https://doi.org/10.1007/978-1-4842-5937-5_8

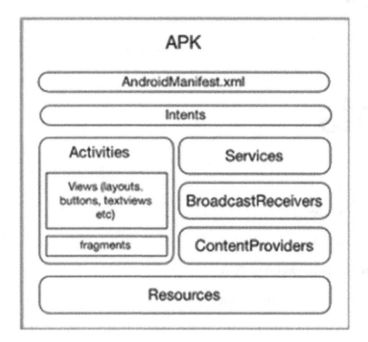

Figure 8-1. *Logical representation of an Android App*

Launching an Activity isn't as simple as creating an instance of a particular Activity class. It's a bit more involved than that. An Activity isn't merely an object; it's a component, and component activation in Android requires the use of Intents.

To launch an Activity, we need to create an Intent object, tell this Intent object what we want to activate, and then launch it. After that, the Android Runtime tries to resolve the Intent, and if successful, the target component gets activated. In code, it looks like this:

```
Intent intent = new Intent(context, target);
startActivity(intent);
```

where

- **context**—Is a reference to the component that wants to initiate or launch the Intent.

- **target**—Is a class object; this is the component you want to launch.

A typical scenario when launching an Activity (usually from the MainActivity) is when a user clicks a button or selects a menu item.

To try this out, you will need a project with two Activities. You already know how to create a project with an empty Activity, so just create that; presumably, the first Activity class' name is MainActivity. To add another Activity, we can use the context menu. On the Project tool window, right-click the app folder (assuming you're on the Android scope, which is the default), then choose **New ➤ Activity ➤ Empty Activity**, as shown in Figure 8-2.

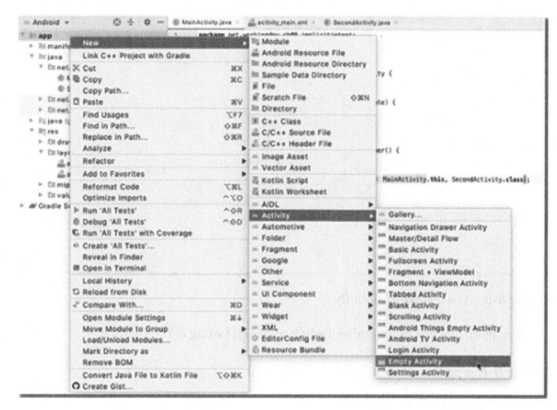

Figure 8-2. *New Empty Activity*

In the window that follows, type the second Activity name, as shown in Figure 8-3. Adopt the suggested layout name (or change it to your liking), and make sure it's on the same Java package and that the source language is Java. Click **Finish** to proceed.

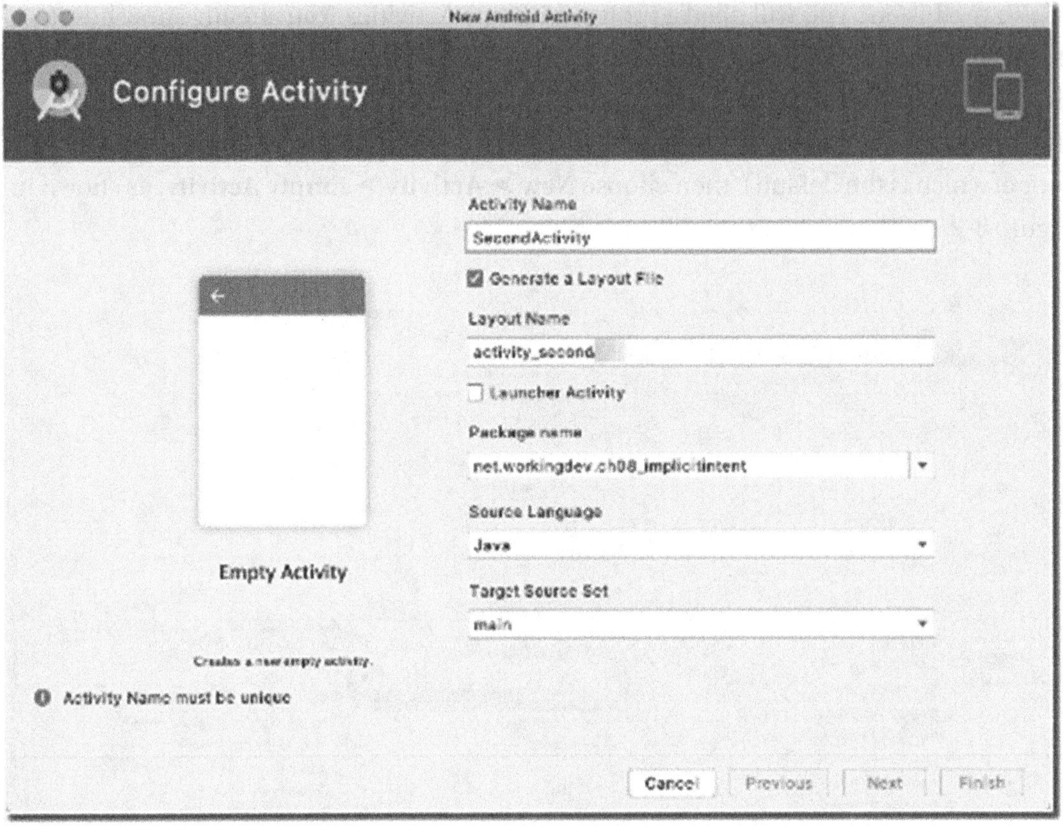

Figure 8-3. *New Android Activity*

Next, open *activity_main.xml* and edit it to match Listing 8-1.

Listing 8-1. app/res/layout/activity_main.xml

```xml
<?xml version="1.0" encoding="utf-8"?>
<androidx.constraintlayout.widget.ConstraintLayout
xmlns:android="http://schemas.android.com/apk/res/android"
  xmlns:app="http://schemas.android.com/apk/res-auto"
  xmlns:tools="http://schemas.android.com/tools"
  android:layout_width="match_parent"
  android:layout_height="match_parent"
  tools:context=".MainActivity">
```

```
<Button
  android:id="@+id/button"
  android:layout_width="wrap_content"
  android:layout_height="wrap_content"
  android:layout_marginTop="78dp"
  android:text="Button"
  app:layout_constraintEnd_toEndOf="parent"
  app:layout_constraintStart_toStartOf="parent"
  app:layout_constraintTop_toTopOf="parent" />
</androidx.constraintlayout.widget.ConstraintLayout>
```

What I've done in the activity_main layout was to remove the default TextView object and replaced it with a Button View (whose **id** is *button*).

Now we can work on MainActivity. We need to attach a click handler to the Button, and on that handler, we create and launch an Intent. Listing 8-2 shows the annotated code to do that.

Listing 8-2. MainActivity

```
import androidx.appcompat.app.AppCompatActivity;
import android.content.Intent;
import android.os.Bundle;
import android.view.View;
import android.widget.Button;

public class MainActivity extends AppCompatActivity {

  @Override
  protected void onCreate(Bundle savedInstanceState) {
    super.onCreate(savedInstanceState);
    setContentView(R.layout.activity_main);

    Button btn = findViewById(R.id.button); ❶
    btn.setOnClickListener(new View.OnClickListener() { ❷
```

```
    @Override
    public void onClick(View view) {
        Intent intent = new Intent(MainActivity.this, SecondActivity.
        class); ❸
        startActivity(intent); ❹
    }
});
}
}
```

---

❶   Let's get a reference to the Button View.

❷   Create an OnClickListener object and bind it to the Button object.

❸   Inside the **onClick()** method, let's create an Intent object. The first parameter is a Context object, which is supposed to refer to MainActivity. I wrote **MainActivity.this** and not merely **this** because currently we're making the call inside a click handler (which is an anonymous class); **this** would refer to the anonymous class' instance and not to MainActivity. To be explicit, we refer to the context of MainActivity as **MainActivity.this**. Alternatively, you can also pass the Application Context as the first parameter. You can get the Application Context using the method getApplicationContext(). The second parameter is the class object of the component we want to launch, which is SecondActivity; so, we pass **SecondActivity.class**.

❹   Finally, we call the **startActivity()** method of MainActivity, and we pass the Intent object as the parameter; this will launch the Intent.

If you run the app now, the SecondActivity will launch when you click the Button on MainActivity. In this example, we told the Intent object what component we wanted to activate (SecondActivity). This kind of Intent object is called an explicit Intent, simply because we're very precise on what we want to activate. Another type of Intent is called an implicit Intent, which is what we'll discuss in the next section.

Implicit Intents

There are two kinds of Intent, an implicit and an explicit one. You can think of the two types of Intent this way; let's imagine asking someone to buy some sugar. If we instruct "could you please buy some sugar" with no further details, this would be equivalent to an implicit Intent because that person could buy the sugar anywhere. On the other hand, if we gave instructions like "could you please go to the ABC store on third street and buy some sugar," this would be equivalent to an explicit Intent. Our earlier example in Listing 8-2 is an explicit Intent because we told the Intent specifically which component to activate.

Implicit Intents, on the other hand, are very powerful because they allow an application to take advantage of other applications. Your app can gain functionalities that you did not write yourself. For example, you can create an Intent that opens the camera, shoots, and saves a photo, without writing any camera-specific code.

The purpose of implicit Intent is for you to use a functionality that doesn't exist within your app, because if the feature exists within your app, you would have used explicit Intents in the first place. Using an implicit Intent is a way to ask the Android Runtime to find an application somewhere on the device that can service your request.

In an explicit Intent, we tell the Intent which specific component to activate. In an implicit Intent, we tell the Intent what we'd like to do instead; for example, if we wanted to launch a browser and navigate to `https://apress.com`, here's how to do it:

1. Create an Intent object.

2. Tell it what to do by specifying some actions, for example, "view a map," "call a number," "take a picture," "view a web page," and so on.

3. Give it some information or data; for example, if we want to launch a browser and navigate to a specific web page, we need to tell the Intent the URI of the web page.

4. Finally, we launch the Intent.

Listing 8-3 shows how to do this in code.

Listing 8-3. Example Intent to browse a web page

```
Intent intent = new Intent(); ❶
intent.setAction(Intent.ACTION_VIEW); ❷
intent.setData(Uri.parse("https://apress.com")); ❸
startActivity(intent); ❹
```

❶   Create the Intent object using the no-arg constructor.

❷   Set the Intent action. In this example, we'd like to view something; it could be a contact, a web page, a map, a picture somewhere, and so on. At this point, the Android Runtime doesn't know yet what you want to view. **ACTION_VIEW** is one of the many Intent Actions you can use. You can find other kinds of Action in the official Android's website: `https://developer.android.com/guide/components/intents-common`.

❸   Set its data. At this point, the Android Runtime has a pretty good idea of what you want to do. In this example, the Uri is a web page. Android is pretty smart to figure out that we'd like to view a web page.

❹   Android will search every app on the device, which will best match this request. If it finds more than one app, it will let the user choose which one. If it finds only one, it will simply launch that app.

Alternatively, you can set the Intent's action and data by passing them to the Intent's constructor, like this:

```
Intent intent = new Intent(Intent.ACTION_VIEW,
Uri.parse("https://apress.com"));
```

Any component that can respond to this Intent does not need to be running to receive the Intent. Remember that all applications need to have a manifest file. Each application declares its capabilities in the manifest file, specifically through the **<intent-filter>** section. Android's package manager has all the info of all the applications installed on the device. Android's runtime only needs the information on the manifest file to see which among the apps are capable or eligible to respond to the Intent. The Android Runtime inspects the Intent object's content and then compares it to the Intent filters of all components. An Intent filter is a way for Android components to declare their capabilities to the Android system.

To see this in action, let's create another project with an empty Activity. Assuming you've already done that, let's work on the MainActivity class. We will create three action triggers; we could use Buttons, but let's use the Options menu for this exercise. Listing 8-4 shows the annotated code for MainActivity.

Listing 8-4. MainActivity

```java
import androidx.annotation.NonNull;
import androidx.appcompat.app.AppCompatActivity;
import android.content.Intent;
import android.net.Uri;
import android.os.Bundle;
import android.util.Log;
import android.view.Menu;
import android.view.MenuItem;

public class MainActivity extends AppCompatActivity {

  private final String TAG = getClass().getName();

  @Override
  protected void onCreate(Bundle savedInstanceState) {
    super.onCreate(savedInstanceState);
    setContentView(R.layout.activity_main);

  }

  @Override
  public boolean onCreateOptionsMenu(Menu menu) { ❶
    menu.add("View Apress"); ❷
    menu.add("View Map");
    menu.add("Call number");
    return super.onCreateOptionsMenu(menu);
  }

  @Override
  public boolean onOptionsItemSelected(@NonNull MenuItem item) { ❸

    Intent intent = null;
    Uri uri;
    switch(item.toString()) {  ❹
      case "View Apress":
        Log.d(TAG, "View Action");
        uri = Uri.parse("https://apress.com");
```

```
      intent = new Intent(Intent.ACTION_VIEW, uri); ❺
      break;
   case "View Map":
     uri = Uri.parse(("geo:40.7113399,-74.0263469"));
     intent = new Intent(Intent.ACTION_VIEW, uri); ❻
     break;
   case "Call number":
     Log.d(TAG, "Call number");
     uri = Uri.parse(("tel:639285083333"));
     intent = new Intent(Intent.ACTION_CALL, uri); ❼
  }
  startActivity(intent);

  return true;
 }
}
```

❶   Let's override the **onCreateOptionsMenu()** callback; this will be called shortly after
    the **onCreate()** callback. Overriding this method allows us to build a dynamic menu
    programmatically.

❷   Add a menu item dynamically.

❸   Whenever the user clicks one of the Menu Items, the **onOptionsItemSelected** is called; this
    is where we will handle the menu clicks.

❹   The item parameter can tell us which Menu Item was clicked. We're converting it to String to
    use it to route our program logic using a switch statement.

❺   Create an Intent and set its action and data to view the Apress website.

❻   Create an Intent and set its action and data to view a location.

❼   Create an Intent and set its action and data to call a specific number.

Figure 8-4 shows the app at runtime.

Figure 8-4. Implicit Intent project, running

Summary

- Intents are used for component activation.

- There are two kinds of Intents, implicit and explicit ones.

- Explicit Intents let us work with multiple activities. You can activate a specific Activity using an explicit Intent.

- Implicit Intents extend the functionality of your application. They allow your application to do things that are outside the functionality of your app.

CHAPTER 9

Fragments

What we'll cover:

- Introduction to Fragments

- The Fragment class and Fragment resource file

- Adding Fragments to Activities dynamically

In the early days of Android, when it ran only on phones, and there weren't any high-resolution screens, activities were sufficient to compose the UI and interact with the user. Then came the tablets and high-resolution displays. It became increasingly difficult to create applications that can run well on both phones and tablets. Developers were faced with hard choices. Either you choose the least capable hardware as the target and make it like the least common denominator or make the app adapt to a range of form factors by removing and adding UI elements in response to the device's capability, which proved to be very difficult to do manually. When API 11 (Honeycomb) came out, Android solved this problem with Fragments; this is the topic of this chapter.

Introduction to Fragments

If we think of an activity as a composition unit for our UI, think of a fragment as a mini-activity—it's a smaller composition unit. You will usually show (and hide) fragments during runtime in response to something that a user did, for example, tilting the device, switching from portrait to landscape orientation, thus making more screen space available. You may even use fragments as a strategy to adapt to device form factors. When the app is running on a smaller screen, you will show only some of the fragments.

Like an activity, a fragment comprises two parts—a Java program and a layout file. The idea is almost the same—define the UI elements in an XML file and then inflate the XML file in a program file so that all the view objects in the XML will become an object.

T. Hagos, *Learn Android Studio 4*, https://doi.org/10.1007/978-1-4842-5937-5_9

After that, we can reference each view object in the XML using the **R.class**. Think of a fragment as an ordinary view object that we can drag and drop on the main layout file.

To create a Fragment, we generally do the following:

1. Create an XML resource file and put it in the **/app/res/layout** folder, just like where we put **activity_main.xml**.

2. Give the new resource file a descriptive name, say fragment_ booktitles.

3. Create the Fragment class; this class must inherit **androidx. fragment.app.Fragment**—all support libraries are now in the **androidx** package.

4. Next, hook up the Fragment class with the XML resource layout. You can inflate the XML resource file in the **onCreate()** method of the Fragment class.

5. Make some changes to MainActivity. The default MainActivity inherits from AppCompatActivity; this is usually fine, but we are using the Fragment class from the support library, which means we need to inherit from FragmentActivity instead of the default AppCompatActivity.

6. Add the newly created Fragment.

Let's do them in Android Studio. First, create a project with an empty Activity, just like all the other projects we've created.

Let's create an XML resource file and put it in **/app/res/layout**. You can do that by right-clicking the project's layout folder, then choosing **New ➤ Layout Resource File**, as shown in Figure 9-1.

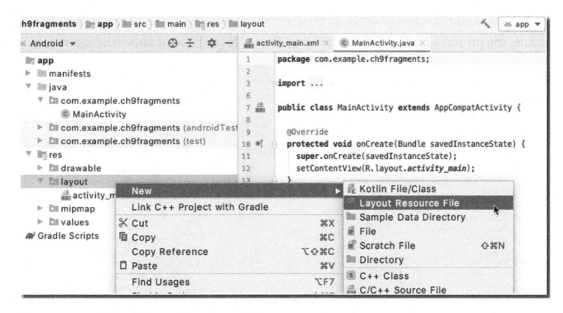

Figure 9-1. *New Layout Resource File*

In the window that follows, type the filename of the new resource file (fragment_ booktitles), as shown in Figure 9-2.

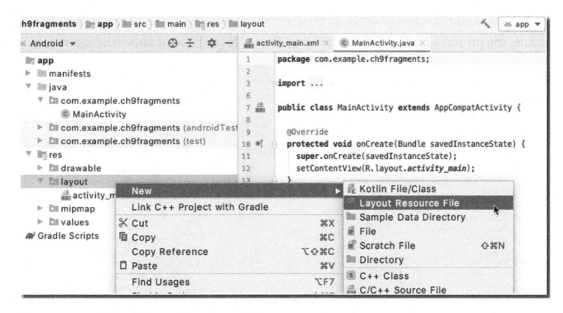

Figure 9-2. *New Resource File*

Next, let's add a fragment class. To do that, add a Java class to the project by right-clicking the project's package, then choosing **New ➤ Java Class**, as shown in Figure 9-3.

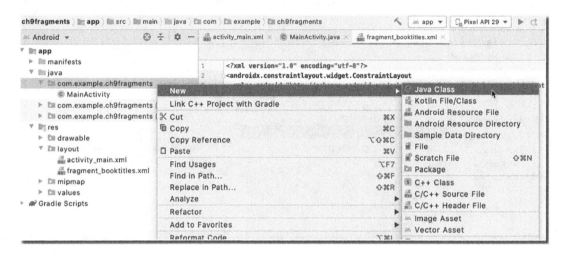

Figure 9-3. *Add a Java class*

In the pop-up window that follows, type the name of the new Java class (BookTitle), as shown in Figure 9-4.

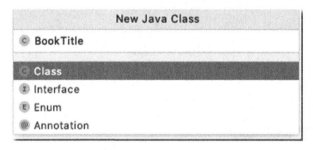

Figure 9-4. *New Java Class*

Edit the fragment_booktitles layout file to match Listing 9-1. You can add whatever View component you want to add; for my purpose, I simply added a TextView object.

Listing 9-1. app/res/layout/fragment_booktitles.xml

```
<?xml version="1.0" encoding="utf-8"?>
<androidx.constraintlayout.widget.ConstraintLayout
xmlns:android="http://schemas.android.com/apk/res/android"
  xmlns:app="http://schemas.android.com/apk/res-auto"
```

```
xmlns:tools="http://schemas.android.com/tools"
android:layout_width="match_parent"
android:layout_height="match_parent">

<TextView
    android:id="@+id/textView"
    android:layout_width="wrap_content"
    android:layout_height="wrap_content"
    android:layout_marginTop="122dp"
    android:text="MyFragment"
    android:textSize="36sp"
    app:layout_constraintEnd_toEndOf="parent"
    app:layout_constraintStart_toStartOf="parent"
    app:layout_constraintTop_toTopOf="parent" />
</androidx.constraintlayout.widget.ConstraintLayout>
```

Next, modify the BookTitle class to match Listing 9-2.

Listing 9-2. BookTitle class

```java
import android.os.Bundle;
import android.view.LayoutInflater;
import android.view.View;
import android.view.ViewGroup;

import androidx.annotation.NonNull;
import androidx.annotation.Nullable;
import androidx.fragment.app.Fragment;
import static com.example.ch9fragments.R.layout.*;

public class BookTitle extends Fragment {

    @Nullable
    @Override
    public View onCreateView(@NonNull LayoutInflater inflater,
                             @Nullable ViewGroup container,
                             @Nullable Bundle savedInstanceState) {
```

```
    final View view = inflater.inflate(fragment_booktitles, container,
    false);
    return view;
  }
}
```

We can associate the fragment layout file (fragment_booktitles) with the fragment class (BookTitle) by inflating the layout file and returning it from within the **onCreateView()** callback.

The **onCreateView()** callback is similar to the **onCreate()** method of the Activity class, but be careful not to refer to any View element here because they won't be available just yet. If you need to refer to any View element contained in the fragment layout file, you have to do that in the **onViewCreated()** callback (not shown here). The reason you can't refer to any View element inside the **onCreateView()** callback is because you have yet to inflate the layout resource file, so, naturally, they won't be there just yet.

Next, let's edit MainActivity. We need to change the parent class of MainActivity from AppCompactActivity to FragmentActivity—because we're using Fragments. Listing 9-3 shows the code for MainActivity.

Listing 9-3. MainActivity

```
import androidx.fragment.app.FragmentActivity;

import android.os.Bundle;
import android.view.View;
import android.widget.Button;

public class MainActivity extends FragmentActivity {

  @Override
  protected void onCreate(Bundle savedInstanceState) {
    super.onCreate(savedInstanceState);
    setContentView(R.layout.activity_main);

  }
}
```

If you want to display the fragment we created, you can edit the activity_main layout file, then drag and drop the **<fragment>** element from the palette (as shown in Figure 9-5). When you run the app, the fragment will appear in the Activity like any other View element.

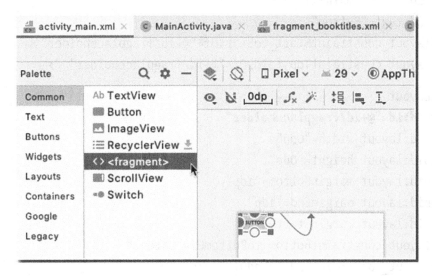

Figure 9-5. *<fragment>*

Alternatively, you can display the fragment programmatically. To do that, we need a placeholder for the fragment and perhaps a Button element (to serve as an action trigger for when we're about to display the fragment). Edit **activity_main.xml** to match Listing 9-4.

Listing 9-4. app/res/layout/activity_main

```
<androidx.constraintlayout.widget.ConstraintLayout
xmlns:android="http://schemas.android.com/apk/res/android"
  xmlns:app="http://schemas.android.com/apk/res-auto"
  xmlns:tools="http://schemas.android.com/tools"
  android:layout_width="match_parent"
  android:layout_height="match_parent"
  tools:context=".MainActivity">
```

```
<Button
  android:id="@+id/button"
  android:layout_width="wrap_content"
  android:layout_height="wrap_content"
  android:layout_marginTop="1dp"
  android:text="Button"
  app:layout_constraintStart_toStartOf="@+id/fragplaceholder"
  app:layout_constraintTop_toTopOf="@+id/fragplaceholder" />

<FrameLayout
  android:id="@+id/fragplaceholder"
  android:layout_width="0dp"
  android:layout_height="0dp"
  android:layout_marginBottom="1dp"
  android:layout_marginEnd="1dp"
  android:layout_marginStart="1dp"
  app:layout_constraintBottom_toBottomOf="parent"
  app:layout_constraintEnd_toEndOf="parent"
  app:layout_constraintHorizontal_bias="1.0"
  app:layout_constraintStart_toStartOf="parent"
  app:layout_constraintTop_toTopOf="parent"
  app:layout_constraintVertical_bias="0.0">

</FrameLayout>
</androidx.constraintlayout.widget.ConstraintLayout>
```

I've added a Button and a FrameLayout container to **activity_main**. I gave the FrameLayout an id of **fragplaceholder** (you can give it any name you like) so I can refer to it later.

Adding a Fragment to the MainActivity (dynamically) requires the use of a FragmentTransaction object. To get a FragmentTransaction object, we also need a FragmentManager object. It's usually done like this:

```
FragmentManager fm = getSupportFragmentManager();
FragmentTransaction ft = fm.beginTransaction();
```

Now, we can make fragment transactions. To add the BookTitle fragment to MainActivity, we need two things:

1. An instance of BookTitle

2. A ViewGroup which to place the fragment; this is our FrameLayout object

In code, it looks like this:

```
BookTitle booktitle = new BookTitle();
FragmentManager fm = getSupportFragmentManager();
FragmentTransaction ft = fm.beginTransaction();
ft.add(R.id.fragplaceholder, booktitle);
ft.commit();
```

To put this all in context, edit MainActivity to match Listing 9-5, which contains the complete code for our small demo app for fragments.

Listing 9-5. MainActivity, complete listing

```
import androidx.fragment.app.FragmentActivity;
import androidx.fragment.app.FragmentManager;
import androidx.fragment.app.FragmentTransaction;

import android.os.Bundle;
import android.view.View;
import android.widget.Button;

public class MainActivity extends FragmentActivity {
  @Override
  protected void onCreate(Bundle savedInstanceState) {
    super.onCreate(savedInstanceState);
    setContentView(R.layout.activity_main);

    Button btn = findViewById(R.id.button);
    btn.setOnClickListener(new View.OnClickListener() {
      @Override
      public void onClick(View v) {
        BookTitle booktitle = new BookTitle();
```

```
        FragmentManager fm = getSupportFragmentManager();
        FragmentTransaction ft = fm.beginTransaction();
        ft.add(R.id.fragplaceholder, booktitle);
        ft.commit();
      }
    });
  }
}
```

When the app runs, it won't show the fragment just yet. When you click the Button, the BookTitle fragment will be displayed.

Figure 9-6 shows the fragment app running in an emulator.

Figure 9-6. *Fragment app*

Summary

- To create a fragment, you need a layout resource file and a Java class (inheriting from **androidx.fragment.app.FragmentActivity**).

- To associate a Fragment class with a fragment layout file, inflate the layout file inside the class' onCreateView() callback method.

- To add Fragments programmatically, you need to use FragmentManager and FragmentTransaction objects.

CHAPTER 10

Navigation

What we'll cover:

- Review of navigation techniques in Android
- Navigation components from Jetpack

Navigation Before Architecture Components

In the early days of Android development, most nontrivial apps have more than one screen, and the UI was partitioned across multiple Activities. That meant you needed the skill to navigate from one Activity to another and back. So, during those days, you might have written something that looks like the code in Listing 10-1.

Listing 10-1. How to launch an Activity

```java
class FirstActivity extends AppCompatActivity
  implements View.OnClickListener {

  public void onClick(View v) {
    Intent intent = new Intent(this, SecondActivity.class);
    startActivity(intent);
  }
}

// SecondActivity.java
class SecondActivity extends AppCompatActivity { }
```

If you needed to pass data from one Activity to another, you might have coded it like the code snippet shown in Listing 10-2.

© Ted Hagos 2020
T. Hagos, *Learn Android Studio 4*, https://doi.org/10.1007/978-1-4842-5937-5_10

Listing 10-2. How to pass data to another Activity

```
Intent intent = new Intent(this, SecondActivity.class);
Intent.putExtra("key", value);
startActivity(intent);
```

This kind of screen management has the following advantages:

- It's simple to do; just call the **startActivity()** method from any Activity.

- The currently running Activity can be closed programmatically by calling the **finish()** method. The user can also close the Activity by pressing the back button.

- The back stack is completely managed by the Android Runtime; see Figure 10-1.

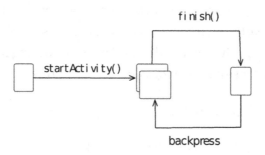

Figure 10-1. *Simple activity workflow*

But not all is well; Activity navigation comes with some baggage. The disadvantages are

- We don't have a clear idea which Activities are on the back stack—because we don't manage it; here is an example of a trait being both an advantage and disadvantage at the same time.

- Each screen requires a new Activity, which drains computing resources.

- Each Activity was declared on the Android manifest file—which Android Studio does for you automatically each time you create an Activity using the wizards, so it's not much of an issue; it was an issue before Android Studio came along.

- It will be difficult for you to use the more modern navigation patterns like bottom navigation bar.

Because of these limitations, another way of screen navigation emerged. Sometime in 2011 when Google released Android 4.0, we got **Fragments**. We just dealt with Fragments in the previous chapter, so I'm sure it's still very fresh for you; an Activity is basically a composition unit for the UI, and the Fragment is just a smaller composition unit.

A Fragment, like an Activity, is comprised of two parts—a Java or Kotlin program and a layout file. The idea is basically the same—define the UI in an XML file and then inflate the XML file during runtime so that all the UI in the XML file become actual Java objects.

The idea is to create multiple fragments and contain them in a single Activity. You would generally hide or show a Fragment depending on either a user action, the orientation of the device, or the form factor of the device; and this is usually done with the *FragmentManager* and *FragmentTransaction* objects. The code snippet in Listing 10-3 is a typical fragment management code.

Listing 10-3. Fragment snippet

```
FragmentManager fm = getFragmentManager();
FragmentTransaction ft = fm.beginTransaction();
Fragment fragment = new FirstFragment();
ft.add(R.id.fragment_container, fragment);
ft.commit();
```

With Fragments, we know exactly what's in the navigation stack, unlike when we're using Activity navigation; but, as you can see in Listing 10-3, it can get cumbersome because we must manually manage the navigation stack.

Thus far, we only had two options for navigation: either we use Activity-based navigation, which was easy and simple to use but we take some performance penalty and we don't have control over the navigation stack, or we use Fragments which offered us full control of the navigation stack, but the API is cumbersome and prone to error.

Fast forward to 2017 when Google introduced the Navigation components. Now we can use Fragments but without the baggage of the complicated API. With Navigation components, all the codes we've written in Listing 10-3 can now be replaced with a single line of code (see Listing 10-4).

Listing 10-4. Navigation component snippet

```
findNavController().navigate(destination);

// WE NO LONGER NEED THE FF CODES
/*
  FragmentManager fm = getFragmentManager();
  FragmentTransaction ft = fm.beginTransaction();
  Fragment fragment = new FirstFragment();
  ft.add(R.id.fragment_container, fragment);
  ft.commit();
*/
```

Navigation Components

Alright, that single line of code reference from the previous section probably got you excited—and relieved. But it's not the savings of keystrokes that's the big picture here, it's the fact that now we can get the best of both Activity-based and Fragment-based navigation. Now, Fragment navigation also has an easy API.

But first, we need to understand a bit about Navigation components. It's a small part of Architecture components, which is in turn a part of a bigger thing called Android Jetpack—we're not getting into Jetpack nor Architecture components in detail here; they are large topics, but a brief background can't hurt.

At Google I/O 2017, Google introduces the Android Architecture components. These libraries are part of a larger collection called Android Jetpack. Together with Architecture components, there were others like Foundation, Behavior, and UI.

Jetpack is a collection of Android software components. It helps us follow the best practices and lets us avoid writing too much boilerplate code. You'll find the Jetpack codes in the **androidx.*** package libraries.

Here's a brief description of the Jetpack components:

Foundation

- **AppCompat**—Lets you write code that degrade gracefully on older versions of Android

- **Android KTX**—So you write more concise, idiomatic Kotlin code, if you're using Kotlin

- **Multidex**—Provides support for apps with multiple DEX files

- **Test**—A testing framework for unit and runtime UI tests

Behavior

- **Download manager**—Lets you write programs that schedule and manage large downloads

- **Media and playback**—Backward-compatible APIs for media playback and routing

- **Notifications**—Provide a backward-compatible notification API with support for wear and auto

- **Permissions**—Compatibility APIs for checking and requesting app permissions

- **Preferences**—Create interactive settings screens

- **Sharing**—Provides a share action suitable for an app's action bar

- **Slices**—Create flexible UI elements that can display app data outside the app

UI

- **Animations and transitions**—Move widgets and transition between screens.

- **Auto**—If you're working on apps that will run in vehicles' infotainment consoles, you'll need this. These are the components that help you build apps for Android Auto.

- **Emoji**—Enables an up-to-date emoji font on older platforms.

- **Fragment**—All the Fragment codes already moved here.

- **Layout**—Layout widgets using different algorithms.

- **Palette**—Pulls useful information out of color palettes.

- **TV**—Components to help develop apps for Android TV.

- **Wear OS by Google**—If you want to work with Android wearables like the watch, this is what you need.

Architecture

- **Data binding**—Declaratively binds observable data to UI elements.

- **Lifecycles**—Manage Activity and Fragment lifecycles.

- **LiveData**—Notify views when underlying database changes.

- **Paging**—Gradually load information on demand from your data source; think when the user is scrolling through a list, this helps you handle the loading of data. It's coupled with the Recycler view.

- **ViewModel**—Manages UI-related data in a lifecycle-conscious way.

- **WorkManager**—Manages background jobs.

- **Navigation**—Implementation of navigation in an app. Passes data between screens. Provides deep links from outside the app.

- **Room**—Think ORM for your SQLite database.

There's a lot to explore in Jetpack, so make sure you check them out.

Going back to our topic, the Navigation components simplify the implementation of, well, navigation between destinations in an app. A destination is any place in your app. It could be an Activity, a fragment inside an Activity, or a custom view; and destinations are managed using a navigation graph.

A navigation graph groups all the destinations and defines the different connections between the destinations; these connections are called **actions**. The graph is simply an XML resource file which represents all your app's navigation paths. You can have more than one navigation graph in your app.

Working with Jetpack Navigation

To get a better appreciation of the Navigation components, it's best if you can work on a small project. So, create a new empty project in Android Studio, as shown in Figure 10-2.

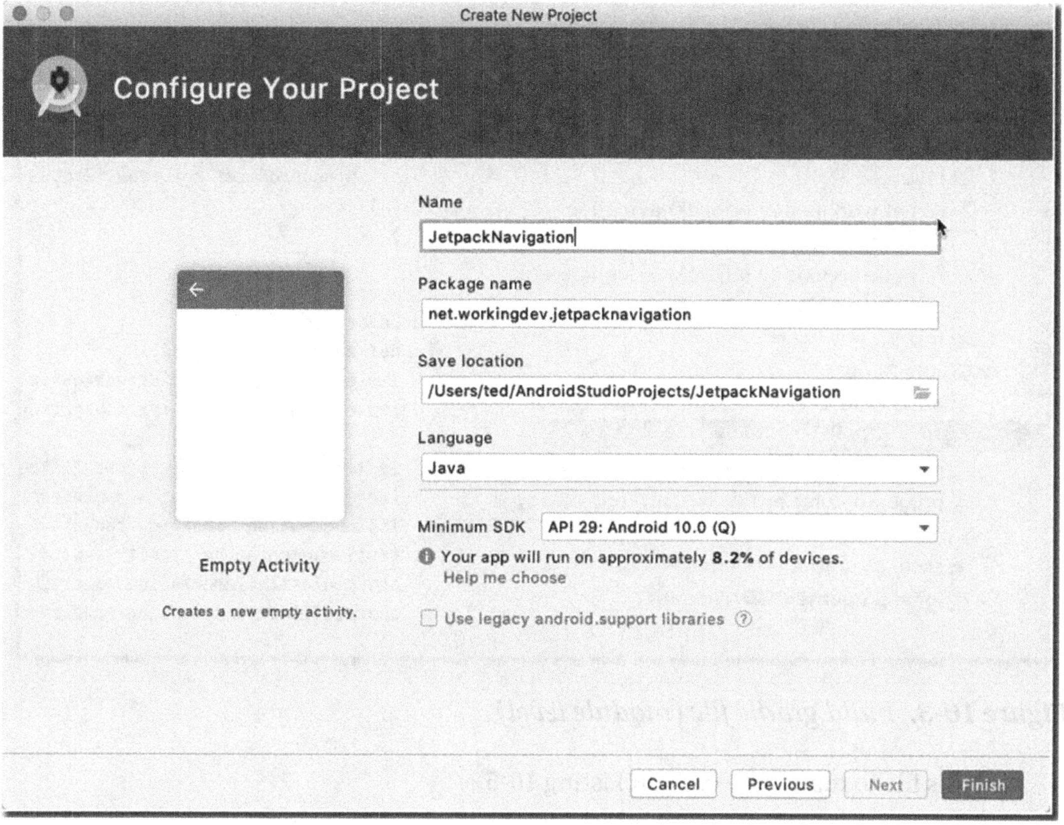

Figure 10-2. *New empty project*

Next, we need to add the Navigation component dependencies. You can do this in the module-level **build.gradle** file (shown in Figure 10-3). Mind that there are two build. gradle files; you want the one that says (Module: app).

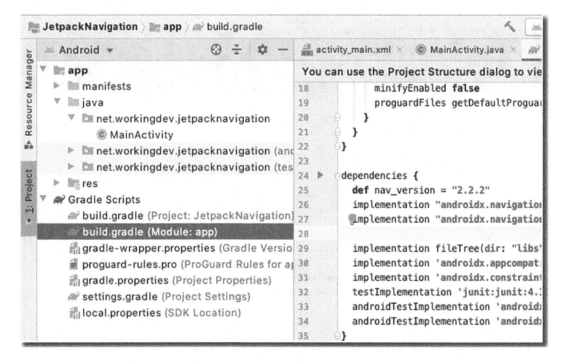

Figure 10-3. *build.gradle file (module level)*

Edit this file to match the code in Listing 10-5.

Listing 10-5. Add navigation to build.gradle

```
dependencies {
    def nav_version = "2.2.2"
    implementation "androidx.navigation:navigation-fragment:$nav_version"
    implementation "androidx.navigation:navigation-ui:$nav_version"

    implementation fileTree(dir: "libs", include: ["*.jar"])
    implementation 'androidx.appcompat:appcompat:1.1.0'
    implementation 'androidx.constraintlayout:constraintlayout:1.1.3'
    testImplementation 'junit:junit:4.12'
    androidTestImplementation 'androidx.test.ext:junit:1.1.1'
    androidTestImplementation 'androidx.test.espresso:espresso-core:3.2.0'
}
```

At the time of writing, the stable release of Navigation components is 2.2.2; there was also a beta release **2.3.0-beta01**. By the time you read this, the version may have moved. Make sure to check the official Android Developers website for more up-to-date information: `https://developer.android.com/jetpack/androidx/releases/navigation`.

Next, let's add a navigation graph to the project. You can create a navigation graph by creating a new resource file; right-click the project's *res* folder, then select **New ➤ Android Resource File**, as shown in Figure 10-4.

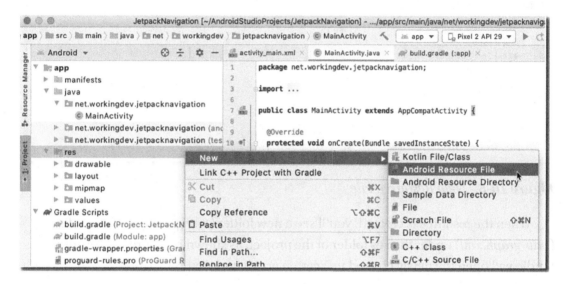

Figure 10-4. *Add a new resource file*

On the "New Resource File" dialog, change the resource type to *Navigation* and supply the filename:

- **Filename**—nav_graph

- **Resource type**—*Navigation* (you must click the down arrow to select it)

In the window that follows (shown in Figure 10-5), click OK.

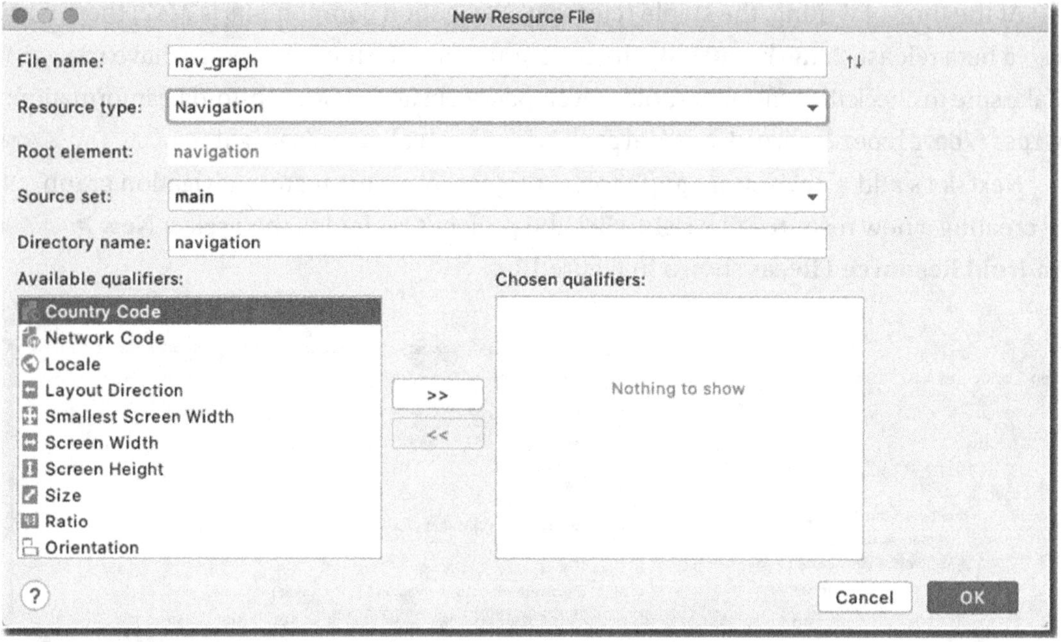

Figure 10-5. *New Resource File*

When the resource is created, you'll see a new folder (*navigation*) and a new file (*nav_graph.xml*) under the **res** folder of the project, as shown in Figure 10-6. Android Studio will open the newly created navigation graph in the editor. Figure 10-6 shows the newly created navigation graph—it's empty, of course.

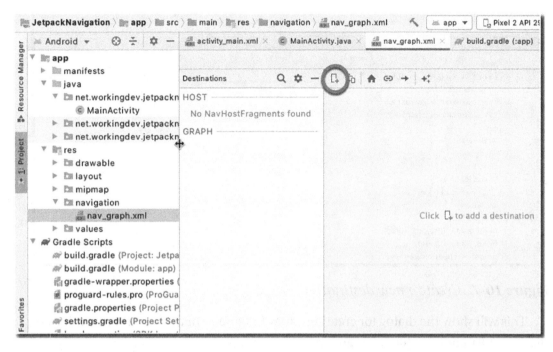

Figure 10-6. *Navigation graph*

When you're using Navigation components, navigation happens as an interaction between destinations. Destinations are what your users can navigate to, and destinations are connected via *actions*. At the moment, we don't have any destination yet; so, let's add one. Click the plus sign on the top panel of the navigation editor, as shown in Figure 10-7, then choose "Create new destination."

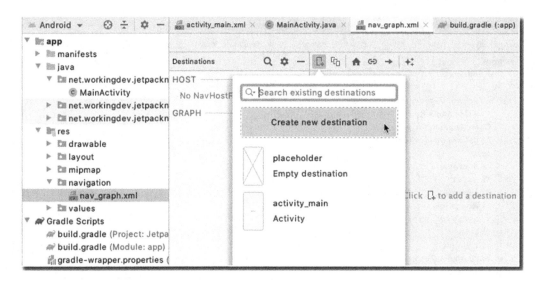

Figure 10-7. *Create a new destination*

This will show the dialog for creating a new Fragment. In the window that follows (Figure 10-8), choose a blank Fragment.

Figure 10-8. *New Android Fragment*

In the window that follows, type the name of the Fragment and the name of the layout file and choose the source language, as shown in Figure 10-9.

- **Fragment Name**—One

- **Fragment Layout Name**—fragment_one

- Keep the source language as **Java**

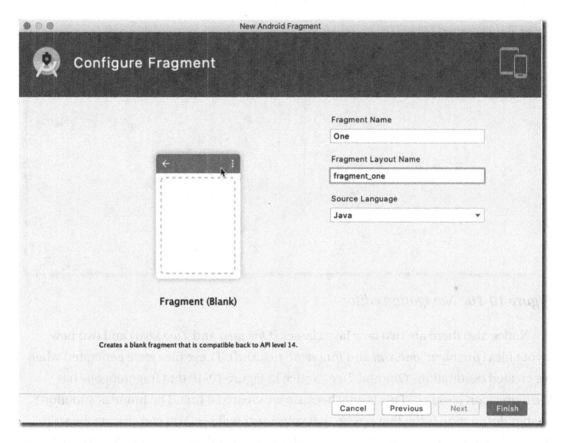

Figure 10-9. *New Android Fragment, details*

Click **Finish** to start the creation of the new Fragment; this Fragment will become one of the destinations in your app. Create another destination and make the Fragment's name "Two." The navigation editor, by now, should look like Figure 10-10.

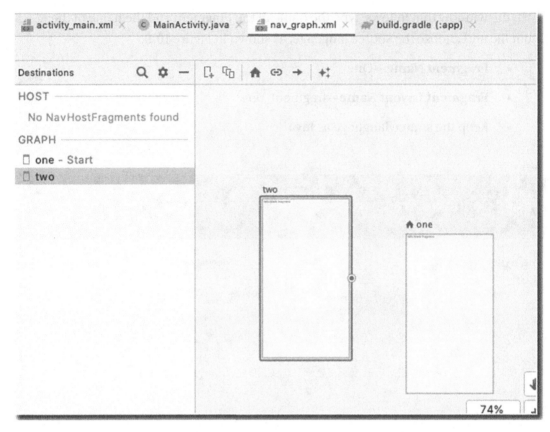

Figure 10-10. *Navigation editor*

Notice also there are two new Java classes (*One.java* and *Two.java*) and two new layout files (*fragment_one.xml* and *fragment_two.xml*). These files were generated when we created destinations *One* and *Two*. Notice in Figure 10-10 that fragment *one* has the home icon beside it. This is only because we created it first. The home destination or start destination is the first screen that your users will see. You can change the start destination any time by right-clicking any destination and then clicking "Set as start destination"; but for now, we'll keep *one* as the start destination.

Our navigation graph doesn't have a **NavHost** yet; it needs one. A NavHost acts like a viewport for all our destinations. It's an empty container where destinations are swapped in and out as the user navigates through the app. The NavHost needs to be in an Activity. We're going to put the NavHost in our *MainActivity*.

Open the layout file for our MainActivity, it's on *res/layout/activity_main.xml*, then edit in text mode. The default *activity_main* contains a single TextView object; remove it and replace it with the code snippet shown in Listing 10-6.

Listing 10-6. Defining a NavHost in activity_main.xml

```
<fragment
  android:layout_width="match_parent"
  android:layout_height="match_parent"
  android:id="@+id/nav_container"   ❶
  android:name="androidx.navigation.fragment.NavHostFragment"   ❷
  app:navGraph="@navigation/nav_graph"   ❸
  app:defaultNavHost="true"      ❹
  >
</fragment>
```

❶   It needs an id, just like any other element in the resource file. I just chose nav_container for this one. You can name what you like.

❷   This is the fully qualified name of the NavHostFragment class. This belongs to the Navigation component, and this will be responsible for making our MainActivity the viewport for all our defined destinations.

❸   The app:navGraph attribute tells the runtime which navigation graph we want to host in the MainActivity. Remember that you can have more than one navigation graph in the app; nav_graph is the name we gave to the navigation graph XML resource earlier.

❹   When you set the defaultNavHost to *true*, this makes sure that the **NavHostFragment** intercepts the system back button; that way, when the user clicks the back button, Android will show you the previous screen in your app, and not an external app's screen which happened to be on the back stack.

Now it's time to connect our two destinations. Open the navigation graph again—it's on *res/navigation/nav_graph*.

We want the user to navigate from destination *one* to destination *two*. So, hover your mouse over to destination one until a small circle appears on its right side. Click and drag this point over to destination two, so that the two destinations can be connected, as shown in Figure 10-11.

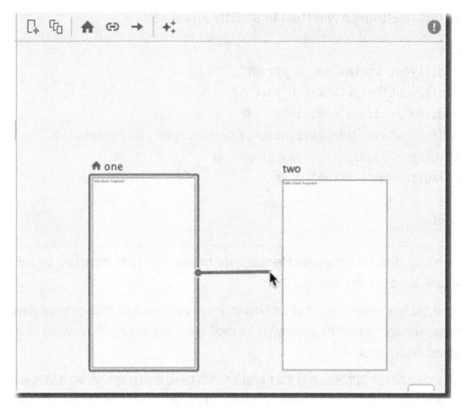

Figure 10-11. *Connect one to two*

Destination one is now connected to destination two. If you select the connection between *one* and *two*, you'll see that it has attributes you can set, as shown in Figure 10-12. We won't deal with the attributes; we just want to connect the two destinations.

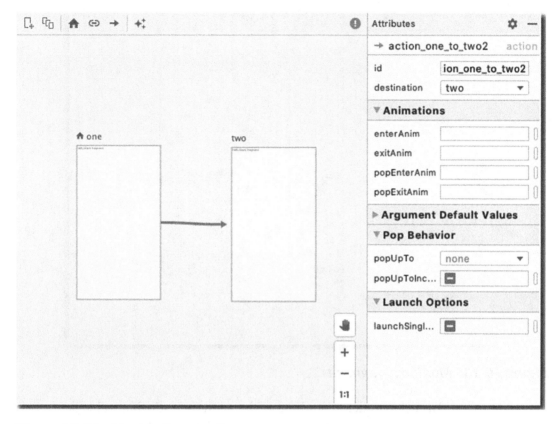

Figure 10-12. *Navigation graph*

To test this small app, I needed an object in the start destination that will trigger an action, like a Button (shown in Figure 10-13). I modified the layout of the two fragments as follows:

fragment_one

- Changed the layout to ConstraintLayout, just because it's easier to work with this kind of layout. Use the layout that's appropriate for you.

- I removed the TextView and replaced it with a button and centered it.

fragment_two

- Like fragment_one, I also changed the layout to ConstraintLayout.

- I changed the text of the TextView and centered it.

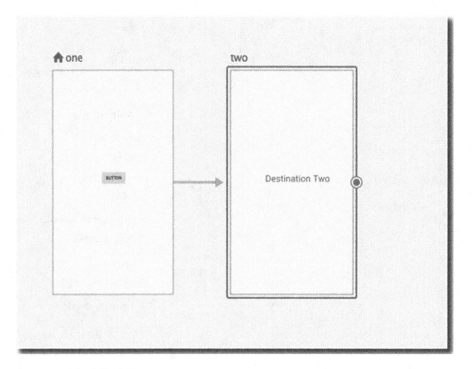

Figure 10-13. *Modified Fragments*

Next, we'll add a click handler to our button, then add the code that will make fragment_one navigate to fragment_two when the button is clicked.

Navigating to a destination is done using a **NavController**; it's an object that manages app navigation within a NavHost. Each NavHost has its own corresponding NavController.

A NavController lets you navigate to destinations in two ways: (1) navigate to a destination using an ID, which is what we will use here, and (2) navigate using a URI—which I will leave it up to you to explore.

To add a click handler to our button, open *One.java*, which contains the Java source file for our *One* destination, and modify its onCreateView() method to match Listing 10-7.

Listing 10-7. Class One.onCreateView()

```
@Override
public View onCreateView(LayoutInflater inflater, ViewGroup container,
                    Bundle savedInstanceState) {
  // Inflate the layout for this fragment
```

```
final View view = inflater.inflate(R.layout.fragment_one, container, false);

Button btn = (Button) view.findViewById(R.id.button);
btn.setOnClickListener(new View.OnClickListener(){

  @Override
  public void onClick(View view) {
    Navigation.findNavController(view).navigate(R.id.action_one_to_two2);
  }
});
  return view;
}
```

The most important line of code in Listing 10-7 is the **navigate()** method of the **NavController** object. We simply passed the ID of the action we created in the navigation graph as a parameter to **navigate()**, and that already did the trick. You can now launch the emulator and test the app.

This chapter merely scratched the surface of Navigation components; there's a lot to discover in this area, so make sure you check them out.

Summary

- You can still use Activity-based or Fragment-based navigation in your app; just remember their pros and cons.

- Navigation components combine the best features of Activity-based and Fragment-based navigation; the API is easy to work with, and we have more control on the back stack.

- Navigation components introduce the concept of *destinations*. *Destinations* can be Fragments, Activities, or custom views; they are what your users will navigate to.

- *Destinations* are grouped using a navigation graph; it's an XML resource file that contains all the *actions* between destinations.

- *Destinations* are connected to each other by *actions*.

- The basic ideas for navigation are to

    1. Create a navigation graph.

    2. Create destinations.

    3. Connect the destinations; each connection becomes an action.

    4. Navigate programmatically from one destination to another using the NavController object. You can navigate using an ID or a URI.

CHAPTER 11

Running in the Background

What we'll cover:

- Basic thread concepts

- The UI thread

- How to create and use Java threads

Knowing how to run codes in the background is an essential skill for every developer. Making adept use of threads can boost your app's performance. Users love that. The bar is very high right now on application performance. No one wants to use an app that runs like molasses. Jittery and janky apps are quickly forgotten nowadays.

In this chapter, we'll explore the wonderful world of Threads.

Basic Concepts

When you launch an app, a process is created, and it's allocated some resources like memory, among other things. It's also given one thread.

A thread, loosely speaking, is a sequence of instructions. It's the thing that executes your code. During the time the app is alive, this thread will utilize the process' resources. It may read or write data to memory, disk, or sometimes even the network I/O. While the thread is interacting with all these, it is just waiting. It can't take advantage of CPU cycles while it's waiting. We can't let all those CPU cycles go to waste. Can we? We can create other threads so that when one or more threads are waiting for something, the other threads can utilize the CPU. This is the case for multithreaded applications.

© Ted Hagos 2020
T. Hagos, *Learn Android Studio 4*, https://doi.org/10.1007/978-1-4842-5937-5_11

When the Android Runtime creates an instance of an app, that process will be given one thread. It's called the main thread; some developers call it the UI thread, but we'll be given just the one thread and no more. The good news is we can create more threads. The UI thread is allowed to spawn other threads.

The UI Thread

The UI thread, also known as the main thread, is responsible for launching the main activity and inflating the (XML) layout file. Inflating the layout file means turning all the View elements into actual Java objects, for example, Buttons, TextViews, and so on. In short, the main thread is responsible for displaying the UI. When we make calls like **setText()** or **setHint()** on a TextView object, these calls aren't executed right away; instead, it is as follows:

1. The call is placed in a MessageQueue.

2. There it will stay until a handler picks it up for execution.

3. Then, it gets executed on the main thread.

The main thread is not only used for displaying UI elements, it's also used for everything else that happens in your app. You may recall that Activity has lifecycle methods like onCreate, onStop, onResume, onCreateOptionsMenu, onOptionsItemSelected, and other methods. Whenever the code runs on these blocks, the runtime cannot process any message in the queue. It's in a *blocked* state; a blocked state means that the main thread is waiting for something to finish before it can continue to go about its business—this is not good for user experience.

Most of the time, the calls we make don't take that much time to run. The calls are cheap, so to speak, in terms of computing resources. So, it's not really a big deal. It becomes a big deal when we make calls that take quite a while to complete. The Android development team's guidance is that we should limit our calls to no more than 15 milliseconds; anything more than that, then we should consider running those codes in a background thread. This guidance was from Project Butter, which was released around the time of Jelly Bean (Android 4.1); it was meant to improve Android apps' performance. When the runtime senses that you're doing too much on the main thread, it'll start dropping frames. When you're not making expensive calls, the app runs at a very smooth 60 frames per second. If you hog the main thread, you will start noticing sluggish performances because the frame rates begin to drop. In the Android world, this is known as jank. Doing too much processing on the main thread will cause slow UI rendering, which results in dropped or skipped frames, which results in the app's perceived stuttering. The app becomes janky.

Note   Before Project Butter, if the UI thread senses that you're doing way too much on the UI thread, for example, opening a large file, creating a network socket, or anything that takes a long time, the runtime may slap you with the ANR (Android Not Responding) screen. ANRs are rarely seen nowadays; jank is more the concern.

If you want to avoid jank, you need to know how to run time-consuming or I/O-related codes in the background.

You don't need to get overexcited and start running everything in the background. Be reasonable and use your judgment. The following call, for example, doesn't need to be in a background thread:

```
txt1.setText(String.format("%d", (2 * 2 * 2)));
```

It is merely setting the Text property of a TextView to a calculated field. The calculation isn't complex.

Even Listing 11-1 isn't considered an expensive code to run. It does some rudimentary calculation of the GCF (greatest common factor), but it uses the Euclidean algorithm to get at the results. This algorithm performs efficiently. The number of loop cycles doesn't grow wildly regardless of how large the input values are; the time complexity doesn't change much whether we're finding the GCF of 12 and 15 or 16,848,662 and 24. So, it's quite okay to put this in the main thread.

Listing 11-1. GCF calculation

```
private void gcfCalculate(int firstNo, int secondNo) {
  int rem, bigno, smallno = 1;

  if (firstNo > secondNo) { bigno = firstNo; smallno = secondNo;}
  else {bigno = secondNo; smallno = firstNo;}
```

```
while(!((rem = bigno  % smallno) == 0)) {
  bigno = smallno;
  smallno = rem;
}
String msg = String.format("GCF = %s", smallno);
Toast.makeText(this, msg, Toast.LENGTH_LONG).show();
}
```

Listing 11-2, on the other hand, is an expensive call. It looks contrived right now, but you'll be surprised to find that these kinds of codes actually exist and are probably more common than you think—when you sit in for code reviews often enough, you'll know what I mean. Anyway, you want to watch out for codes like this because, even if it doesn't have any network or I/O call, it hogs the UI thread to calculate a Cartesian product—a Cartesian product mathematical set that's the result of multiplying other sets. A code that's similarly structured is best placed in a background thread.

Listing 11-2. Nested calls

```
private void nestedCall() {
  for(int i = 1; i < 10000; i++) {
    for(int j = 1; j < 10000; j++) {
      for(int k = 1; k < 10000; k++) {
        System.out.printf("%d", i * j * k);
      }
    }
  }
}
```

Another example of code that needs to run in the background is Listing 11-3. It uses the Internet to fetch information from GitHub.

Listing 11-3. Get GitHub info

```
private String fetch(String gitHubId) {

  String userInfo = "";
  String url = String.format("https://api.github.com/users/%s", gitHubId);

  OkHttpClient client = new OkHttpClient();
```

```
Request request = new Request.Builder()
    .url(url)
    .build();

try(Response response = client.newCall(request).execute()) {
  userInfo = response.body().string();
}
catch(IOException ioe) {
  Log.e(TAG, ioe.getMessage());
}
return userInfo;
}
```

The Android Runtime will smack you with a **NetworkonMainThreadException** if you try to run this on the UI thread. Any code that uses network connectivity can't run in the UI thread.

When you find yourself in a situation where you either need to (1) fetch or write data using the network, (2) fetch or write data using file I/O, or (3) perform a resource-intensive operation (like in Listing 11-2), you need to run that code in a background thread. There are a couple of ways to do that; see the list that follows:

- **Java threads**, which are from Java

- **AsyncTask**, which is part of the Android framework

- **Handlers and Messages**, which are also part of the Android framework

Whichever technique you use, the principle will remain the same; and that is

1. Spawn a background thread when executing long-running or resource-consuming tasks.

2. If you need to do something in the UI thread (like setting the property of a View) while inside a background thread, you have to find a way to go back to the UI thread before working on the View element.

Of all the ways to run codes in the background, the Thread will be the most familiar with Java programmers, but it will also be the most rudimentary.

Threads and Runnables

We can run statements in the background by spawning new threads. Thread objects are created either by extending the **java.lang.Thread** class or by implementing the Runnable interface. A thread object describes a single thread of execution, and that execution happens inside the Thread class' **run()** method.

Extending the Thread class is the simplest way to create a thread object. Listing 11-4 shows the typical structure of a Thread class.

Listing 11-4. class Worker

```
class Worker extends Thread {
  public void run() {
    // things you want to run in
    // background
  }
}
```

The Worker class simply extends **java.lang.Thread**. You need to override the **run()** method of the thread and put all the statements you want to run in the background inside it. After that, what's left to do is to instantiate Worker and run it, as shown in Listing 11-5.

Listing 11-5. How to create and run a thread

```
Worker worker = new Worker(); ❶
worker.start(); ❷
```

---

❶   Create an instance of the Thread class.

❷   Invoke the **start()** method. If you forget this, the thread won't run. Calling the **start()** method
     kickstarts the thread.

Another way to create a thread is by implementing the Runnable interface, as shown in Listing 11-6.

Listing 11-6. The Worker class implements the Runnable interface

```
class Worker implements Runnable {
  @Override
  public void run() {
    // things you want to run in
    // background
  }
}
```

As you can see, it's not that different from our previous sample; instead of extending the Thread, we simply implemented the Runnable interface. You still need to override the **run()** method and put the statement you'd like to run in the background in the **run()** method. The difference won't be in the Worker class structure, but in how the Worker class is instantiated and ran, which is shown in Listing 11-7.

Listing 11-7. How to use a Runnable object

```
Worker worker = new Worker(); ❶
Thread thread = new Thread(worker); ❷
thread.start(); ❸
```

❶   Create an instance of the Worker.

❷   Create an instance of a Thread class by passing an instance of the Runnable class (the Worker instance) to the Thread's constructor.

❸   Now we can kickstart the thread by calling the **start()** method.

Now that we have a conceptual idea on how to use Threads, let's use it to fetch user information from GitHub. Listing 11-8 shows the steps on how to call the GitHub API using OkHttpClient.

Listing 11-8. fetchUserInfo

```
private String fetchUserInfo(String gitHubId) { ❶
  String userInfo = "";
  String url = String.format("https://api.github.com/users/%s", gitHubId); ❷
  Log.d(TAG, String.format("URL: %s", url));
```

```
OkHttpClient client = new OkHttpClient(); ❸
Request request = new Request.Builder()
    .url(url)
    .build();

try(Response response = client.newCall(request).execute()) { ❹
  userInfo = response.body().string();  ❺
}
catch(IOException ioe) {
  Log.e(TAG, ioe.getMessage());
}
return userInfo;
}
```

---

❶   We want to take the GitHub **userid** as a parameter.

❷   Let's construct a String URL that incorporates the GitHub userid.

❸   We'll use the **OkHttpClient** from Square, Inc. OkHttpClient is an open source project designed to be an efficient HTTP client. It supports the SPDY protocol. SPDY is the basis for HTTP 2.0 and allows multiple HTTP requests to be multiplexed over one socket connection; you can learn more about SPDY at https://en.wikipedia.org/wiki/SPDY. As of Android 5.0, OkHttpClient is a part of the Android platform and is used for all HTTP calls. This example is lifted from OkHttpClient's web page at https://square.github.io/okhttp/.

❹   Let's use the **try with resources** block, so we don't have to worry about cleaning up later; when the **try block** goes out of scope, all the resources we opened within that block will be automatically closed.

❺   If all our previous setup went well, we could get the response from the GitHub API.

We want to run the **fetchUserInfo()** method in a background thread to get the **NetworkonMainThreadException** error. Let's create a small demo project for this. Create a project with an empty Activity. Let's build a simple UI with the following' elements:

• **EditText**—Where we can input the GitHub userid.

• **Button**—Which will trigger the user action.

- **TextView**—Where we will display the results of our fetch call from GitHub.

- **ScrollView**—We will wrap the TextView here, so that the displayed text is multiline, and it can scroll.

Figure 11-1 shows the app's layout.

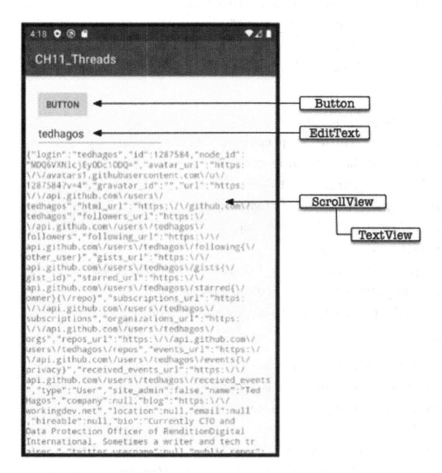

Figure 11-1. *The layout of the app*

Open **activity_main.xml** for editing and modify it to match Listing 11-9.

Listing 11-9. activity_main.xml

```xml
<?xml version="1.0" encoding="utf-8"?>
<androidx.constraintlayout.widget.ConstraintLayout
xmlns:android="http://schemas.android.com/apk/res/android"
  xmlns:app="http://schemas.android.com/apk/res-auto"
  xmlns:tools="http://schemas.android.com/tools"
  android:layout_width="match_parent"
  android:layout_height="match_parent"
  tools:context=".MainActivity">

  <Button
    android:id="@+id/button"
    android:layout_width="wrap_content"
    android:layout_height="wrap_content"
    android:layout_marginStart="18dp"
    android:layout_marginTop="21dp"
    android:layout_marginBottom="46dp"
    android:text="Button"
    app:layout_constraintBottom_toTopOf="@+id/scrollView"
    app:layout_constraintStart_toStartOf="parent"
    app:layout_constraintTop_toTopOf="parent" />

  <EditText
    android:id="@+id/txtName"
    android:layout_width="wrap_content"
    android:layout_height="wrap_content"
    android:ems="10"
    android:inputType="textPersonName"
    app:layout_constraintStart_toStartOf="@+id/button"
    app:layout_constraintTop_toBottomOf="@+id/button" />

  <ScrollView
    android:id="@+id/scrollView"
    android:layout_width="0dp"
    android:layout_height="0dp"
    android:layout_marginStart="1dp"
```

```
      android:layout_marginEnd="1dp"
      android:layout_marginBottom="1dp"
      app:layout_constraintBottom_toBottomOf="parent"
      app:layout_constraintEnd_toEndOf="parent"
      app:layout_constraintStart_toStartOf="parent"
      app:layout_constraintTop_toBottomOf="@+id/button">

      <TextView
        android:id="@+id/textView"
        android:layout_width="match_parent"
        android:layout_height="wrap_content"
        android:textAlignment="viewStart"
        android:typeface="monospace" />
  </ScrollView>

</androidx.constraintlayout.widget.ConstraintLayout>
```

Next, let's take care of the manifest file. We need to access the Internet when we call the GitHub API; so, let's declare that in the **AndroidManifest** file. Insert the INTERNET uses permission in the manifest, as shown in Listing 11-10.

Listing 11-10. AndroidManifest.xml

```
<?xml version="1.0" encoding="utf-8"?>
<manifest xmlns:android="http://schemas.android.com/apk/res/android"
  package="net.workingdev.ch11_threads">

  <uses-permission android:name="android.permission.INTERNET" />

  <application>
    ...
  </application>
</manifest>
```

Next, let's deal with the Gradle file. There are two changes we need to make on the app module's Gradle file. First, we need to add the dependency entry for OkHttpClient. Second, we need to add an entry to enable View binding.

We don't have to use View binding for this example, but I thought it's a good way to introduce new features that can make our programming lives easier. View binding lets us write code that interacts with the Views. Once View binding is enabled in a module, it generates a *binding class* for each XML layout file present in that module. An instance of a binding class contains direct references to all views with an ID in the corresponding layout. In most cases, View binding replaces **findViewByID**. Edit the module's Gradle file and modify it to match Listing 11-11.

Listing 11-11. build.gradle (Module:app)

```
apply plugin: 'com.android.application'

android {

  buildFeatures {  ❶
    viewBinding = true
  }

  compileSdkVersion 29

  defaultConfig {
    ...
  }

  buildTypes {
    release {
      ...
    }
  }
}

dependencies {
  implementation 'com.squareup.okhttp3:okhttp:4.7.2'  ❷
  ...
}
```

❶   Insert this block to enable View binding. Setting the **viewBinding** to *true* allows View binding for this module.

❷   Insert this dependency so we can use OkHttpClient.

You will need to sync the Gradle file after editing it.

Since Android Studio 3.6, you can already replace **findViewById** calls with View binding; when it's enabled for a module, it generates a binding class for each XML layout file that the module contains. Each binding class contains references to the root view and all views that have an ID. The name of the binding class is generated by converting the XML file's name to camel case and adding the word "Binding" to the end—for example, in our project, we only have **activity_main.xml**; so, a class called **ActivityMainBinding** will be generated for us.

Listing 11-12 shows the annotated use of View binding in the MainActivity class.

Listing 11-12. MainActivity

```
import androidx.appcompat.app.AppCompatActivity;
import okhttp3.OkHttpClient;
import okhttp3.Request;
import okhttp3.Response;
import android.os.Bundle;
import android.util.Log;
import android.view.View;
import android.widget.TextView;
import net.workingdev.ch11_threads.databinding.ActivityMainBinding;
import org.json.JSONException;
import org.json.JSONObject;
import java.io.IOException;

public class MainActivity extends AppCompatActivity {

  private final String TAG = getClass().getName();
  private TextView txtUserInfo;    ❶
```

```
@Override
protected void onCreate(Bundle savedInstanceState) {
  super.onCreate(savedInstanceState);

  final ActivityMainBinding binding = ActivityMainBinding.
  inflate(getLayoutInflater()); ❷
  View view = binding.getRoot(); ❸
  setContentView(view); ❹

  txtUserInfo = binding.textView; ❺

  binding.button.setOnClickListener(new View.OnClickListener() { ❻
    @Override
    public void onClick(View view) {
      Log.d(TAG, "Click");
      String username = binding.txtName.getText().toString(); ❼
      new RunBackground(username).start(); ❽
    }
  });
}

}
```

---

❶   I declared the TextView as a member because we will use this later, outside of the **onCreate()** method.

❷   Call the **inflate()** method (statically) to create an instance of the binding class for MainActivity to use.

❸   Get a reference of the root view by calling **getRoot()**.

❹   Instead of passing the name of the layout file (activity_main), pass the root view instead.

❺   Let's get a reference to the TextView object; this is where we will send the results of the GitHub API call.

❻   Let's set up a click listener for the Button.

❼   Get the content of the EditText.

❽   Then, instantiate the Thread object and kickstart it. We haven't defined the Thread object yet; we will do that shortly. Listing 11-13 shows the **RunBackground** class implemented as an inner class in MainActivity.

Listing 11-13. RunBackground inner class

```java
public class MainActivity extends AppCompatActivity {

  private final String TAG = getClass().getName();
  private TextView txtUserInfo;

  @Override
  protected void onCreate(Bundle savedInstanceState) {
    super.onCreate(savedInstanceState);
    ...
  }

  class RunBackground extends Thread {  ❶
    String userName;
    RunBackground(String userName) {  ❷
      this.userName = userName;
    }
    public void run() {  ❸
      String userInfo = fetchUserInfo(userName);  ❹
      Log.d(TAG, userInfo);
      Log.d(TAG,"Run in thread");
      try {
        final JSONObject jsonreader = new JSONObject(userInfo);  ❺
        Log.d(TAG, jsonreader.toString());
        runOnUiThread(new Thread() {  ❻
          public void run() {
            Log.d(TAG, "runOnUiThread");
            txtUserInfo.setText(jsonreader.toString());  ❼
          }
        });
      }
      catch(JSONException e) {
        Log.e(TAG, e.getMessage());
      }
    }
  }
}
```

```
private String fetchUserInfo(String gitHubId) {
    ...
  }
}
```

---

❶   Let's extend the Thread class because we want this to run in the background. We're implementing this also as an inner class to have access to the members of the outer class (MainActivity).

❷   Let's take the GitHub username as a parameter to this class' constructor.

❸   Override the **run()** method. Everything inside this method is what will run in the background.

❹   Let's call the **fetchUserInfo()** method.

❺   The GitHub API will return the result as a String. If you need to work with the returned object as JSON, you need to use **JSONObject**, as shown here. This way, if you want to extract specific parts of the userInfo, you can make calls like userInfo.getString("id").

❻   While you're in a background thread, you cannot make calls to any UI element, for example, if you want to set the text of either TextView or an EditText, you won't be able to do that. To make changes to the UI element while running in a background thread, you have to go back to the UI thread; and the way to do that is by calling the **runOnUiThread()** method. The **runOnUiThread()** method takes a Thread object as a parameter; override this Thread object's **run()** method, and that is where you write the codes to make changes to the UI (as shown here).

❼   Now we can write the results of the GitHub call to the TextView.

Now, run the application either in an emulator or a device and try to fetch your own GitHub info.

Summary

- When you try to do too much on the main thread, the runtime may start dropping frame rates, which results in jank.

- The UI thread is responsible for creating the UI elements, among other things. Don't overburden this thread. If you need to do some time-consuming or resource-consuming tasks, spawn a background thread and do that task there.

CHAPTER 12

Debugging

What we'll cover:

- Kinds of errors you'll encounter
- Logging debug statements
- Using the debugger

All but the most trivial programs are without errors. Dealing with errors will be a big part of your life as a developer. This chapter will discuss the kinds of errors you've faced and will still face in the foreseeable future. We will also discuss how you can use Android Studio to ease the difficulty of dealing with these errors.

Types of Errors

The three most common errors you'll face in programming are

- Syntax errors
- Runtime errors
- Logic errors

Syntax Errors

Syntax errors are exactly what you think they are, errors in the syntax. It happens because you wrote something in the code that's not allowed in the set of rules of the Java compiler. The compiler doesn't understand it. The error can be as simple as forgetting to close a parenthesis or a missing pair of a curly brace. It can also be complex like passing the wrong type of argument to a function or a parameterized class when using generics.

© Ted Hagos 2020
T. Hagos, *Learn Android Studio 4*, https://doi.org/10.1007/978-1-4842-5937-5_12

You can catch syntax errors with Android Studio with ease. Whenever you see red squiggly lines in on the main editor, like Figure 12-1. It means something is syntactically wrong with the code. Android Studio puts the red squiggly lines very near the offending code. If you hover your mouse on the red squiggly line, most of the time, Android Studio can tell you, with a high degree of accuracy, what's wrong with the code. What's more, you can quickly fix these kinds of errors using a technique that's aptly named "quick fix."

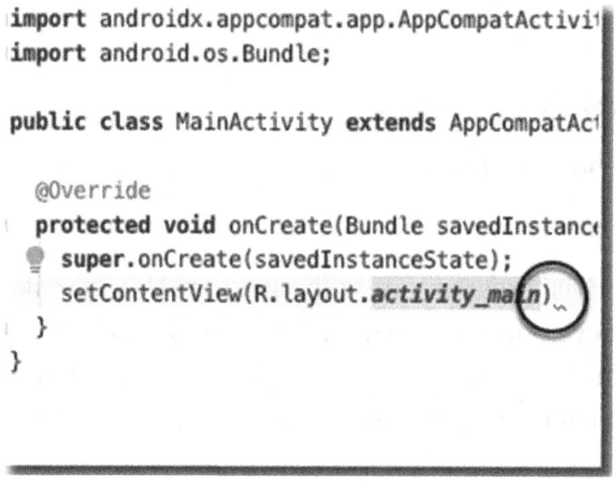

```
import androidx.appcompat.app.AppCompatActivit
import android.os.Bundle;

public class MainActivity extends AppCompatAct

    @Override
    protected void onCreate(Bundle savedInstance
        super.onCreate(savedInstanceState);
        setContentView(R.layout.activity_main)
    }
}
```

Figure 12-1. *Main editor showing error indicators*

To do a quick fix, bring the cursor anywhere within the red squiggly lines, then press **Alt + Enter** (if you're on Windows or Linux) or **Option + Enter** (if you're on macOS), and the IDE takes care of the rest; if there's more than one way to fix the error, the IDE will show you some options.

Runtime Errors

Runtime error happens when your code hits a situation it doesn't expect. As the name implies, this error happens only when your program is running. It's not something you'll see during compilation.

Java has two types of Exceptions, *checked* and *unchecked*. Android Studio gives you lots of assistance with checked Exceptions. Figure 12-2 shows what happens in the main editor when you try to call a method that throws a checked Exception; with unchecked Exceptions, however, you're still on your own.

There are two ways to resolve the error shown in Figure 12-2; we can enclose the openFileOutput() method call inside a *try-catch* structure or we add an Exception to the method signature, as shown in Figure 12-3.

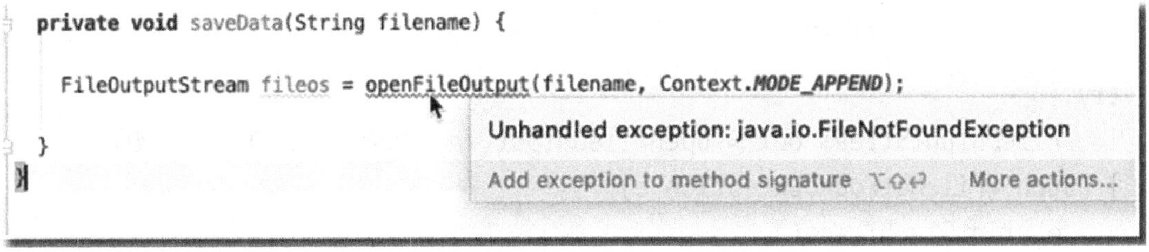

Figure 12-2. *IDE reminder that you need to handle the Exception*

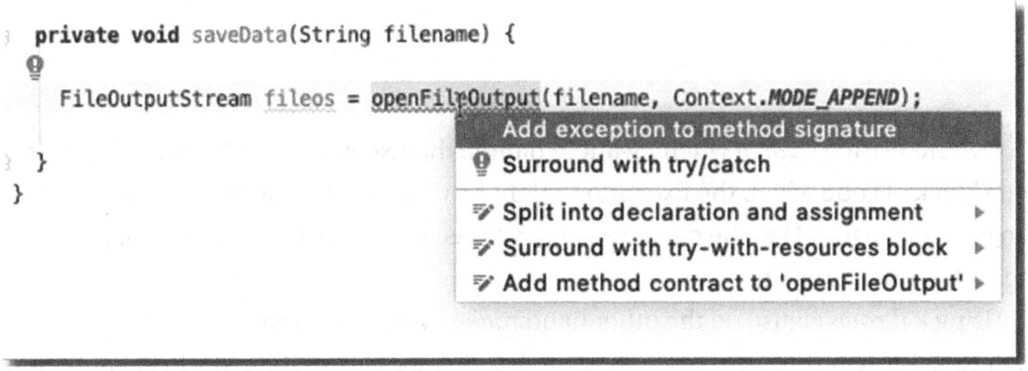

Figure 12-3. *Quick fix*

Listing 12-1 shows how to handle the FileNotFoundException by adding a throws clause to the method signature.

Listing 12-1. FileNotFoundException thrown in saveData()

```
import java.io.FileNotFoundException;
...
void saveData() throws FileNotFoundException {
  String fn = "somefile.txt";

  FileOutputStream out = openFileOutput(fn, Context.MODE_APPEND);
}
```

Listing 12-2 shows the code for handling the same Exception using a *try-catch* block.

Listing 12-2. Handling an Exception using try-catch

```
void saveData() {
  String fn = "somefile.txt";

  try {
      FileOutputStream out = openFileOutput(fn, Context.MODE_APPEND);
  } catch (FileNotFoundException e) {
      e.printStackTrace();
  }
  finally {
      ...
  }
}
```

I would use a *try-catch* when I want to handle the Exception locally, meaning in the same block of code where the Exception might be thrown. Most of the time, the only things to do are to (1) log the error and (2) try to recover from the error, if at all possible, and let the user try again.

Using a *throws* clause on the other hand means you don't want to handle the error on the local block; you'd like the calling method to take care of the error instead. If the calling method also uses a throws clause in its signature, then the error handling is passed along up the call stack.

Logic Errors

Logic errors are the hardest to find. As its name suggests, it's an error on your logic. When your code is not doing what you thought it should be doing, that's logic error. There are many ways to cope with it, but in this section, we'll take a look at two—printing debugging statements in certain places of your code and walking through your code using the debugger.

As you inspect your codes, you will recognize certain areas where you're pretty sure about what's going on, and then there are areas where you are not so sure—you can place debugging statements in these areas. It's like leaving breadcrumbs for you to follow. There are a couple of ways to print debugging statements. You can either use **println**, **Log**, or the **Logger** class.

When you set Logcat's mode to verbose, info, or debug, you will see all the messages that Android's runtime generates. If you want to be able to filter our messages, for example, warn or error, you need to use either the Log or the Logger class.

The Log class has five static methods; the usage is shown as follows:

```
Log.v(TAG, message) // verbose
Log.d(TAG, message) // debug
Log.i(TAG, message) // info
Log.w(TAG, message) // warning
Log.e(TAG, message) // error
```

In each case, **TAG** is a String literal or variable, typically the name of the class where Log is called. The **message** is also a String literal or variable which contains what you actually want to see in the log. Listing 12-3 shows a typical use of the Log class in code.

Listing 12-3. Typical use of the Log class

```
import androidx.appcompat.app.AppCompatActivity;
import android.content.Context;
import android.os.Bundle;
import android.util.Log;
import java.io.FileOutputStream;
import java.io.IOException;

public class MainActivity extends AppCompatActivity {

  private final String TAG = getClass().getName();

  @Override
  protected void onCreate(Bundle savedInstanceState) {
    super.onCreate(savedInstanceState);
    setContentView(R.layout.activity_main);

    Log.d(TAG, "onCreate");
  }

  @Override
  protected void onStart() {
    super.onStart();
    Log.d(TAG, "onStart");
  }
```

```
@Override
protected void onResume() {
  super.onResume();
  Log.d(TAG, "onResume");
}

private void saveData(String fn) throws IOException {

  try (FileOutputStream fileos = openFileOutput(fn, Context.MODE_APPEND))
{

    Log.d(TAG, "Doing something with the file");
  }
  catch(IOException ioe) {
    Log.e(TAG, ioe.getMessage());
    // you can still re-throw the Exception here
    // or do some recovery
  }
}
}
```

When the app runs, you can see the Log messages in the **Logcat** window, as shown in Figure 12-4. You can get to the Logcat window either by clicking its tab in the menu strip at the bottom of the IDE or from the main menu bar, **View ➤ Tool Windows ➤ Logcat**.

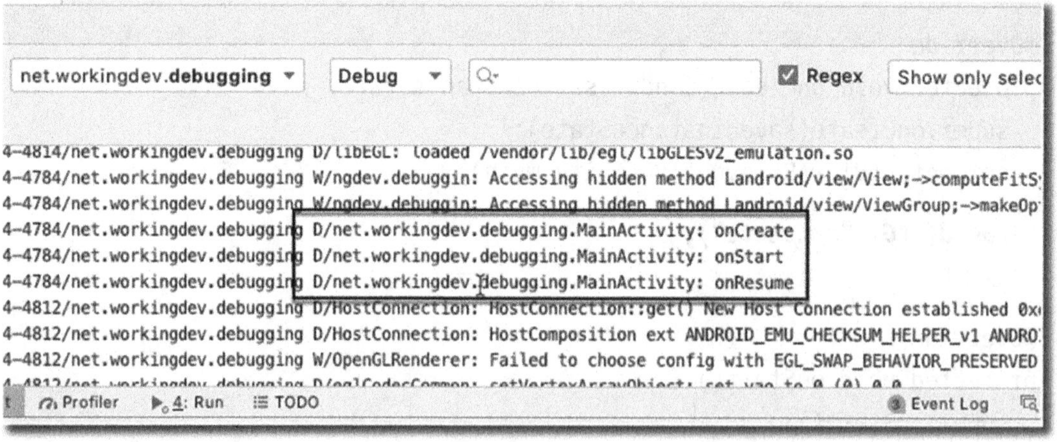

Figure 12-4. *Logcat tool window*

Debugger

Android Studio includes an interactive debugger which allows you to walk and step through the code while it's running. With the interactive debugger, you can inspect snapshots of the application—values of variables, running threads, and so on—at specific locations in the code and at specific points in time. These specific locations in the code are called *breakpoints*; you get to choose these breakpoints.

To set a breakpoint, choose a line that has an executable statement and then click its line number in the gutter. When you set a breakpoint, there will be a pink circle icon in the gutter, and the whole line is lit in pink—as shown in Figure 12-5.

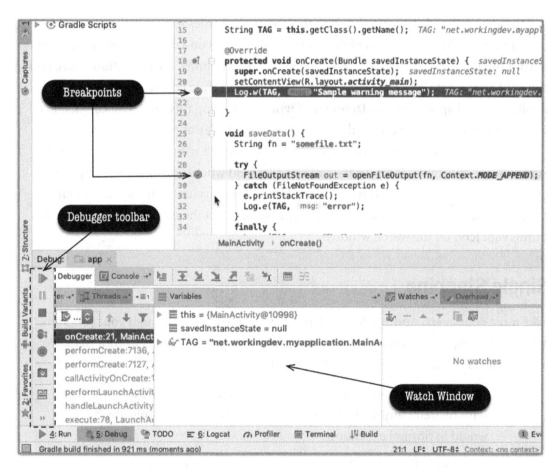

Figure 12-5. *Debugger window*

After the breakpoints are set, you have to run the app in debug mode. Stop the app if it is currently running, and then from the main menu bar, click **Run ➤ Debug App**.

Note   Running the app in debug mode isn't the only way to debug the app. You can also attach the debugger process in a currently running application. There are situations where this second technique is useful; for example, when the bug you are trying to solve occurs on very specific conditions, you may want to run the app for a while, and when you think you are close to the point of error, you can then attach the debugger.

Use the application as usual. When the execution comes to a line where you set a breakpoint, the line turns from pink to blue. This is how you know the code execution is at your breakpoint. At this point, the debugger window opens, the execution stops, and Android Studio gets into interactive debugging mode. While you are here, the state of the application is displayed in the **Debug tool window**. During this time, you can inspect values of variables and even see the threads running in the app.

You can even add variables or expression in the watch window by clicking the plus sign with the spectacles icon. There will be a text field where you can enter any valid expression. When you press **Enter**, Android Studio will evaluate the expression and show you the result. To remove a watch expression, select the expression and click the minus sign icon on the watch window.

Single Stepping

Like most debuggers, Android Studio lets you step line by line through your program. When the debugger stops at a breakpoint, you have a couple of tools at your disposal. You'd typically want to know how to do the following:

- **Resume**—Resumes execution until you get to the next breakpoint. If there aren't any more breakpoints, then the program runs like it would in normal execution.

- **Step into**—If the next line has a method call, this will jump to the method and pause it at the first line.

- **Step over**—Executes whatever happens on the next line and then jumps to the next line.

- **Step out**—Executes the remainder of the current method and then pauses at the next statement after the method. It essentially gets out of the method.

You can get to these actions from the main menu bar under the **Run** menu. You can also get to them from the Debugger toolbar (shown in Figure 12-6).

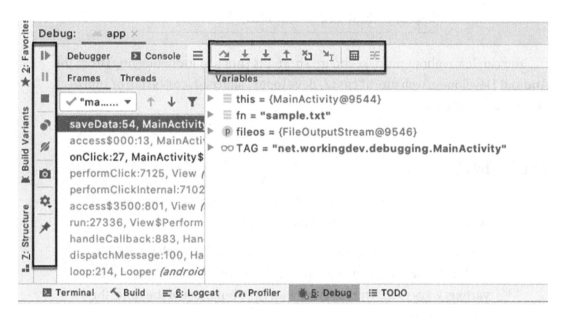

Figure 12-6. *Debugger toolbar*

Lastly, you can get the single-step actions via keyboard shortcuts, as shown in Table 12-1.

Table 12-1. *Debugger keyboard shortcuts*

	Windows/Linux	macOS
Debug	Shift + F9	Ctrl + D
Resume	F9	Command + Option + R
Step into	F7	F7
Step over	F8	F8
Step out	Shift + F8	Shift + F8

You can learn about more keyboard shortcuts (not just for debugging) from the Android Developers website: `https://developer.android.com/studio/intro/keyboard-shortcuts`.

Summary

- The three kinds of errors you may encounter are compile type or syntax errors, runtime errors, and logic errors.

- Syntax errors are the easiest to fix; Android Studio itself bends over backward for you so you can quickly spot syntax errors. There are various ways to fix syntax errors with AS3, but most of the time, the **quick fix** should do it.

- You can walk through your code line by line by setting breakpoints and using the single-step actions.

CHAPTER 13

Testing

What we'll cover:

- Types of testing

- Unit testing

- Testing basics

- About instrumented testing

- How to create UI test interactions

- Basic test interactions

- Implementing test verifications

- Test recording

We've done a bit of programming work in the previous chapters. Next, we go through some testing concepts and techniques. The development lifecycle goes through a testing phase to find all errors and inconsistencies in the code. A polished app doesn't have rough edges. We need to test it, debug it, and make sure it doesn't hog computing resources.

Types of Testing

Functional testing. Functional testing is a standard way of testing an app. It's called *functional* because we're testing the app's features (also known as functionalities) as they are specified in the requirement specification—the requirement specification is something you or a business analyst would have written during the planning stages of the app. The requirement specifications would have been written in a document (usually called functional requirement specification). Examples of what you might find in a functional specification are "user must log in to the server before entering the app," "user

© Ted Hagos 2020
T. Hagos, *Learn Android Studio 4*, https://doi.org/10.1007/978-1-4842-5937-5_13

must provide a valid email for registration," and so on. The testers, usually called QA or QC (short for quality assurance and quality control, respectively), are the ones who carry out these tests. They will create test assets, craft a test strategy, execute them, and eventually report on the executions' results. Failing tests are usually assigned back to the developer (you) to fix and resubmit. What I'm describing here is a typical practice for a development team that has a separate or dedicated testing team; if you're a one-person team, the QA will most likely be you as well. Testing is an entirely different skill, and I strongly encourage you to enlist other people, preferably those who have experience in testing, to help you out.

Performance testing. You could probably guess what this type of testing does just from its name. It pushes the app to its limits and sees how it performs under stress. What you want to see here is how the app responds when subjected to above-normal conditions. **Soak testing or endurance testing** is a kind of performance testing; usually, you leave the app running for a long time and in various modes of operation, for example, leave the app for a long time while it's paused or at the title screen. You're trying to find here how the app responds to these conditions and how it utilizes system resources like the memory, CPU, network bandwidth, and so on; you will use tools like the *Android Profiler* to carry out these measurements.

Another form of performance testing is **volume testing**; if your app uses a database, you might want to find out how it will respond when data is loaded to the database. What you're checking is how the system responds under various loads of data.

Spike testing or scalability testing is also another kind of performance testing. If the app depends on a central server, this test will usually raise the number of users (device endpoints) connected to the central server. You'd want to observe how a spike in the number of users affects the user experience—is the app still responsive, was there an effect on frames per second, are there lags, and so on.

Compatibility testing is where you check how the app behaves on different devices and configurations of hardware/software. This is the situation where AVDs (Android Virtual Devices) will come in handy; because AVDs are simply software emulators, you don't have to buy different devices. Use the AVDs whenever you can. Some apps will be difficult to test reliably on emulators; when you're in that situation, you have to fork over money for testing devices.

Compliance or conformance testing. If you're building a game app, this is where you check the game against Google Play guidelines on apps or games; make sure you read Google Play's Developer Policy Center at `https://bit.ly/developerpolicycenter`.

Ensure you are also acquainted with PEGI (Pan European Game Information) and ESRB (Entertainment Software Rating Board). If the game app has objectionable content that's not aligned with a specific rating, they need to be identified and reported. Violations could be a cause for rejection, which may result in costly rework and resubmission. If you're collecting data from the users, you might want to audit the app to check if it is compliant with applicable data privacy regulations.

Localization testing is essential, especially if the app is for global markets. App titles, contents, and texts need to be translated and tested in the supported languages.

Recovery testing. This is taking edge case testing to another level. Here, the app is forced to fail, and you're observing how the application behaves as it fails and how it comes back after it fails. It should give you insight into whether you've written enough **try-catch-finally** blocks or not. Apps should fail gracefully, not abruptly. Whenever possible, runtime errors should be guarded by try-catch blocks; when the exception happens, try to write a log and save the app's state.

Penetration or security testing. This kind of testing tries to discover the weaknesses of the app. It simulates the activities that a would-be attacker will do to circumvent all the security features of the app; for example, if the app uses a database to store data, especially user data, a pen tester (a professional who practices penetration testing) might use the app while Wireshark is running—Wireshark is a tool that inspects packets; it's a network protocol analyzer. If you stored passwords in clear text, it would show up in these tests.

Sound testing. If your app uses sounds, check if any errors are loading the files; also, listen to the sound files if there's a cracking sound and so on.

Developer testing. This is the kind of testing you (the programmer) do as you add layers and layers of code to the app. This involves writing test codes (in Java as well) to test your actual program. This is known as unit testing. Android developers usually perform JVM testing and instrumented testing; we'll discuss unit testing more in the following sections.

Unit Testing

Unit testing is a functional testing that a developer performs, not the QA or QC. A unit test is simple; it's a particular thing that a method might do or produce. An application typically has many unit tests because each test is a very narrowly defined set of behavior. So, you'll need lots of tests to cover the complete functionality. Android developers usually use JUnit to write unit tests.

JUnit is a regression testing framework written by Kent Beck and Erich Gamma. You might remember them as the one who created extreme programming and the other from Gang of Four (GoF, Design Patterns), respectively, among other things.

Java developers have long used JUnit for unit testing. Android Studio comes with JUnit and is very well integrated into it. We don't have to do much by way of setup. We only need to write our tests.

JVM Test vs. Instrumented Test

If you look at any Android application, you'll see that it has two parts: a Java-based and an Android-based one.

The Java part is where we code business logic, calculations, and data transformations. The Android part is where we interact with the Android platform. This is where we get input from users or show results to them. It makes perfect sense to test the Java-based behavior separate from the Android part because it's much quicker to execute. Fortunately, this is already the way it's done in Android Studio. When you create a project, Android Studio creates two separate folders, one for the JVM tests and another for the instrumented tests. Figure 13-1 shows the two test folders in the Android view, and Figure 13-2 shows the same two folders in the Project view.

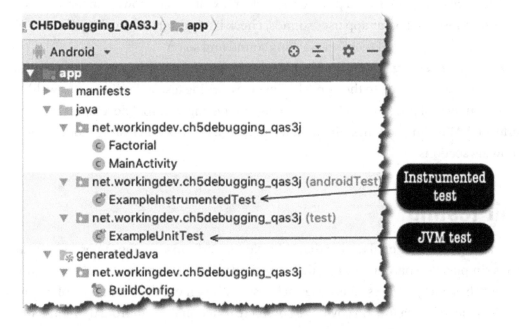

Figure 13-1. *JVM test and instrumented test in Android view*

Figure 13-2. *JVM test and instrumented test in Project view*

As you can see from either Figure 13-1 or 13-2, Android Studio went the extra mile to generate sample test files for both the JVM and instrumented tests. The example files are there to serve as just quick references; it shows us what unit tests might look like.

A Simple Demo

To dive into this, create a project with an empty Activity. Add a Java class to the project and name the class **Factorial.java**; edit this class to match Listing 13-1.

Listing 13-1. Factorial.java

```java
public class Factorial {
  public static double factorial(int arg) {
    if (arg == 0) {
      return 1.0;
    }
    else {
      return arg + factorial(arg - 1);
    }
  }
}
```

Ensure that **Factorial.java** is open in the main editor, as shown in Figure 13-3; then, from the main menu bar, go to **Navigate ➤ Test**. Similarly, you can also create a test using the keyboard shortcut (**Shift + Command + T** for macOS and **Ctrl + Shift + T** for Linux and Windows).

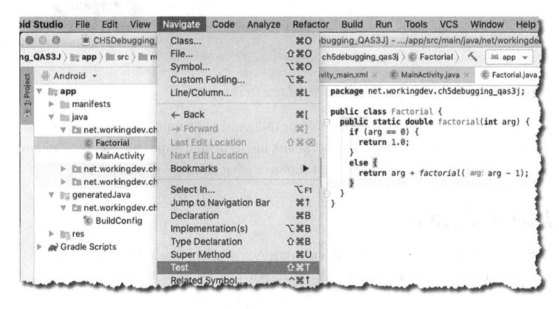

Figure 13-3. *Create a test for Factorial.java*

Right after you click **Test**, a pop-up dialog (Figure 13-4) will prompt you to click another link—click **Create New Test**, as shown in Figure 13-4.

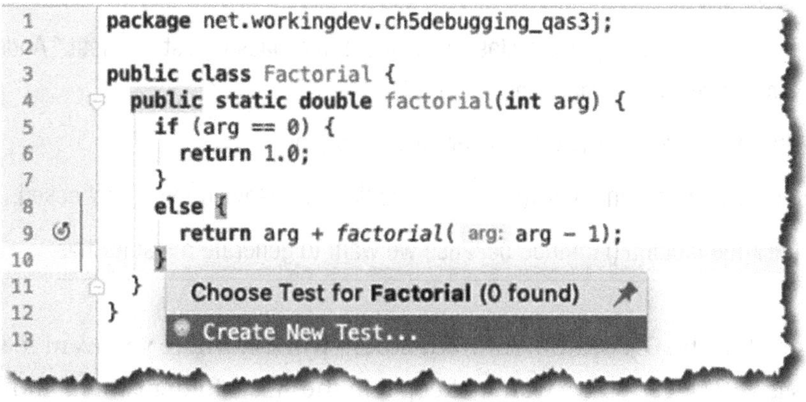
package net.workingdev.ch5debugging_qas3j;
public class Factorial {
public static double factorial(int arg) {
if (arg == 0) {
return 1.0;
}
else {
return arg + factorial(arg: arg - 1);
}
}
}
Choose Test for Factorial (0 found)
Create New Test...

Figure 13-4. *Create New Test pop-up*

Right after creating a new test, you'll see another pop-up dialog.

In the window that follows (shown in Figure 13-5), create the new test.

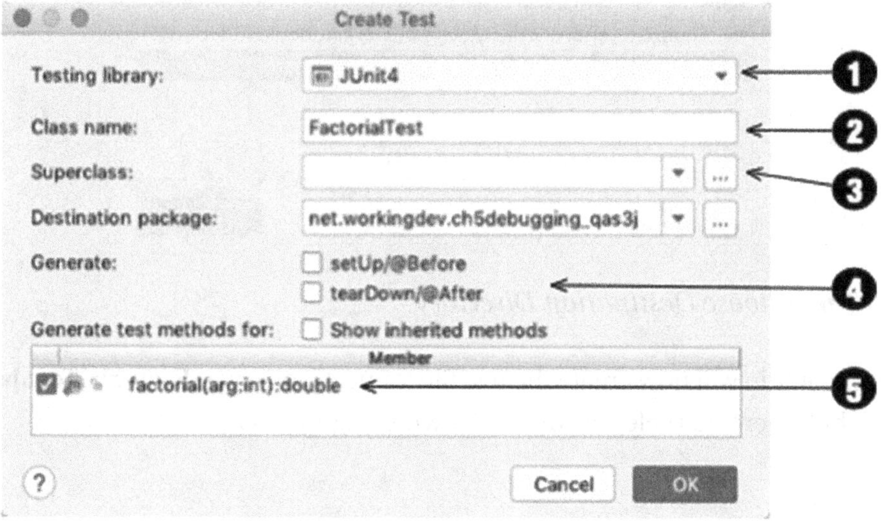
Create Test
Testing library:
JUnit4
Class name:
FactorialTest
Superclass:
Destination package:
net.workingdev.ch5debugging_qas3j
Generate:
setUp/@Before
tearDown/@After
Generate test methods for:
Show inherited methods
Member
factorial(arg:int):double
Cancel
OK
1
2
3
4
5

Figure 13-5. *Create FactorialTest*

❶   You can choose which testing library you want to use. You can choose JUnit 3, 4, or 5. You can even choose Groovy JUnit, Spock, or TestNG. I used JUnit4 because it comes installed with Android Studio.

❷   The convention for naming a test class is "name of the class to test" + "Test." Android Studio populates this field using that convention.

❸   Leave this blank; we don't need to inherit from anything.

❹   We don't need setUp() and tearDown() routines, for now, leaving them unchecked.

❺   Let's check the factorial() method because we want to generate a test for this.

When you click the **OK** button, Android Studio will ask where you want to save the test file. This is a JVM test, so we want to keep it in the "test" folder (not in androidTest). See Figure 13-6. Click "OK."

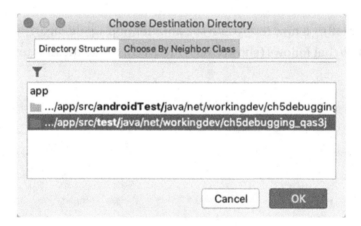

Figure 13-6. *Choose Destination Directory*

Android Studio will now create the test file for us. If you open **FactorialTest.java**, you'll see the generated skeleton code— shown in Figure 13-7.

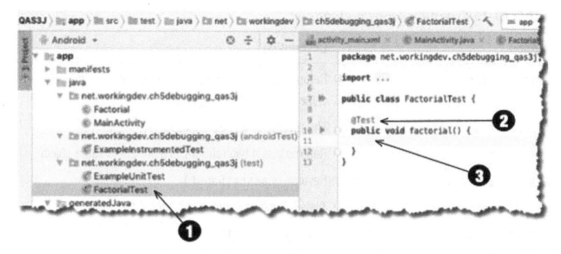

Figure 13-7. FactorialTest.java in Project view and main editor

❶   The file *Factorial.java* was created under the *test* folder.

❷   A **factorial()** method was created, and it's annotated as @Test. This is how JUnit will know that this method is a unit test. You can prepend your method names with "test," for example, **testFactorial()**, but that is not necessary; the @Test annotation is enough.

❸   This is where we put our assertions.

See how simple that was? Creating a test case in Android Studio doesn't involve that much in terms of setup and configuration. All we need to do now is write our test.

Implementing the Test

JUnit supplies several static methods that we can use in our test to make assertions about our code's behavior. We use assertions to show an expected result, which is our control data. It's usually calculated independently and is known to be true or correct—that's why you use it as a control data. When the expected data is returned from the assertion, the test passes; otherwise, the test fails. Table 13-1 shows the common assert methods you might need for your code.

Table 13-1. *Common assert methods*

Method	Description
assertEquals()	Returns true if two objects or primitives have the same value
assertNotEquals()	The reverse of assertEquals()
assertSame()	Returns true if two references point to the same object
assertNotSame()	Reverse of assertSame()
assertTrue()	Tests a Boolean expression to see if it's true
assertFalse()	Reverse of assertTrue()
assertNull()	Tests for a null object
assertNotNull()	Reverse of assertNull()

Now that we know a couple of assert methods, we're ready to write some tests. Listing 13-2 shows the code for FactorialTest.java.

Listing 13-2. FactorialTest.java

```java
import org.junit.Test;
import static org.junit.Assert.*;

public class FactorialTest {

  @Test
  public void factorial() {
    assertEquals(1.0, Factorial.factorial(1),0.0);
    assertEquals(120.0, Factorial.factorial(5), 0.0);
  }
}
```

Our FactorialTest class has only one method because it's for illustration purposes only. Real-world codes would have many more methods than this, to be sure.

Notice that each test (method) is annotated by **@Test**. This is how JUnit knows that factorial() is a test case. Notice also that assertEquals() is a method of the Assert class, but we're not writing the fully qualified name here because we've got a static import on Assert—it certainly makes life easier.

The **assertEquals()** method takes three parameters; they're illustrated in Figure 13-8.

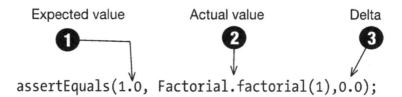

Figure 13-8. assertEquals method

---

❶   The **Expected** value is your control data; this is usually hard-coded in the test.

❷   The **Actual** value is what your method returns. If the expected value is the same as the actual value, the assertEquals() passes—your code behaves as expected.

❸   **Delta** is intended to reflect how close the *actual* and *expected* values can be and still be considered equal. Some developers call this parameter the "fuzz" factor. When the difference between the expected and actual values is higher than the "fuzz factor," then assertEquals() will fail. I used 0.0 here because I don't want to tolerate any kind of deviation. You can use other values like 0.001, 0.002, and so on; it depends on your use case and how much fuzz your app is willing to tolerate.

Now, our code is complete. You can insert a couple more asserts in the code so you can get into the groove of things if you prefer.

There are a couple of things I did not include in this sample code. I did not override the **setUp()** and **tearDown()** methods because I didn't need it. You will typically use the **setUp()** method to set up database connections, network connections, and so on. Use the **tearDown()** method to close whatever it is you opened in the **setUp()**.

Now, we're ready to run the test.

Running a Unit Test

You can run just one test or all the tests in the class. The little green arrows in the gutter of the main editor are clickable. When you click the small arrow beside the class' name, that will run all the tests in the class. When you click the one beside the test method's name, that will run only that test case. See Figure 13-9.

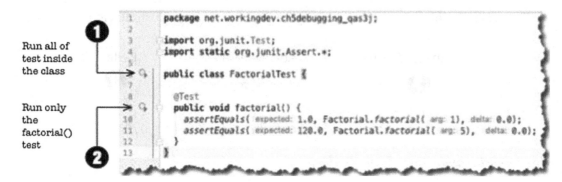

Run all of test inside the class

Run only the factorial() test

```
1    package net.workingdev.ch5debugging_qas3j;
2
3    import org.junit.Test;
4    import static org.junit.Assert.*;
5
6    public class FactorialTest {
7
8        @Test
9        public void factorial() {
10           assertEquals( expected: 1.0, Factorial.factorial( arg: 1), delta: 0.0);
11           assertEquals( expected: 120.0, Factorial.factorial( arg: 5), delta: 0.0);
12       }
13   }
```

Figure 13-9. *FactorialTest.java in the main editor*

Similarly, you can also run the main menu bar test and go to **Run ➤ Run**. Figure 13-10 shows the result of the test execution.

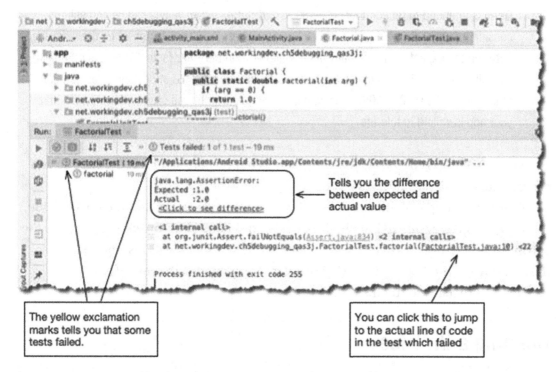

The yellow exclamation marks tells you that some tests failed.

Tells you the difference between expected and actual value

You can click this to jump to the actual line of code in the test which failed

Figure 13-10. *Result of running FactorialTest.java*

Android Studio gives you plenty of cues so you can tell if your tests are passing or failing. Our first run tells us that there's something wrong with *Factorial.java*; the **assertEquals()** has failed.

> **Tip**   When a test fails, it's best to use the debugger to investigate the code. **FactorialTest.java** is no different than any other class in our project; it's just another Java file; we can debug it. Put some breakpoints on your test code's strategic places, and then instead of "running" it, run the "debugger" so you can walk through it.

Our test failed because the factorial of 1 isn't 2, it's 1. If you look closer at *Factorial.java*, you'll notice that the factorial value isn't calculated correctly.

Edit the *Factorial.java* file, then change this line

```
return arg + factorial(arg - 1);
```

to this line

```
return arg * factorial(arg - 1);
```

If we rerun the test, we see successful results, as shown in Figure 13-11.

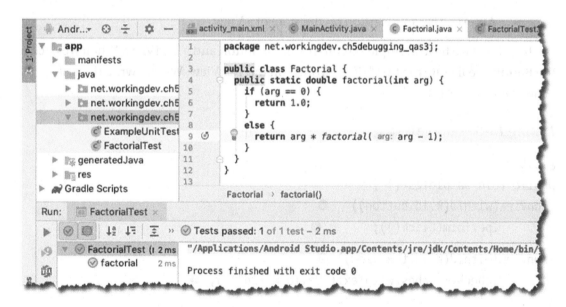

Figure 13-11.   *Successful test*

Instead of yellow exclamation marks, we now see green checkmarks. Instead of seeing "Test failed," we now see "Test passed." Now we know that our code works as expected.

Instrumented Testing

Unit testing that interacts with the Android platform is known as instrumented testing; we will use the Espresso framework to do this.

Espresso is a testing framework for Android to make it easy to write reliable and concise user interface tests. Google released the Espresso framework in 2013. Since its 2.0 release, Espresso became part of the Android Support Repository.

Espresso automatically synchronizes your test actions with the user interface of your application. The framework also ensures that your activity is started before the tests run. It also lets the test wait until all observed background activities have finished.

The general steps when working with Espresso tests are the following:

- **Match**—Use a matcher to target a specific component, for example, a button or textview. A *ViewMatcher* lets you find a View object in the hierarchy.

- **Act**—Use a *ViewAction* object to perform an action, for example, a click, on a targeted View object.

- **Assert**—Use an assertion on the state of a View.

Imagine if we have a simple screen that has a Button and a TextView. When we click the Button, we'll write the text "Hello World" on the TextView. We can write the test, as shown in Listing 13-3.

Listing 13-3. sampleTest

```
@Test
public void sampleTest() {
  onView(withId(R.id.button))     ❶
        .perform(Click());        ❷

  onView(withId(R.id.textview)) ❸
        .check(matches(withText("Hello World"))); ❹
}
```

❶   Use a *ViewMatcher* to find a View object. We're looking for a View with an id of button. Remember that when you're using onView(), Espresso waits until all synchronization conditions are met before performing the corresponding UI action.

❷   When we find it, use a *ViewAction* to do something with it; in this case, we want to click it.

❸   Once again, we use a ViewMatcher to find a View object; this time, we're trying to find a TextView with an id of textview.

❹   When we find it, we want to check if its text property matches "Hello World."

Setting Up a Simple Test

Let's set up a simple project, something that has an empty Activity. Listing 13-4 shows the XML layout code, and Listing 13-5 shows the MainActivity code.

Listing 13-4. activity_main.xml

```xml
<?xml version="1.0" encoding="utf-8"?>
<android.support.constraint.ConstraintLayout
xmlns:android="http://schemas.android.com/apk/res/android"
  xmlns:app="http://schemas.android.com/apk/res-auto"
  xmlns:tools="http://schemas.android.com/tools"
  android:layout_width="match_parent"
  android:layout_height="match_parent"
  tools:context=".MainActivity">

  <TextView
    android:id="@+id/textView"
    android:layout_width="241dp"
    android:layout_height="wrap_content"
    android:layout_marginTop="147dp"
    android:text="TextView"
    android:textSize="36sp"
    app:layout_constraintEnd_toEndOf="parent"
    app:layout_constraintStart_toStartOf="parent"
    app:layout_constraintTop_toTopOf="parent" />
```

```
<Button
    android:id="@+id/btnhello"
    android:layout_width="146dp"
    android:layout_height="wrap_content"
    android:layout_marginTop="20dp"
    android:onClick="onClick"
    android:text="hello"
    android:textSize="36sp"
    app:layout_constraintEnd_toEndOf="@+id/textView"
    app:layout_constraintHorizontal_bias="0.494"
    app:layout_constraintStart_toStartOf="@+id/textView"
    app:layout_constraintTop_toBottomOf="@+id/textView" />

<Button
    android:id="@+id/btnworld"
    android:layout_width="wrap_content"
    android:layout_height="wrap_content"
    android:layout_marginTop="8dp"
    android:onClick="onClick"
    android:text="world"
    android:textSize="36sp"
    app:layout_constraintEnd_toEndOf="@+id/btnhello"
    app:layout_constraintHorizontal_bias="0.0"
    app:layout_constraintStart_toStartOf="@+id/btnhello"
    app:layout_constraintTop_toBottomOf="@+id/btnhello" />
</android.support.constraint.ConstraintLayout>
```

The layout code is fairly simple, as you can see; it has one TextView and two Buttons. Both Buttons will call the **onClick()** method in MainActivity when the user clicks it.

Listing 13-5. MainActivity

```
public class MainActivity extends AppCompatActivity {

    TextView txtview;

    @Override
    protected void onCreate(Bundle savedInstanceState) {
```

```
    super.onCreate(savedInstanceState);
    setContentView(R.layout.activity_main);
    txtview = (TextView) findViewById(R.id.textView);
  }

  public void onClick(View view) {
    switch(view.getId()) {
      case R.id.btnhello:
        txtview.setText("hello");
        break;
      case R.id.btnworld:
        txtview.setText("world");
        break;
    }
  }
}
```

The **onClick()** method in MainActivity tries to get the Button's id that got clicked and routes program logic according to that. If *btnhello* were clicked, we would set the text content of the TextView to "hello," and if *btnworld* were clicked, we'd set the content to "world"—it's simple enough. To verify this behavior, we can set up an instrumented test.

In the previous chapter, we wrote the test class in *src/test* because those were the JVM test. We will then write the test class inside *src/androidTest*; this will be an instrumented test. Listing 13-6 shows the code for our instrumented test class.

Listing 13-6. MainActivityTest

```
import android.support.test.rule.ActivityTestRule;
import android.support.test.runner.AndroidJUnit4;
import org.junit.Rule;
import org.junit.Test;

import static android.support.test.espresso.Espresso.onView;  ❶
import static android.support.test.espresso.action.ViewActions.click;
import static android.support.test.espresso.assertion.ViewAssertions.
matches;
import static android.support.test.espresso.matcher.ViewMatchers.withId;
import static android.support.test.espresso.matcher.ViewMatchers.withText;
```

```
public class MainActivityTest {

  @Rule ❷
  public ActivityTestRule<MainActivity> mActivityTestRule = new
  ActivityTestRule<>(MainActivity.class);

  @Test ❸
  public void buttonHelloTest() {
    onView(withId(R.id.btnhello)) ❹
        .perform(click());          ❺

    onView(withId(R.id.textView)) ❻
        .check(matches(withText("hello"))); ❼
  }

  @Test
  public void buttonWorldTest() {
    onView(withId(R.id.btnworld))
        .perform(click());

    onView(withId(R.id.textView))
        .check(matches(withText("world")));
  }
}
```

❶   You'd want to import the Espresso matchers, actions statically, and *asserts* so you won't have to qualify them later in the code fully.

❷   This just intercepts our test method calls and makes sure that the Activity is launched before we perform any test.

❸   You need to annotate each test method with @Test.

❹   Find the *btnhello* object using the **withId()** method.

❺   Then we simulate a click using a **ViewAction.click()**.

❻   Then we find the TextView, using a **withId()** method again.

❼   Finally, we assert if the TextView contains the text "hello."

You can run the instrumented test the same way you run the JVM test. You can either

- Click the arrows in the IDE gutter.

- Right-click the test and use the context-sensitive menu, then choose "Run MainActivityTest." or

- Go to the main menu bar, choose Run ➤ Run, then select MainActivityTest.

Recording Espresso Tests

Android Studio includes a feature where you can run your app, record the interaction, and create an Espresso test using the recording. Go to the main menu bar, then **Run ➤ Record Espresso Test**, as shown in Figure 13-12.

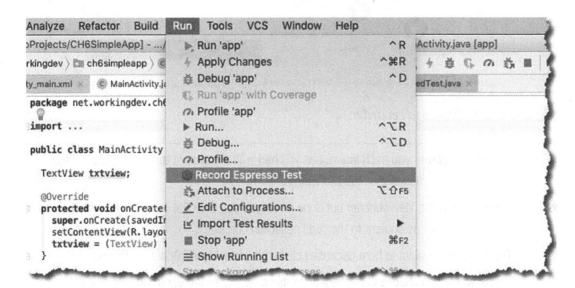

Figure 13-12. *Record Espresso Test*

After choosing the "Record Espresso Test," you can now interact with the app, like usual, but this time, the interaction is recorded. If you click one of the buttons, say the "HELLO" button, the test recorder screen will pop up, as shown in Figure 13-13.

Figure 13-13. *Espresso recorder*

❶   This section shows you each interaction you had with the app. At this point, I clicked the app once only; I clicked the "HELLO" button.

❷   This section is the *ViewMatcher* but done visually. If you click the TextView, like what I did here, it goes over as an item to the "Edit Assertion" section.

❸   The TextView is selected here because I clicked it in the ViewMatcher section (item 2).

❹   This is where you choose the assertion. In this case, we're merely using the "text is."

❺   This shows the actual value of the TextView we'd like to assert.

You can click "Save and Add Another" if you'd like to add another test or "Save Assertion" and finish the recording. Figure 13-14 shows the next screen.

Figure 13-14. *Espresso recorder, assertion saved*

When you click OK, the recorder will prompt the class' name, where it will save the recording as a test class, as shown in Figure 13-15.

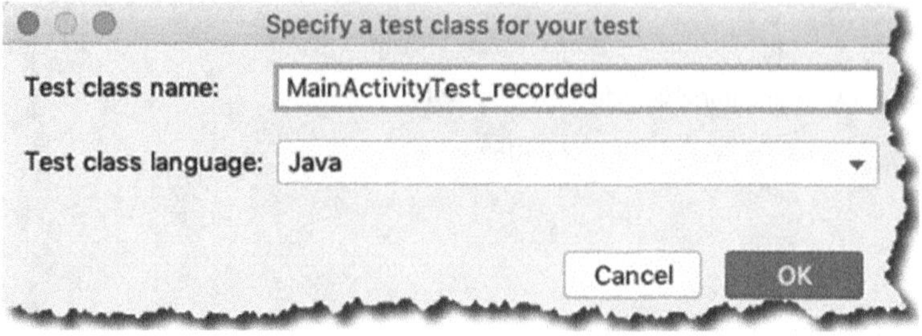

Figure 13-15. *Espresso test, test saved*

When you go to the src/androidTest folder, you'll find the newly generated test class from your recording. You can now run the generated test, the same way you ran MainActivityTest earlier.

Note Two factoids about Espresso: (1) The Espresso recorder is one of the most used tools when using Espresso, according to Android Studio analytics; (2) Espresso recorder was originally named "cassette."

More on Espresso Matchers

Espresso has a variety of matchers, but the one that's commonly used is the ViewMatchers—it's what we used in the earlier examples. Here are the other matchers in Espresso:

- **CursorMatchers**—You can use this for Android Adapter Views that are backed by Cursors to match specific data rows.

- **LayoutMatchers**—To match and detect typical layout issues, for example, TextViews that have ellipsis or multiline texts.

- **RootMatchers**—To match Root objects that are dialogs or Roots that can receive touch events.

- **PreferenceMatchers**—To match Android Preferences and let us find View components based on their key, summary text, and so on.

- **BoundedMatchers**—To create your custom matcher for a given type.

In the previous examples, we used the ViewMatcher to find Views via their ids. We can find Views using other things such as

- **Its value**—You can use the **withText()** method to find a View that matches a certain String expression.

- **The number of its child**—Using the **hasChildCount()** method, you can match a View with a particular child count.

- **Its class name**—Using the **withClassName()** method

ViewMatchers can also tell us whether a View object is

- **Enabled**—By using the **isEnabled()** method

- **Focusable**—By using the **isFocusable()** method

- **Displayed**—isDisplayed()

- **Checked**—isChecked()

- **Selected**—isSelected()

There are plenty more methods you can use in the ViewMatchers class, so make sure to check them out at `https://developer.android.com/reference/android/support/test/espresso/matcher/ViewMatchers`.

Espresso Actions

Espresso Actions let you interact with View objects programmatically during a test. We've used the click earlier, but there's a lot more that ViewActions will let you do. The method names are very descriptive, so they don't need further explanations; you can see what they do. Here are a few of them:

- clearText()

- closeSoftKeyboard()

- doubleClick()

- longClick()

- openLink()

- pressBack()—Presses the back button

- replaceText(String arg)

- swipeDown()

- swipeRight()

- swipeUp()

- typeText(String arg)

There are more actions available, so make sure you visit the API documentation for the ViewAction object.

Before we close the chapter, make sure you visit the official documentation for Espresso on the Android Developers website: `https://bit.ly/androidstudioespresso`; we've only scratched the surface of Espresso here.

Summary

- We've talked about various kinds of testing you can do for your apps; you don't have to do them all, but make sure you do the test that applies to your app.

- Dev testing (unit testing) should be a core development task; try to get into the habit of writing your test cases and your actual codes.

- Put JVM tests in *src/test* and put instrumented tests in *src/androidTest*.

- You can use Espresso to create instrumented tests; the two things you'll need in Espresso are the **ViewMatchers** and **ViewActions**.

- The general steps for writing Espresso tests are as follows: (1) find the View object using ViewMatchers, (2) perform an action on the View with ViewActions, and (3) do your assertions.

- An easy way to create Espresso tests is to use the Espresso recorder.

CHAPTER 14

Working with Files

What we'll cover:

- Introduction to file I/O of Android

- Internal vs. external storage

- How to use internal storage

When you need to work with video, audio, json, or just plain text files, you can use the Java file I/O for local files. You'll use the same **File**, **InputStream**, and **OutputWriter**, and other **I/O** classes in Java—if you've worked with them before. What will be different in Android is where you save them. In a Java desktop application, you can put your files practically anywhere you want. That's not the case in Android. Just like in a Java web application, Android apps are not free to create and read files just about anywhere. There are certain places where your app has read and write access.

Internal and External Storage

Android differentiates between internal and external storage. The *internal* storage refers to that part of a flash drive that's shared among all installed applications. The *external* storage refers to a storage space that can be mounted by the user—it's typically an sdcard, but it doesn't have to be. As long as the user can mount it, it could be anything; it could even be a portion of the internal flash drive.

Each option has pros and cons, so you need to consider your app's needs and each option's limitation. The following list shows some of these pros and cons.

© Ted Hagos 2020
T. Hagos, *Learn Android Studio 4*, https://doi.org/10.1007/978-1-4842-5937-5_14

Internal storage

- The memory is always available to your app. There is no danger of a user unmounting the sdcard or whatever device. It's guaranteed to be there always.

- The storage space will be smaller in size than external storage because your app will be allocated only a portion of the flash storage shared by all the other apps. This was a concern in earlier versions of Android, but it's less of a concern now. According to the Android Compatibility Definition, as of Android 6.0, an Android phone or tablet must have at least 1.5GB of nonvolatile space reserved for user space (the /data partition). This space should be plenty for most apps. You can read the compatibility definition here: `https://bit.ly/android6compatibilitydefinition`.

- When your app creates files in this space, only your app can access them; except when the phone is rooted, but most users don't root their phones, so generally it isn't much of a concern.

- When you uninstall your app, all the files it created will be deleted.

External storage

- It typically has more space than internal storage.

- It may not always be available, for example, when the user removes the sdcard or mounted as a USB drive.

- All files here are visible to all applications and the user. Anybody and any app can create and save files here. They can also delete files.

- When an app creates a file in this space, it can outlive the app; when you uninstall the app, the files it created won't be removed.

Cache Directory

Whether you choose internal or external storage, you may still have to make one more decision on a file location. You can put your files on a cache directory or somewhere more permanent. The Android OS or third-party apps may reclaim files in a cache directory if space is needed. All files that are not in the cache directory are pretty safe unless you delete them manually. In this chapter, we won't work with cache directories or external storage. We will use only the internal storage, and we'll put the files in the standard location.

How to Work with Internal Storage

As said earlier, working with file storage in Android is like working with the usual classes in Java I/O. There are few options to use like **openFileInput()** and **openFileOutput()** or other ways to use **InputStreams** and **OutputStreams**. You just need to remember that these calls will not let you specify the file paths. You can only provide the filename; if you're not concerned with that, go ahead and use them—it's what we will use in this chapter. If, on the other hand, you need more flexibility, you can use the **getFilesDir()** or **getCacheDir()** to get a **File** object that points to the root of your file locations—use **getCacheDir()** if you want to work with the cache directories of the internal storage. When you have a **File** object, you can create your directory and file structure from there.

That's the general lay of the territory when it comes to Android file storage. Again, in this chapter, we'll only work with internal storage in the standard location (not cache).

Writing to a file requires a few simple steps. You need to

1. Decide on a filename

2. Get a FileOutputStream object

3. Convert your content to a ByteArray

4. Write the ByteArray using the FileOutputStream

5. Don't forget to close the file

Listing 14-1 shows an annotated code snippet on how to save String data to a file.

Listing 14-1. Saving String data to a file

```
String filename = "myfile.txt"; ❶
String str = "The quick brown fox jumped over the head"; ❷
try (FileOutputStream out = openFileOutput(filename, Context.MODE_PRIVATE))
{ ❸
  out.write(str.getBytes()); ❹
```

```
} catch (IOException e) {
  e.printStackTrace();
}
```

---

❶　　Choose a filename.

❷　　This is the String we want to save to a file. In a real app, you may be getting this from the contents of an EditText component.

❸　　**openFileOutput()** returns a FileOutputStream; we need this object so we can write to a file. The first parameter of the call is the name of the file you want to create. The second parameter is a **Context mode**. We're using **MODE_PRIVATE** because we want the file to be private to the app. We're using the try-with-resources block here; this way, we don't have to bother closing the file. When the block exits, it will close the file object for us automatically.

❸　　The write method expects a ByteArray. So, we need to convert the String to a byte array. The **getBytes()** method should do that just fine.

Reading from a file involves more steps than writing to it. You generally need to do the following:

1.   Get a FileInputStream.

2.   Read from the stream, one byte at a time.

3.   Keep on reading until there's nothing more to read. You'll know when you're at the end of the file if the value of the last byte you've read is **-1**. It's time to stop by then.

4.   As you work your way to the end of the file, you need to store the bytes you're taking from the stream into a temporary container. A StringBuilder or a StringBuffer should do the trick. Building a String object using the plus operator is wasteful and inefficient because Strings are immutable. Each time you use the **plus** operator, it creates a new String object; if your file has 2000 characters, you would have created 2000 String objects. This will be the case if you're reading a text file. If you're reading something else like an audio or video file, you'll use a different data structure.

5. When you reach the end of the file, stop reading. Do what you
    need to do with what you've read, and don't forget to close it.

Listing 14-2 shows an annotated code snippet on how to read String data from a file.

Listing 14-2. Reading from a file

```
String filename = "myfile.txt";
StringBuilder sb = new StringBuilder(); ❶
String output = "";
try (FileInputStream in = openFileInput(filename)) { ❷
  int read = 0;
  while ((read = in.read()) != -1) { ❸
    sb.append((char) read); ❹
  }
  output = sb.toString(); ❺
}
catch(IOException ie) {
  Log.e(TAG, ie.getMessage());
}
```

❶   We won't be able to read the entire file in one fell swoop. We'll read it by chunks. As we get
      some chunks, we'll store them inside the StringBuilder object.

❷   **openFileInput()** returns a FileInputStream; this is the object we need to read from a file.
      The only parameter it takes is the name of the file to read. Using the try-with-resources
      here spares us from writing the boilerplate codes for closing files.

❸   The **read()** method reads a byte of data from the input stream and returns it as an integer.
      We need to keep reading from the stream one byte at a time until we reach the end of file
      (EOF) marker. When there are no more bytes to read from the stream, the EOF is marked
      as -1. We will use this as the condition for the while loop. Until the **read()** method doesn't
      return **-1**, we keep on reading.

❹   The **read()** method returns an int; it's the ASCII value of each letter in the file, returned as
      an integer. We have to cast it to a **char** before we can put it in the StringBuilder.

❺   When we run out of bytes to read, we'll get out of the loop and get the String out of the
      StringBuilder. Now, you can work with the contents of the file as a String.

Let's build a small project to put all these things together. Create a project with an empty Activity. Our small app will have the following View components:

- **EditText**—This will allow us to input some text.

- **TextView**—When we read data from a file, we will display the contents using this component.

- **Button**—This will trigger a user action to save the contents of the EditText to a file.

Edit /app/res/layout/activity_main.xml to match the contents of Listing 14-3.

Listing 14-3. app/res/layout/activity_main.xml

```xml
<?xml version="1.0" encoding="utf-8"?>
<androidx.constraintlayout.widget.ConstraintLayout
xmlns:android="http://schemas.android.com/apk/res/android"
  xmlns:app="http://schemas.android.com/apk/res-auto"
  xmlns:tools="http://schemas.android.com/tools"
  android:layout_width="match_parent"
  android:layout_height="match_parent"
  tools:context=".MainActivity">

  <Button
    android:id="@+id/btn"
    android:layout_width="wrap_content"
    android:layout_height="wrap_content"
    android:layout_marginBottom="13dp"
    android:layout_marginStart="17dp"
    android:text="save"
    app:layout_constraintBottom_toBottomOf="parent"
    app:layout_constraintStart_toStartOf="parent"
    tools:ignore="MissingConstraints" />

  <EditText
    android:id="@+id/txtinput"
    android:layout_width="0dp"
    android:layout_height="wrap_content"
    android:layout_marginTop="80dp"
```

```
   android:ems="10"
   android:inputType="textMultiLine"
   app:layout_constraintEnd_toEndOf="parent"
   app:layout_constraintHorizontal_bias="0.0"
   app:layout_constraintStart_toStartOf="parent"
   app:layout_constraintTop_toTopOf="parent" />

<TextView
   android:id="@+id/txtoutput"
   android:layout_width="0dp"
   android:layout_height="wrap_content"
   android:layout_marginTop="372dp"
   android:inputType="textMultiLine"
   android:text="TextView"
   app:layout_constraintEnd_toEndOf="parent"
   app:layout_constraintHorizontal_bias="0.0"
   app:layout_constraintStart_toStartOf="parent"
   app:layout_constraintTop_toTopOf="parent" />

</androidx.constraintlayout.widget.ConstraintLayout>
```

Next, edit MainActivity to match the contents of Listing 14-4.

Listing 14-4. MainActivity

```
import android.content.Context;
import android.os.Bundle;
import android.util.Log;
import android.view.View;
import android.widget.Button;
import android.widget.EditText;
import android.widget.TextView;

public class MainActivity extends AppCompatActivity {

  private Button btn;   ❶
  private TextView txtoutput;
  private EditText txtinput;
```

```
private String filename = "myfile.txt";
private String TAG = getClass().getName();

@Override
protected void onCreate(final Bundle savedInstanceState) {
  super.onCreate(savedInstanceState);
  setContentView(R.layout.activity_main);

  txtoutput = findViewById(R.id.txtoutput); ❷
  txtinput = findViewById(R.id.txtinput);

  btn = findViewById(R.id.btn);
  btn.setOnClickListener(new View.OnClickListener() { ❸
    @Override
    public void onClick(View v) {
      // this is where we trigger saving the data
    }
  });
  }
}
```

---

❶   Declare the Button, EditText, TextView, the filename variable, and the TAG variable as class members; we will refer to them later.

❷   Initialize the TextView and EditText variables inside the onCreate() callback.

❸   Bind the Button to a listener object. When the Button is clicked, we will call a method that will contain the codes for saving the contents of **txtinput** to a file.

Next, add a method to MainActivity and name it **saveData()**. Edit it to match the codes, as shown in Listing 14-5. These are mostly the same codes as in Listing 14-1; the only difference is that we're reading the String content from the EditText (txtinput) component.

Listing 14-5. saveData()

```
private void saveData() {
  String str = txtinput.getText().toString();
  try (FileOutputStream out = openFileOutput(filename, Context.MODE_
  PRIVATE)) {
    out.write(str.getBytes());
    loadData();
  } catch (IOException e) {
    Log.e(TAG, e.getMessage());
  }
}
```

Next, add another method to MainActivity and name it loadData(); the codes are shown in Listing 14-6. These are the same codes as in Listing 14-2, but this time, we're setting the text of txtinput and txtoutput to the contents of the file we just read.

Listing 14-6. loadData()

```
private void loadData() {
  StringBuilder sb = new StringBuilder();
  try (FileInputStream in = openFileInput(filename)) {
    int read = 0;
    while ((read = in.read()) != -1) {
      sb.append((char) read);
    }
    txtoutput.setText(sb.toString());
    txtinput.setText(sb.toString());

  }
  catch(IOException ie) {
    Log.e(TAG, ie.getMessage());
  }
}
```

We want the contents of "myfile.txt" to be displayed when the app opens. We can do this by calling loadData() inside the **onResume()** callback of MainActivity. Override the **onResume()** callback and call the **loadData()** method, as shown in Listing 14-7.

Listing 14-7. onResume()

```
@Override
protected void onResume() {
  super.onResume();
  loadData();
}
```

At this point, we're pretty much done. Figure 14-1 shows our app running in an emulator.

Figure 14-1. *Our finished app*

You can view the contents of the local file using the Device Explorer. From the main menu bar, choose **View ➤ Tool Windows ➤ Device Explorer**. The Device Explorer tool window pops up in the IDE, as shown in Figure 14-2.

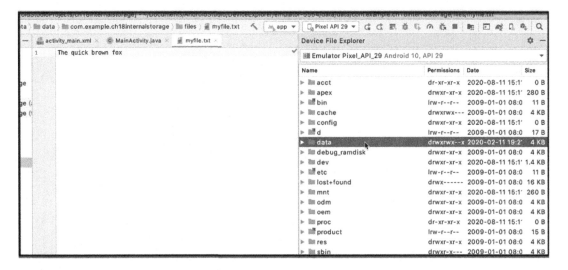

Figure 14-2. *Device Explorer*

Drill down to **data ➤ data ➤** (package name of the app) **➤ files**. You can view the file contents by double-clicking it; Android Studio will display the contents.

Summary

- You can store your file either in the always-available-but-limited internal storage or in the larger-but-may-be-dismounted external storage.

- Java I/O calls throw Exceptions; handle them appropriately.

CHAPTER 15

BroadcastReceivers

What we'll cover:

- Introduction to BroadcastReceivers

- Custom and system broadcasts

- Manifest and Context registered receivers

Android's application model is unique in many ways, but what makes it stand out is how it lets you build an app using the functionalities of other apps that you didn't make yourself—I don't mean just libraries, I mean full apps. In Chapter 8, we learned how to use Intents to activate Activities. In this chapter, we will learn how to send and receive broadcast messages using Intents.

A broadcast is an Intent that is sent either by the Android Runtime or other apps (your apps included) so that every application or component can hear it. Most applications will ignore the broadcast, but you can make your app listen to it. You can tune in to the message so you can respond to the broadcast. That is the topic of this chapter.

Introduction to BroadcastReceivers

Android apps can send or receive broadcast messages from the Android system and other apps (including ours). These broadcasts are sent when something interesting happens, for example, when the system boots up, when the device starts charging, when a file has finished downloading. This type of messaging model is called a *publish-subscribe* pattern; in this pattern, senders of messages (called publishers) do not target specific receivers (called subscribers), but instead categorize messages into classes without knowledge of which subscribers may be listening (if there are any at all). Similarly, subscribers express interest in one or more classes of messages by registering to listen to them without the publishers' knowledge.

© Ted Hagos 2020
T. Hagos, *Learn Android Studio 4*, https://doi.org/10.1007/978-1-4842-5937-5_15

System Broadcast vs. Custom Broadcast

A broadcast can be sent either by the OS (system broadcast) or by applications. A system broadcast is sent by the OS whenever something interesting happens, for example, when WiFi is turned on (or off), when the battery goes down to a specified threshold, a headset is plugged, the device was switched to airplane mode, and so on. Some examples of broadcast actions from the system are as follows:

- android.app.action.ACTION_PASSWORD_CHANGED

- android.app.action.ACTION_PASSWORD_EXPIRING

- android.bluetooth.a2dp.profile.action.CONNECTION_STATE_
  CHANGED

- android.bluetooth.a2dp.profile.action.PLAYING_STATE_CHANGED

- android.bluetooth.adapter.action.CONNECTION_STATE_CHANGED

- android.intent.action.BATTERY_CHANGED

- android.intent.action.BATTERY_LOW

- android.intent.action.BATTERY_OKAY

There are about 150+ of these listed on the documentation. You can find them on the **BROADCAST_ACTIONS.TXT** file in the Android SDK.

A custom broadcast, on the other hand, is something you make up. These are intents that you send to notify some of your app's components (or other apps that are tuned in) that something "interesting" happened, for example, a file has finished downloading, or you've finished calculating prime numbers, and so on.

Two Ways to Register for Broadcast

If you want to follow the coding examples, you need to create a project (with an empty Activity).

To respond to broadcast, you need to listen to it, and to do that, you need to register a receiver. A receiver is a class that extends the BroadcastReceiver class; you need to add a class like this in your app to respond to a broadcast message.

There are two ways to register: via the manifest or the Context.

Manifest registration, as the name implies, is done via the application's manifest file. To listen to broadcast messages via manifest registration, we need to do the following:

1. Add the **<receiver>** element in the application's AndroidManifest file; Listing 15-1 shows an annotated manifest file.

2. Add a class (that extends the BrodcastReceiver class) to the project, then override the **onReceive()** method. Listing 15-2 shows a sample BroadcastReceiver class that logs and displays the contents of the broadcast. You can add a BroadcastReceiver class in either one of two ways; you can right-click the project's package name (in the Project tool window), then choose **New ➤ Java Class**, as shown in Figure 15-1, and then add the necessary code to subclass BroadcastReceiver. Alternatively, you can right-click the application's package name, then choose **New ➤ Other ➤ BroadcastReceiver**. Whichever method you choose to add the BroadcastReceiver class, just make sure the class name is **MyReceiver**, if you want to follow the code examples in Listings 15-1 and 15-2.

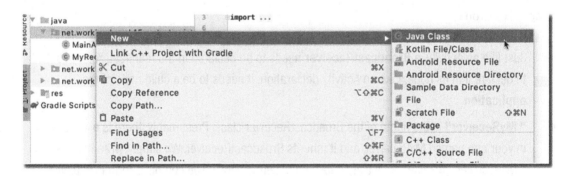

Figure 15-1. *Create a new Java class*

Listing 15-1. Manifest registration

```xml
<?xml version="1.0" encoding="utf-8"?>
<manifest xmlns:android="http://schemas.android.com/apk/res/android"
  package="net.workingdev.ch15_broadcastreceiver">
<application
  android:allowBackup="true"
  android:icon="@mipmap/ic_launcher"
```

```
android:label="@string/app_name"
android:roundIcon="@mipmap/ic_launcher_round"
android:supportsRtl="true"
android:theme="@style/AppTheme">
<activity android:name=".MainActivity">
  <intent-filter>
    <action android:name="android.intent.action.MAIN" />
    <category android:name="android.intent.category.LAUNCHER" />
  </intent-filter>
</activity>

<receiver ❶
  android:name=".MyReceiver"   ❷
  android:exported="true">
  <intent-filter> ❸
    <action android:name="android.intent.action.BOOT_COMPLETED"/>
    <action android:name="android.intent.action.INPUT_METHOD_CHANGED" />
  </intent-filter>
</receiver>
</application>
```

---

❶   Just like an Activity, a **BroadcastReceiver** needs to be declared in the manifest. You have
    to declare it in its node. Like an Activity declaration, it needs to be a child node of the
    application.

❷   **".MyReceiver"** is the name of the BroadcastReceiver class. Presumably, there is a class
    in your app named MyReceiver, and it inherits BroadcastReceiver. We simply write it as
    ".MyReceiver" just like the Activity above it (".MainActivity"). The complete form is actually
    net.workingdev.ch15_broadcast.MyReceiver, but we can use the short form because
    the package name is already declared earlier; look at the second line of the manifest, and
    you'll find the complete name of the package. Any subsequent classes that need to be
    declared in the manifest can simply use the short form, like ".MyReceiver" or ".MainActivity".

❸   The **intent-filter** is how we register. We're telling Android that we're interested in the events
    android.intent.action.BOOT_COMPLETED and android.intent.action.INPUT_
    METHOD_CHANGED. In case those Intents are broadcasted, our app would like to respond to it.

Listing 15-2. BroadcastReceiver class

```java
import android.content.BroadcastReceiver;
import android.content.Context;
import android.content.Intent;
import android.util.Log;
import android.widget.Toast;

public class MyReceiver extends BroadcastReceiver { ❶
  private final String TAG = getClass().getName();
  @Override

  public void onReceive(Context context, Intent intent) { ❷
    StringBuilder sb = new StringBuilder();
    sb.append("Action: " + intent.getAction() + "\n");
    sb.append("URI: " + intent.toUri(Intent.URI_INTENT_SCHEME).toString() +
    "\n");
    String log = sb.toString();
    Log.d(TAG, log);
    Toast.makeText(context, log, Toast.LENGTH_LONG).show();
  }
}
```

❶   Extend the BroadcastReceiver class. This class' name has to be consistent with the **android:name** attribute in the **<receiver>** node of the manifest file in Listing 15-1.

❷   Override the **onReceive()** method and implement your program logic in response to the broadcast message. In our case, we're only displaying a Toast message.

When you declare a BroadcastReceiver in the manifest file, the runtime will launch your app (if it isn't already running when the broadcast is sent).

When a user installs this app on a device, Android's package manager will register this app. The receiver then becomes a separate entry point into your app, which means the runtime can start the app and deliver the broadcast if your app isn't currently running.

The system creates a new BroadcastReceiver component object to handle each broadcast that it receives. This object is valid only for the duration of the call to **onReceive()**. Once your code returns from this method, the system considers the component no longer active.

Now that we've seen how to register a BroadcastReceiver via the manifest, let's see how to register a BroadcastReceiver via the Context. Context registration means registering programmatically—using either the Activity context or the Application context.

Let's create another project (with an empty Activity) for this, then add a Java class that extends the BroadcastReceiver, just like what we did in the previous project. You can name the BroadcastReceiver class MyReceiver as well. Open the MyReceiver class and edit it to match Listing 15-3.

Listing 15-3. MyReceiver class

```
import android.content.BroadcastReceiver;
import android.content.Context;
import android.content.Intent;
import android.widget.Toast;

public class MyReceiver extends BroadcastReceiver {

  @Override
  public void onReceive(Context context, Intent intent) {
    Toast.makeText(context, "Got it", Toast.LENGTH_LONG).show();
  }
}
```

MyReceiver is very simple; it will display a "Got it" Toast message in response to a broadcast.

To register the MyReceiver object via the Context, we will declare a member variable of type MyReceiver as a member of MainActivity, like so:

```
MyReceiver receiver = null;
```

We're making it a member variable because we need to refer to it from a couple of Activity lifecycle callbacks.

Inside the **onCreate()** callback of MainActivity, we will create an instance of the MyReceiver class, like this:

```
receiver = new MyReceiver();
```

We want to listen to broadcast messages only while the Activity is alive. When the Activity isn't visible to the user, we don't want to receive the messages. We will put the registration code inside the **onResume()** method of MainActivity; this method is called when the Activity is visible to the user. We will put the code to unregister the receiver inside the **onPause()** method of MainActivity because this method is called when the user is navigating away from the MainActivity.

Let's edit the MainActivity class. Listing 15-4 shows the annotated MainActivity class.

Listing 15-4. MainActivity

```
import androidx.appcompat.app.AppCompatActivity;
import android.content.IntentFilter;
import android.os.Bundle;

public class MainActivity extends AppCompatActivity {

  MyReceiver receiver = null; ❶

  @Override
  protected void onCreate(Bundle savedInstanceState) {
    super.onCreate(savedInstanceState);
    setContentView(R.layout.activity_main);

    receiver = new MyReceiver(); ❷
  }

  @Override
  protected void onResume() {
    super.onResume();

    IntentFilter filter = new IntentFilter("com.workingdev.
    SOMETHINGHAPPENED"); ❸
    registerReceiver(receiver, filter); ❹
  }
```

```
@Override
protected void onPause() {
  super.onPause();
  unregisterReceiver(receiver); ❺
  }
}
```

---

❶   Let's create an instance of the MyReceiver class. We're setting it to null because we won't instantiate here just yet.

❷   We create an instance of the MyReceiver class inside the **onCreate()** method.

❸   This statement is the programmatic equivalent of the `<intent-filter>` node we've seen earlier in Listing 15-1. To create an IntentFilter object, pass a broadcast action to its constructor. The broadcast action is the event you'd like to subscribe to. In this case, we'd like to be notified when the Intent whose action is `com.workingdev.SOMETHINGHAPPENED` is sent out; this Intent is an example of custom broadcast, not a system broadcast. As I mentioned previously, a custom broadcast action is just something you make up. As you can see in this example, the broadcast action is just a String object.

❹   Use the **registerReceiver()** method of the Activity to register the receiver. The method takes two arguments:
   1. An instance of BroadcastReceiver
   2. An instance of an IntentFilter

❺   Let's call the **unregisterReceiver()** inside the **onPause()** callback. We don't want to receive broadcast messages when MainActivity isn't visible to the user.

To test our app, we need to do two things:

1.   Run our app in an emulator

2.   Send the custom broadcast message `com.workingdev.SOMETHINGHAPPENED`

We can send the custom broadcast in either one of two ways. Firstly, we can programmatically send the custom broadcast message via an Intent object, like this:

```
Intent intent = new Intent("com.workingdev.SOMETHINGHAPPENED");
sendBroadcastIntent(intent);
```

You can put the two statements inside the click handler of a Button in an Activity class. You can put it inside the MainActivity of the current project or create a separate project for it altogether.

Secondly, we can send the custom broadcast message via the Android Debug Bridge or **adb** for short. It's a command-line tool that allows you to communicate with a device (physical or emulated). The **adb** can do quite a range of things like installing/uninstalling APKs, displaying logs, running Linux commands on the device, simulating phone calls, and many more. For our purpose, we'll use the **adb** to send a broadcast Intent. You can find the **adb** program inside the **platform-tools** folder of the Android SDK. If you've forgotten where your Android SDK is located, go to Android Studio's Settings (Windows or Linux) or Android Studio's Preferences (macOS). You can do that by pressing the keys **Ctrl + Alt + S**, for Windows and Linux, or **Command + ,** (comma) for macOS; alternatively, you can also get to them using the main menu bar.

The window that follows goes to **Appearance and Behavior ➤ System Settings ➤ Android SDK**, as shown in Figure 15-2.

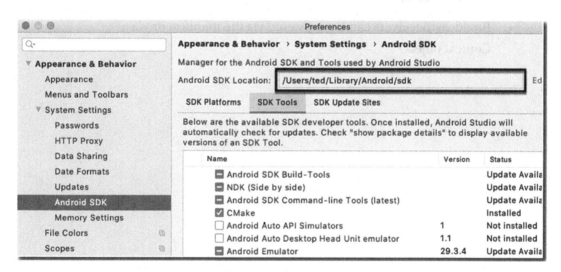

Figure 15-2. *Location of the Android SDK*

Open a command-line window and switch to the directory of the Android SDK. From there, cd to **platform-tools**, run the following command:

```
adb shell: a com.workingdev.SOMETHINGHAPPENED
```

If you're on macOS or Linux, you may have to prepend the command with a dot and forward slash, like this:

```
./adb shell am broadcast -a com.workingdev.SOMETHINGHAPPENED
```

Summary

- You can use BroadcastReceivers and Intents to create truly decoupled apps.

- You can make your app listen to a specific broadcast and do something interesting when the broadcast is sent.

- BroadcastReceivers can be used to route program logic in your app. You can make the app behave in specific ways as a response to the changes in the runtime environment, for example, low battery, no WiFi connection.

- BroadcastReceivers can be registered via the manifest or via a Context object.

CHAPTER 16

Jetpack, LiveData, ViewModel, and Room

What we'll cover:

- Lifecycle aware components

- ViewModel

- LiveData

- Room

We saw a bit of the Architecture components in Chapter 10. In this chapter, we'll look at some other libraries in the Architecture components, namely, Room; it's a persistence library that sits on top of SQLite. If you've used an ORM before (Object Relational Mapper), you can think of Room as something similar to that.

In this chapter, we'll also explore some more libraries in the Architecture components that go hand in hand with the Room libraries. We'll look at lifecycle aware components, LiveData, and ViewModel; these, together with Room, are some of the libraries you'll need to build a fluid and fluent database application.

Lifecycle Aware Components

Lifecycle aware components perform actions in response to a change in the lifecycle status of another component. If you're familiar with the *observable-observer* design pattern, lifecycle aware components operate like that.

© Ted Hagos 2020
T. Hagos, *Learn Android Studio 4*, https://doi.org/10.1007/978-1-4842-5937-5_16

We need to deal with some new vocabularies:

- **Lifecycle owner**—A component that has a lifecycle like an Activity or a Fragment; it can enter various states in its lifecycle, for example, *CREATED, RESUMED, PAUSED, DESTROYED*, and so on. A lifecycle observer can tap into a lifecycle owner and be notified when the lifecycle status changes, for example, when the Activity enters the CREATED state—after it enters **onCreate()**, for example; I sometimes refer to the lifecycle owner as an observable.

- **Lifecycle observer**—An object that listens to the changes in the lifecycle status of a **lifecycle owner**. It's a class that implements the *LifecycleObserver* interface.

With the lifecycle aware components, we can observe a component like Activity and perform actions as it enters any of its lifecycle statuses.

It's helpful to create a new project so you can follow the discussion in this chapter. Create a project with an empty Activity, then create another class named MainActivityObserver. You can create this class by right-clicking the project (as shown in Figure 16-1), then choosing **New ➤ Java Class**.

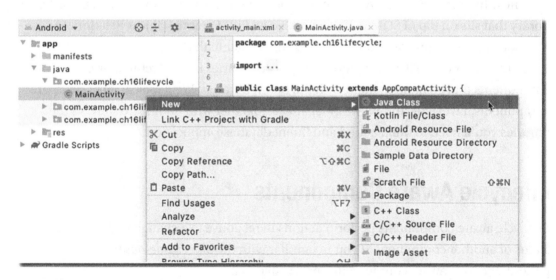

Figure 16-1. *Add a Java class to the project*

Name the new class "MainActivityObserver."

Next, we need to add a dependency on the **build.gradle** file (module level). Edit the project's Gradle file to match Listing 16-1.

Listing 16-1. build.gradle file, module level

```
dependencies {
    def lifecycle_version = "2.2.0"
    implementation "androidx.lifecycle:lifecycle-extensions:$lifecycle_
    version"
    annotationProcessor "androidx.lifecycle:lifecycle-compiler:$lifecycle_
    version"
    ...
}
```

Note   The lifecycle_version at the time of writing is "2.2.0"; this will be different for you since you'll be reading this at a later time. You can visit `https://bit.ly/lifecyclerelnotes` to find out the current version of the lifecycle libraries.

Your project needs to refresh after editing the Gradle file.

To demonstrate the lifecycle concepts, we will examine two classes:

- **MainActivity**—This is a simple Activity, pretty much like any other Activity that the IDE generates when you create a project with an empty Activity. The code sample is shown in Listing 16-2.

- **MainActivityObserver**—A Java class that will implement the LifecycleObserver interface; this will be our listener object. The code is listed and annotated in Listing 16-1.

The classes MainActivity and MainActivityObserver show an example of setting up an *observer-observable* relationship between a *lifecycle owner* (MainActivity) and a *lifecycle observer* (MainActivityObserver). Edit the MainActivityObserver class to match Listing 16-2.

Listing 16-2. MainActivityObserver class

```
import androidx.lifecycle.Lifecycle;
import androidx.lifecycle.LifecycleObserver;
import androidx.lifecycle.OnLifecycleEvent;

public class MainActivityObserver implements LifecycleObserver {   ❶

  @OnLifecycleEvent(Lifecycle.Event.ON_CREATE) ❷
  public void onCreateEvent() {  ❸
    System.out.println("EVENT: onCreate Event fired");   ❹
  }

  @OnLifecycleEvent(Lifecycle.Event.ON_PAUSE)
  public void onPauseEvent() {
    System.out.println("EVENT: onPause Event fired");
  }

  @OnLifecycleEvent(Lifecycle.Event.ON_RESUME)
  public void onResumeEvent() {
    System.out.println("EVENT: onResume Event fired");
  }
}
```

---

❶   If you want to observe other components' lifecycle changes, you need to implement the
     LifecycleObserver interface. This line makes this class an *observer*.

❷   Use the OnLifecycleEvent annotation to tell the Android Runtime that the decorated method
     is supposed to be called when the lifecycle event happens; in this case, we're listening to the
     ON_CREATE event of the observed object. The parameter to the decorator indicates which
     lifecycle event we're listening to.

❸   This is the decorated method. It gets called when the object it is observing enters the
     ON_CREATE lifecycle status. You can name this method anything you want; I just named it
     onCreateEvent() because it's descriptive. Otherwise, you're free to name it to your liking;
     the method's name doesn't matter because you already decorated it, and the annotation is
     sufficient.

❹   This is where you do something interesting in response to a lifecycle status change.

Next, edit the MainActivity class to match Listing 16-3.

Listing 16-3. MainActivity class

```
public class MainActivity extends AppCompatActivity {

  @Override
  protected void onCreate(Bundle savedInstanceState) {
    super.onCreate(savedInstanceState);
    setContentView(R.layout.activity_main);

    getLifecycle().addObserver(new MainActivityObserver()); ❶

  }
}
```

---

❶   From the point of view of the MainActivity (it's the one being observed), the only thing
      we need to do here is to add an observer object using the **addObserver()** method of the
      LifeCycleOwner interface—yes, the AppCompatActivity implements LifeCycleOwner; that's
      the reason we can call the **getLifecycle()** method within our Activity. You simply need to pass
      an instance of an observer class (in our case, it's the MainActivityObserver) to set up lifecycle
      awareness between an Activity and a regular class.

The application doesn't do much. It merely logs messages to the Logcat window
every time there is a change in the lifecycle state of MainActivity. Still, it demonstrates
how we can add an observer to the lifecycle of any Activity.

ViewModel

The Android framework manages the lifecycle of UI controllers like *Activities* and
Fragments; it may decide to destroy or re-create an Activity (or Fragment) in response to
some user actions, for example, clicking the back button, or device events, for example,
rotating the screen. These configuration changes are out of your control.

If the runtime decides to destroy the UI controller, any transient UI-related data that
you're currently storing in them will be lost.

It's best to create another project (with an empty Activity) to follow the discussion in this section; then add a Java class to the project and name it "RandomNumber." Listings 16-4, 16-5, and 16-6 show a simple app that displays a random number every time the Activity is created.

Listing 16-4 shows the code for the random number generator. It only has the two methods **getNumber()** and **createRandomNumber()**; each method leaves a Log statement, so we can inspect when and how many times the methods were called. The logic for the **getNumber()** method is simple—if the **minitialized** variable is false, that means we're creating an instance of the RandomNumber class for the first time; so, we'll create the random number and then simply return it. Otherwise, we'll return whatever is the current value of the **minitialized** variable.

Listing 16-4. RandomNumber class

```java
import android.util.Log;
import java.util.Random;

public class RandomNumber   {

  private String TAG = getClass().getSimpleName();

  int mrandomnumber;
  boolean minitialized = false;

  String getNumber() {
    if(!minitialized) {
      createRandomNumber();
    }
    Log.i(TAG, "RETURN Random number");
    return mrandomnumber + "";
  }

   void createRandomNumber() {
    Log.i(TAG, "CREATE NEW Random number");
    Random random = new Random();
    mrandomnumber = random.nextInt(100);
    minitialized = true;
  }
}
```

Listing 16-5 shows the code for our MainActivity. Everything happens inside the **onCreate()** method. When MainActivity enters the *CREATED* state, we create an instance of the RandomNumber class; we call the **getNumber()** method, and we set the value of the TextView to the result of the **getNumber()** method.

Listing 16-5. MainActivity class

```java
public class MainActivity extends AppCompatActivity {

  @Override
  protected void onCreate(Bundle savedInstanceState) {
    super.onCreate(savedInstanceState);
    setContentView(R.layout.activity_main);

    RandomNumber data = new RandomNumber();

    ((TextView) findViewById(R.id.txtrandom)).setText(data.getNumber());
  }
}
```

Listing 16-6 shows the layout code for activity_main.

Listing 16-6. activity_main.xml

```xml
<?xml version="1.0" encoding="utf-8"?>
<android.support.constraint.ConstraintLayout
xmlns:android="http://schemas.android.com/apk/res/android"
  xmlns:app="http://schemas.android.com/apk/res-auto"
  xmlns:tools="http://schemas.android.com/tools"
  android:layout_width="match_parent"
  android:layout_height="match_parent"
  tools:context=".MainActivity">

  <TextView
    android:id="@+id/txtrandom"
    android:layout_width="wrap_content"
    android:layout_height="wrap_content"
    android:text="Hello World!"
    android:textSize="36sp"
```

```
   app:layout_constraintBottom_toBottomOf="parent"
   app:layout_constraintLeft_toLeftOf="parent"
   app:layout_constraintRight_toRightOf="parent"
   app:layout_constraintTop_toTopOf="parent" />
```

```
</android.support.constraint.ConstraintLayout>
```

When you run this code for the first time, you'll see a random number displayed on the TextView, no surprises there. You'll also see the Log entries for **createNumber()** and **getNumber()** in the Logcat window; no surprises there either. Now, while the app is running on the emulator, try to change the device's orientation—you'll notice that every time the screen orientation changes, the displayed number on the TextView changes as well. You'll also see that additional logs for the **createNumber()** and **getNumber()** methods show up in Logcat. This is because the runtime destroys and re-creates the MainActivity every time the screen orientation changes. Our RandomNumber object also gets destroyed and re-created along with the MainActivity—our UI data cannot survive across orientation changes.

This is a good case for using the ViewModel library so that the UI data can survive the destruction and re-creation of the Activity class. We only need to do three things to implement ViewModel:

1. Add the lifecycle extensions to our project's dependencies, like what we did earlier. Go back to Listing 16-1 for instructions.

2. To make the RandomGenerator class a *ViewModel*, we will extend the ViewModel class from the AndroidX lifecycle libraries.

3. From the MainActivity, we'll get an instance of the RandomNumber class using the factory method of the ViewModelProviders class, instead of merely creating an instance of the RandomNumber class.

Listing 16-7 shows the changes in the RandomNumber class; the RandomNumber class is transformed automatically to a *ViewModel* object by extending the ViewModel class.

Listing 16-7. RandomNumber extends ViewModel

```java
import java.util.Random;
import androidx.lifecycle.ViewModel;

public class RandomNumber extends ViewModel {

  private String TAG = getClass().getSimpleName();

  int mrandomnumber;
  boolean minitialized = false;

  String getNumber() {
    if(!minitialized) {
      createRandomNumber();
    }
    Log.i(TAG, "RETURN Random number");
    return mrandomnumber + "";
  }

  void createRandomNumber() {
    Log.i(TAG, "CREATE NEW Random number");
    Random random = new Random();
    mrandomnumber = random.nextInt(100);
    minitialized = true;
  }
}
```

The class remains mostly the same as its previous version shown in Listing 16-4; the only difference is that now it extends *ViewModel*.

Now, let's implement the changes on the MainActivity; Listing 16-8 shows the modified MainActivity which uses ViewModelProviders to get an instance of the RandomNumber class—which is our ViewModel object.

Listing 16-8. MainActivity and ViewModelProviders

```java
import androidx.lifecycle.ViewModelProviders;
import android.os.Bundle;
import android.widget.TextView;
```

```
public class MainActivity extends AppCompatActivity {

  @Override
  protected void onCreate(Bundle savedInstanceState) {
    super.onCreate(savedInstanceState);
    setContentView(R.layout.activity_main);

    RandomNumber data;
    data = ViewModelProviders.of(this).get(RandomNumber.class); ❶

    ((TextView) findViewById(R.id.txtrandom)).setText(data.getNumber());
  }
}
```

---

❶   This is the only change we need to do in MainActivity. Instead of directly managing the
     ViewModel object (the RandomNumber class) by creating an instance of it inside the
     onCreate() method, we'll let the ViewModelProviders class manage the scope of our
     ViewModel object.

LiveData

Going back to our RandomNumber example, we have an app that shows a random
number every time the app is launched. The app uses ViewModel already, so we don't
have the problem of losing data every time the Activity is destroyed and re-created. The
basic data flow is shown in Figure 16-2.

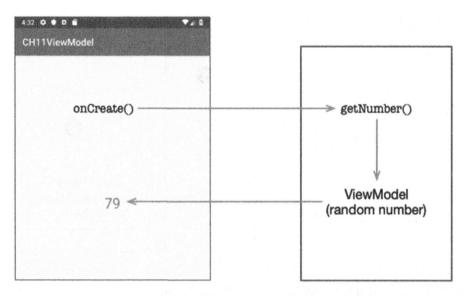

Figure 16-2. *Data flow for the RandomNumber example*

But what if you need to fetch another number? For that, we may add a trigger on the
MainActivity, like a Button, and then it will call **getNumber()** on the ViewModel—but
how are we going to refresh the TextView in the MainActivity? There are already a couple
of ways to do this, and you might have encountered them already. One way to facilitate
data exchange between our ViewModel and Activity is the creative use of interfaces (but
we won't discuss that here) or by using an EventBus like Otto (we also won't discuss that
here)—but now, thankfully, because of Architecture components, we can use LiveData.
The new data flow is depicted in Figure 16-3.

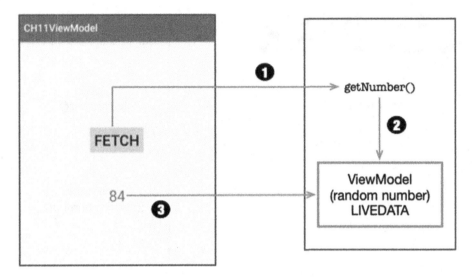

Figure 16-3. *RandomNumber sample with LiveData*

❶   The user clicks the **FETCH** button, which calls the **getNumber()** function; actually, we're going to call the **createNumber()** first, then call the **getNumber()**. This way, we're fetching a new random number. There are ways to do this more elegantly, but this is the quickest way to do it, so bear with me.

❷   Our ViewModel object gets a new random number. This isn't a simple String anymore; we're going to change it to a MutableLiveData to become *observable*.

❸   From the MainActivity, we'll get an instance of the LiveData coming from our ViewModel object and write some codes to *observe* it; next, we simply react to changes on the LiveData.

Let's see how that works in code. Listings 16-9 and 16-10 show the code for our ViewModel and MainActivity, respectively.

Listing 16-9. ViewModel with LiveData

```
import androidx.lifecycle.MutableLiveData;
import androidx.lifecycle.ViewModel;

public class RNModel extends ViewModel {
  private String TAG = getClass().getSimpleName();

  MutableLiveData<String> mrandomnumber = new MutableLiveData<>(); ❶
  boolean minitialized = false;
```

```
MutableLiveData<String> getNumber() { ❷
  if(!minitialized) {
    createRandomNumber();
  }
  Log.i(TAG, "RETURN Random number");
  return mrandomnumber;
}

void createRandomNumber() {
  Log.i(TAG, "CREATE NEW Random number");
  Random random = new Random();

  mrandomnumber.setValue(random.nextInt(100) + ""); ❸
  minitialized = true;
}
}
```

❶   The value of mrandomnumber is what we return to the MainActivity. We want this to be an *observable* object. To do this, we change its type from *int* to *MutableLiveData*.

❷   We have to make that type change here too since mrandomnumber is now *MutableLiveData*; this function has to return *MutableLiveData*.

❸   To set the value of the *MutableLiveData*, use the setValue() method.

Now we can move on to the changes in MainActivity. Listing 16-10 shows the modified and annotated code for MainActivity.

Listing 16-10. MainActivity

```
import androidx.appcompat.app.AppCompatActivity;
import androidx.lifecycle.MutableLiveData;
import androidx.lifecycle.Observer;
import androidx.lifecycle.ViewModelProviders;
import android.os.Bundle;
import android.view.View;
import android.widget.Button;
import android.widget.TextView;
```

```java
public class MainActivity extends AppCompatActivity {

  @Override
  protected void onCreate(Bundle savedInstanceState) {
    super.onCreate(savedInstanceState);
    setContentView(R.layout.activity_main);

    final RNModel data;
    data = ViewModelProviders.of(this).get(RNModel.class);

    final TextView txtnumber = (TextView) findViewById(R.id.txtrandom);
    MutableLiveData<String> mnumber = data.getNumber(); ❶

    Button btn = (Button) findViewById(R.id.button);  ❷
    btn.setOnClickListener(new View.OnClickListener() {
      @Override
      public void onClick(View v) {
        data.createRandomNumber();
        data.getNumber();
      }
    });

    mnumber.observe(this, new Observer<String>() { ❸
      @Override
      public void onChanged(String val) { ❹
        txtnumber.setText(val);
      }
    });
  }
}
```

---

❶   Let's fetch the random number from the ViewModel. The random number isn't of String type anymore; it's MutableLiveData.

❷   This is the boilerplate code for a button click. We need this trigger to fetch a random number from the ViewModel.

❸   To *observe* a LiveData, we call the **observe()** method; the method takes two arguments. The first argument is the lifecycle owner (MainActivity, so we pass *this*); the second argument is an Observer object. We used an anonymous class here to create the Observer object.

❹   This **onChanged()** method is called every time the value of the random number (mrandomnumber) in the ViewModel changes; so, when it changes, we set the value of the TextView accordingly.

Cool, right? If you're still not sold on using LiveData, here are a couple of things to consider. When you use LiveData

- You're sure the UI **always matches the data** state. You've already seen this from the example. LiveData follows the Observer pattern; it notifies the observer when its value changes.

- There are **no memory leaks**. Observers are bound to lifecycle objects. If, for example, our MainActivity enters the paused state (for whatever reason, maybe another Activity is on the foreground), the LiveData won't be observed; if the MainActivity is destroyed, the LiveData again won't be observed, and it will clean up after itself—which also means we won't need to handle the lifecycles of MainActivity and the ViewModel manually.

Room

If you want to include database functionalities to your app, you might want to look at **Room**. Before Room, the two popular ways to build database apps were either using Realm or just using good ole SQLite. Dealing with SQLite was considered to be a bit low level; it felt too close to the metal and, as such, was a bit cumbersome to use. **Realm** was quite popular among developers, but it wasn't a first-party solution, no matter the popularity. Thankfully, we now have Room.

Room is an abstraction on top of SQLite; if you've used an ORM before, like Hibernate, it's similar to that. Room has several advantages over using plain vanilla SQLite; with Room

- You don't have to deal with raw queries for basic database operations.

- It verifies the SQL queries at compile time, so you don't need to worry about SQL injection—remember those?

- There is no impedance mismatch between your database objects and Java objects. Room takes care of it; you only need to deal with Java objects.

Room has three major components, the **Entity**, the **Dao**, and the **Database** component. Their relationship with the application is shown in Figure 16-4.

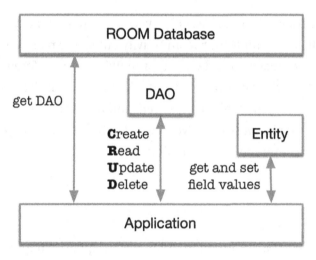

Figure 16-4. *Room components*

- **Entity**—An Entity is used to represent a database table. You code it as a class that's decorated by the @Entity annotation.

- **Dao** or Data Access Object is a class that contains methods to access the tables in the database. This is where you code your CRUD (create, read, update, and delete). This is an *interface* that's decorated by the @Dao annotation.

- **Database**—This component holds a reference to the database. It's an abstract class that is annotated by the @Database annotation.

Before you can use Room in a project, you need to add its dependencies to the *build. gradle* file (module level), as shown in Listing 16-11.

Listing 16-11. Room dependencies

```
dependencies {
    def room_version = "2.1.0-alpha07"
    implementation "androidx.room:room-runtime:$room_version"
    annotationProcessor "androidx.room:room-compiler:$room_version"

    . . .

}
```

Listings 16-12, 16-13, 16-14, and 16-15 show the four Java source files that demonstrate Room's basic usage.

Listing 16-12. Person class, the Entity

```
import androidx.annotation.NonNull;
import androidx.room.Entity;
import androidx.room.PrimaryKey;

@Entity(tableName = "person") ❶
public class Person {
  @PrimaryKey(autoGenerate = true) ❷
  @NonNull public int uid;

  @ColumnInfo(name="last_name") ❸
  public String last_name;
  public String first_name;

  public Person(String lname, String fname) {
    last_name = lname;
    first_name = fname;
  }

  public Person() {}
}
```

❶   The @Entity annotation makes this an Entity. If you don't pass the *tableName* argument, the table's name will default to the name of the decorated class. You will only need to pass this argument if you want the table's name to be different from the decorated class. So, what I wrote here is unnecessary and redundant because I set the value of *tableName* to "person," which is the same as the decorated class name.

❷   We're making the uid member variable the primary key; we're also saying it can't be null.

❸   The member variables of the class will automatically become the fields on the table. The column names on the table will take after the member variables' names unless you use the @ColumnInfo annotation. If you want the name of the table field (column) to be different from the name of the member variable, use the @ColumnInfo decoration, as shown here, and set the *name* to your preferred column name.

Listing 16-13. PersonDAO, the Data Access Object

```
import java.util.List;
import androidx.room.Dao;
import androidx.room.Delete;
import androidx.room.Insert;
import androidx.room.Query;
import androidx.room.Update;

@Dao ❶
interface PersonDAO { ❷
  @Insert   ❸
  void insertPerson(Person person);

  @Update
  void updatePerson(Person person);

  @Delete
  void deletePerson(Person person);

  @Query("SELECT * FROM person") ❹
  public List<Person> listPeople();
}
```

❶   A DAO needs to be annotated by the @Dao decorator.

❷   Daos have to be written as interfaces.

❸   Use the @Insert decorator to indicate that the decorated method will be used for inserting
      records to the table. Similarly, you will decorate methods for update, query, and delete with
      @Update, @Query, and @Delete, respectively.

❹   Use the @Query to write SQL select statements. Each @Query is verified at compile time; if
      there is a problem with the query, a compilation error occurs instead of a runtime error. That
      should put your mind at ease.

Listing 16-14. AppDatabase, the database holder

```
import android.content.Context;
import androidx.room.Database;
import androidx.room.Room;
import androidx.room.RoomDatabase;

@Database(entities = {Person.class}, version = 1) ❶
public abstract class AppDatabase extends RoomDatabase { ❷

  private static AppDatabase minstance;
  private static final String DB_NAME = "person_db";

  public abstract PersonDAO getPersonDAO(); ❸

  public static synchronized AppDatabase getInstance(Context ctx) { ❹
    if(minstance == null) {
      minstance = Room.databaseBuilder(ctx.getApplicationContext(), ❺
          AppDatabase.class,
          DB_NAME)
          .fallbackToDestructiveMigration()
          .build();
    }
    return minstance;
  }
}
```

❶   Use the @Database to signify that this class is the database holder. Use the *entities* argument to specify the Entities that are in the database. If you have more than one Entity, use commas to separate the list. The second argument is the *version*; this is an integer value that specifies the version of your DB.

❷   A Database class is *abstract* and extends the RoomDatabase.

❸   You need to provide an abstract class that will return an instance of the DAO object.

❹   You need to provide a static method to get an instance of the Database. It doesn't have to be a singleton, like what we did here, but I imagine you don't want more than one instance of the Database class.

❺   Use the **databaseBuilder()** method to create an instance of the RoomDatabase. There are three arguments to the builder method: (1) an application context; (2) the abstract class, which is annotated by @Database; and (3) the name of the database file. This will be the filename of SQLite dB.

Now that all our Room components are in place, we can use them from our app. Listing 16-15 shows how to use Room components from an Activity.

Listing 16-15. MainActivity

```
public class MainActivity extends AppCompatActivity {

  private AppDatabase db;

  @Override
  protected void onCreate(Bundle savedInstanceState) {
    super.onCreate(savedInstanceState);
    setContentView(R.layout.activity_main);

    Button btn = (Button) findViewById(R.id.button);
    btn.setOnClickListener(new View.OnClickListener() {
      @Override
      public void onClick(View v) {
        saveData();
        System.out.println("Clicked");
      }
    });
```

```java
  db = AppDatabase.getInstance(this); ❶
  }

  private void saveData() {
    final String mlastname = ((TextView) findViewById(R.id.txtlastname)).
    getText().toString();
    final String mfirstname = ((TextView) findViewById(R.id.txtfirstname)).
    getText().toString(); ❷

    new Thread(new Runnable() { ❸
      @Override
      public void run() {
        Person person = new Person(mlastname, mfirstname); ❹
        PersonDAO dao = db.getPersonDAO(); ❺
        dao.insertPerson(person); ❻
        List<Person> people = dao.listPeople(); ❼

        for(Person p:people) { ❽
          System.out.printf("%s , %s\n", p.last_name, p.first_name );
        }
      }
    }).start();
  }
}
```

---

❶ To begin using the RoomDatabase, get an instance of using the factory method we coded in the AppDatabase earlier.

❷ Let's collect the data from the TextViews.

❸ Room follows best practices, so it won't allow you to run any database query on the main UI thread. You need to create a background thread and run all your Room commands in there. Here, I used a quick and dirty Thread and Runnable objects, but you're free to use any other means of background execution, for example, AsyncTask.

❹ Create a Person object using the inputs from the TextViews.

❺ Let's get an instance of the DAO.

❻ Do an *insert* using the insertPerson() method we coded in the DAO earlier.

❼   Let's do a *SELECT*.

❽   And list all entries in our person table.

In a real app, you probably wouldn't access the database from a UI controller like an Activity; you might want to put in a ViewModel class. That way, the UI controller's responsibility is strictly to present data and not to act as a model.

If you use Room with ViewModel and LiveData, it can provide a more responsive UI experience. I didn't cover it here, but it's a great exercise to pursue after this chapter.

Summary

- AppCompatActivity objects are now lifecycle owners. You can write another class and listen to the lifecycle changes of a lifecycle owner, then react accordingly; Fragments too are lifecycle owners—don't forget to use *AndroidX artifacts* on your project when working with lifecycle aware components.

- ViewModel makes your UI data resilient to the destruction and re-creation of UI controllers (like Activities and Fragments).

- LiveData makes the relationship between your UI object and model data bidirectional. A change in one is automatically reflected in the other.

- Room is an ORM for SQLite. It's a first-party solution and it's part of the Architecture components—there's little reason we shouldn't use it.

CHAPTER 17

Distributing Apps

What we'll cover:

- Preparing for release
- Signing the app
- Google Play
- App bundle

You can distribute your app quite freely and without much restrictions; you can let your users download it from your website, Google Drive, Dropbox, and so on. You may even email the app directly to the users, if you wish; but many developers choose to distribute their app on a marketplace like Google or Amazon to maximize reach. Another reason to put your app on the trusted digital marketplaces is, well, they're trusted. When an app is not downloaded from a trusted source, the apps won't be instantly usable; they will get a notification that the app is not from a trusted source.

In this chapter, we'll discuss the things you need to do to get your app out in Google Play.

Prepare the App for Release

A couple of things you need to mind when releasing an app to the public are

1. Prepare the material and assets for release
2. Configure the app for release
3. Build a release-ready app

© Ted Hagos 2020
T. Hagos, *Learn Android Studio 4*, https://doi.org/10.1007/978-1-4842-5937-5_17

Prepare Material and Assets for Release

Your code is great, and you might even think it's clever, but the user will never see it. What they will see are your View objects, the icons, and the other graphical assets. You should polish them.

If you think the app's icon isn't a big deal, that could be a mistake. The icons help the users identify your app as it sits on the home screen. This icon also appears on other areas like the launcher window and the download section, and more importantly, it appears on the store where the app was published. The app's icon holds a lot of sway when creating the first impressions about an app. It's a good idea to put some work into this and read Google's guidelines regarding icons; you can read about it at `http://bit.ly/androidreleaseiconguidelines`. While you're at it, also visit `https://romannurik.github.io/AndroidAssetStudio/`—this resource will save you plenty of time when generating assets for your app.

You also need to pay attention to the graphical assets like screen captures and the text for promotional copy. Make sure you read Google's guidelines for graphical assets; you can read it here: `http://bit.ly/androidreleasegraphicassets`.

Configure the App for Release

1. **Check the package name**—The app may have started as an exercise or throwaway code, and then it grew and took on a life of its own. You may want to check the package name of the app. Make sure it isn't still **com.example.myapp**. The package name makes the app unique across the Google marketplace; and once you decide on a package name, you can't change it anymore. So, give it some thought. You already know how to change this; we covered this in the Gradle chapter; remember?

2. **Deal with the debug information**—Make sure the android:debuggable attribute in the `<application>` tag of the Manifest is removed; you just need to check, really, because Android Studio would have removed this automatically when you change the mode to "release."

3. **Remove the Log statements**—Different developers do this differently. Some would go through the code and remove the statements (painfully) manually. Some would write *sed* or *awk* programs to strip away the log statements. Some would use *ProGuard* and others would use third-party tools like *Timber* to take care of logging activities. It's up to you which you will use; but make sure that your users won't accidentally see the log information—if you haven't made up your mind yet, I would really urge you to try *Timber*.

4. **Check the application's permissions**—Sometime during development, you may have experimented on some features of the application, and you may have set permissions on the manifest like permission to use the network, write to external storage, and so on. Review the `<uses-permission>` tag on the manifest and make sure that you don't grant permissions that the application does not need.

5. **Check remote servers and URLs**—If your application relies on web APIs or cloud services, make sure that the release build of the app is using production URLs and not test paths. You may have been given sandboxes and test URLs during development; you need to switch them up to the production version.

Build a Release-Ready Application

During development, Android Studio did quite a few things for you; it

1. Created a debug certificate

2. Assembled all your project's assets, config files, and runtime binaries into an APK

3. Signed the APK using a debug certificate

4. Deployed the APK to an emulator or a connected device

All these things happened in the background; you didn't have to do anything else but write your codes. Now, you need to take care of that certificate. Google Play and other similar marketplaces won't distribute an app signed with a debug certificate. It needs to be a proper certificate. You don't need a certificate authority like Thawte or Verisign; a self-signed certificate will suffice.

In the next steps, we'll generate a signed bundle or APK. You already know what an APK is—it's the package that contains your application. It's what you upload to Google Play. A bundle, on the other hand, is a lot like an APK, but it's a newer upload format. Like the APK, it also includes all your app's compiled code and resources, but it defers APK generation. It's a new app serving model called Dynamic Delivery. It uses your app bundle to generate and serve optimized APK for each user's device configuration—so they download only the code and resources that are needed to run your app. You don't have to build, sign, and manage multiple APKs anymore.

In Android Studio, the steps to generate an APK and a bundle are almost identical. In the following steps, we'll see how to generate both the bundle and an APK.

Launch Android Studio, if it isn't open yet. Open the project, then from the main menu bar, go to **Build ➤ Generate Signed Bundle or APK**, as shown in Figure 17-1.

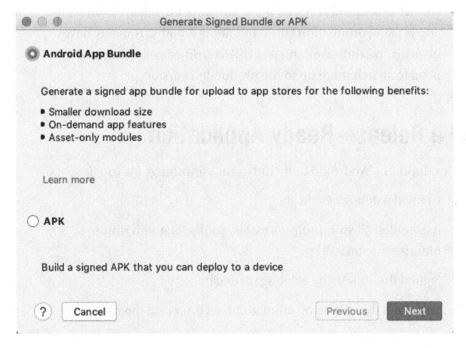

Figure 17-1. *Generate signed APK*

Choose either Bundle or APK, then click Next; in this example, I chose to create a bundle. When you click Next, you will see the "Keystore" dialog, as shown in Figure 17-2.

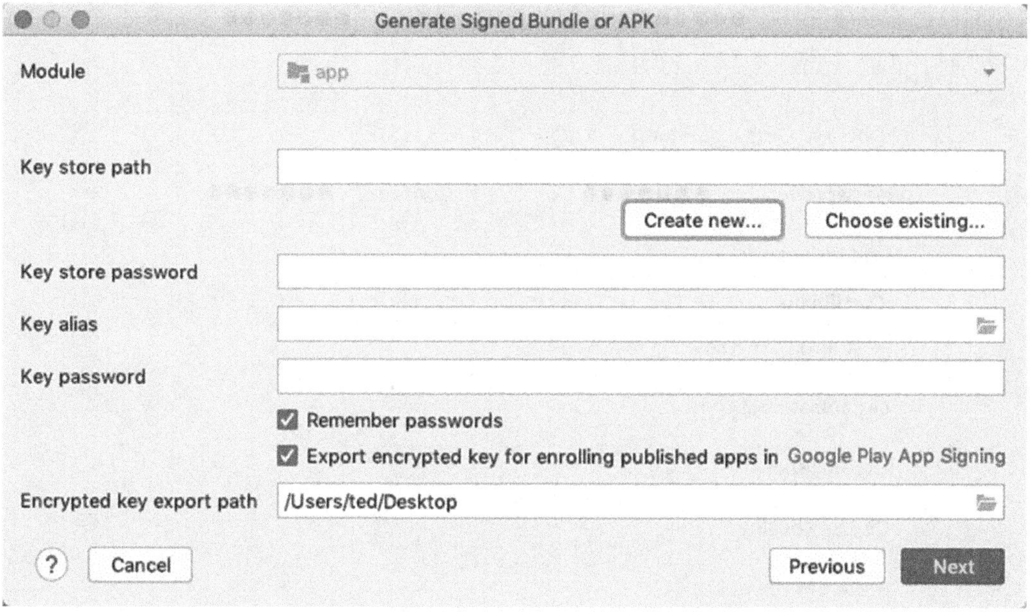

Figure 17-2. *Keystore dialog*

The **Key store path** is asking where our Java Keystore (JKS) file is. At this point, you don't have it yet. So, click **Create New**. You'll see the dialog window for creating a new keystore, as shown in Figure 17-3.

Figure 17-3. *New keystore*

Table 17-1 shows the description for the input items of the keystore.

Table 17-1. *Keystore items and description*

Keystore items	Description
Keystore path	The location where you want to keep the keystore. This is entirely up to you. Just make sure you remember this location
Password	This is the password for the keystore; don't lose this, and make sure you remember this one—otherwise, you'll need to create another keystore file
Alias	This alias identifies the key. It's just a friendly name for it
(Key) Password	This is the password for the key. This is NOT the same password as the keystore's (but you can use the same password if you like)
Validity, in years	The default is 25 years; you can just accept the default. If you publish on Google Play, the certificate must be valid until October of 2033—so, 25 years should be fine
Other information	Only the first and last name fields are required

When you're done filling up the New Key Store dialog, click OK. This will bring you back to the Generate Signed Bundle or APK window, as shown in Figure 17-4; but now, the JKS file is created and the Keystore dialog is populated with it.

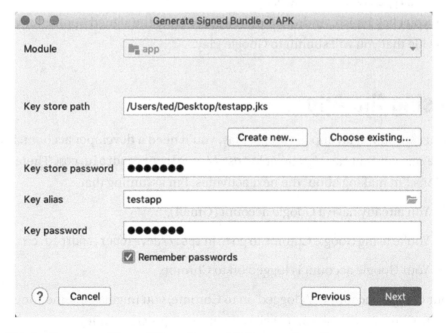

Figure 17-4. *Generate Signed Bundle or APK, populated*

Click Next. Now we choose the destination of the signed bundle as shown in Figure 17-5.

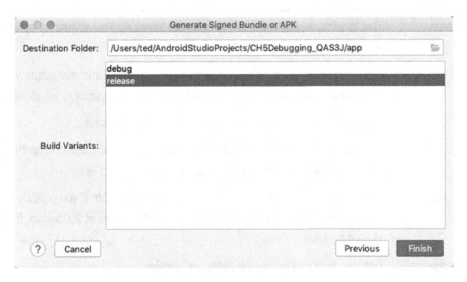

Figure 17-5. *Signed APK, APK destination folder*

You need to remember the location of the "Destination Folder," as shown in Figure 17-5. This is where Android Studio will store the signed bundle. Also, make sure that the **Build type** is set to "release."

When you click Finish, Android Studio will generate the signed bundle for your app. This is the file that you will submit to Google Play.

Releasing the App

Before you can submit an app to Google Play, you'll need a developer account. If you don't have one yet, you can sign up at https://developer.android.com. There's a lot of assumptions I'm making about the next activities. I'm assuming that

1. You already have a Google account (Gmail).

2. You're using Google Chrome to go to https://developer.android.com.

3. Your Google account is logged on to Chrome.

If your Google account isn't logged on to Chrome, you might see something like Figure 17-6. Chrome will ask you to select an account (or create one).

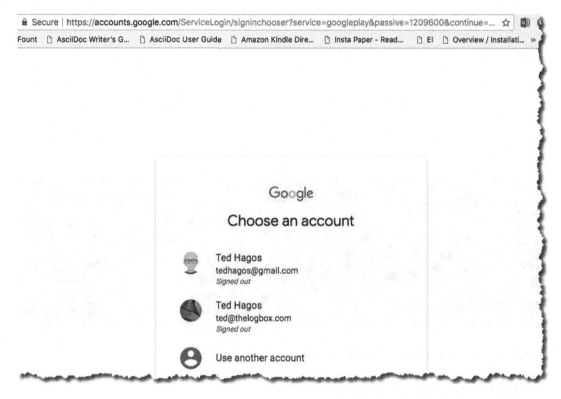

Figure 17-6. *Choose an account*

When you get your Google account sorted out, you'll be taken to the `https://developer.android.com` website, as shown in Figure 17-7.

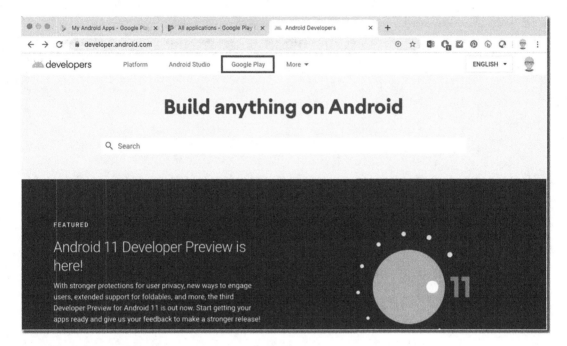

Figure 17-7. *Android Developers website*

Click **Google Play**, as shown in Figure 17-7.

Click **Launch Play Console**, as shown in Figure 17-8.

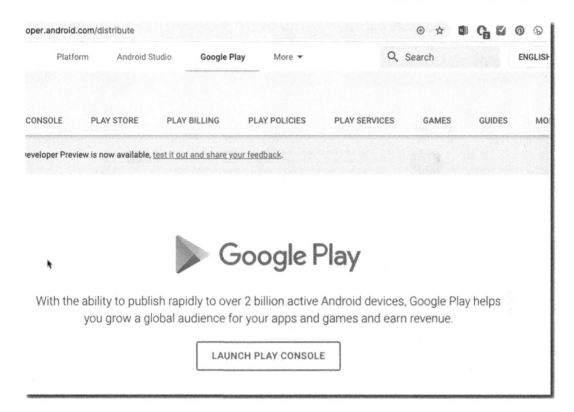

Figure 17-8. *Launch Play Console*

You need to go through four steps to complete the registration (shown in Figure 17-9):

1. Sign in with your Google account.

2. Accept the developer agreement.

3. Pay the registration fee.

4. Complete your account details.

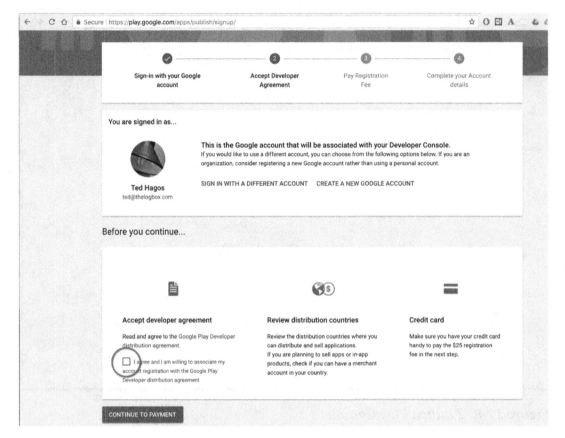

Figure 17-9. *Google Play Console, sign up*

Once you have completed the registration and one-time payment, you will now have access to the Google Play Console, as shown in Figure 17-10.

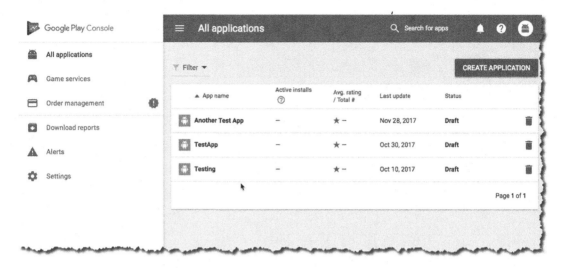

Figure 17-10. *Google Play Console*

This is where you can start the process of submitting your app to the store. Click the "Create Application" button to get started.

Summary

- Before the users can experience your app, they will see the icons and other graphical assets first—make sure the graphical assets are just as polished as your code.

- Strip your code of all debug info and log statements before you build a release.

- Code review your own work. If you have buddies or other people who can review the code with you, that's much better. If your app uses servers, RESTful URLs, and so on, make sure they are production ready and not sandboxes.

- Before you can upload your app to Google Play, you need to sign your app with a proper certificate.

- You'll need a Google Play account if you want to sell your apps on Google Play. I paid a one-time fee of 25 USD, but that was a couple of years ago.

- Don't forget to test your app on a real device.

CHAPTER 18

Short Takes

What we'll cover:

- How to import sample codes

- Refactoring

- Code generators

- Live templates

- Code editor preferences

- Keyboard shortcuts

We're at the end of the book, but before we conclude, I'd like to point out some features of Android Studio that make coding life a bit easier.

Productivity Features

What we usually mean when talking about productivity is that we want to do what we need to do in the shortest possible time; that means keyboard shortcuts, templates, snippets, and so on. In this section, we'll take a peek at some of what Android Studio has to offer to give our productivity a little boost. We won't go into detail; that's not the goal, but rather just to show you what's available.

Importing Samples

A key part of boosting your productivity is to actually learn how to create things and discover how they work in Android. So, our first productivity tip is learn how to use the "import sample" feature. You can get to this feature from the main menu bar, **File ➤ New ➤ Import Sample**. Figure 18-1 shows the "Import Sample" screen.

© Ted Hagos 2020
T. Hagos, *Learn Android Studio 4*, https://doi.org/10.1007/978-1-4842-5937-5_18

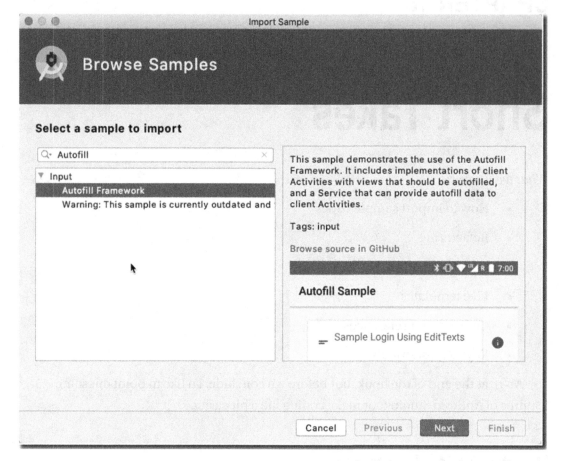

Figure 18-1. *Import Sample*

What you see in Figure 18-1 is a list of code samples you can either browse or create as a local project.

Let's say I'd like to learn something about the Autofill Framework—like what you see in Figure 18-1, you can see a preview of what it looks like, and you can also click the "Browse source in GitHub" link. When you click *Next*, you'll see a dialog that's somewhat similar to when creating a new project, as shown in Figure 18-2.

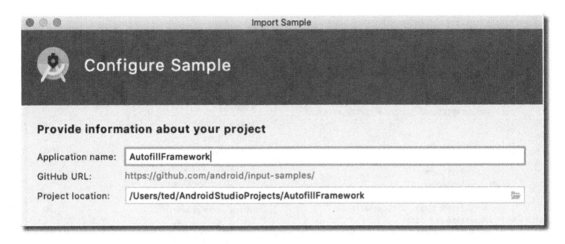

Figure 18-2. *Import Sample, next window*

If you click "Finish" on the "Import Sample" dialog, Android Studio will create a new project locally and download the sample file from GitHub so you can take a closer look at it and work on right away.

Refactoring

Refactoring is basically rewriting and improving your source code without creating a new functionality; this practice helps keep the code SOLID and DRY (don't repeat yourself) and hence easier to maintain.

Note   I spelled SOLID in all caps because it's also an acronym which stands for **S**ingle Responsibility, **O**pen-Closed Principle, **L**iskov Substitution Principle, **I**nterface Segregation and **D**ependency Inversion Principle—these are principles for object-oriented design which was popularized by Robert C. Martin.

Android Studio has some nifty refactoring capabilities. It's easy to get started; just select a piece of code that you'd like to refactor, then use the context-sensitive right-click, as shown in Figure 18-3. Alternatively, you can also use the keyboard shortcuts—**Ctrl + T** for macOS and **Ctrl + Alt + Shift + T** if you're on Windows/Linux.

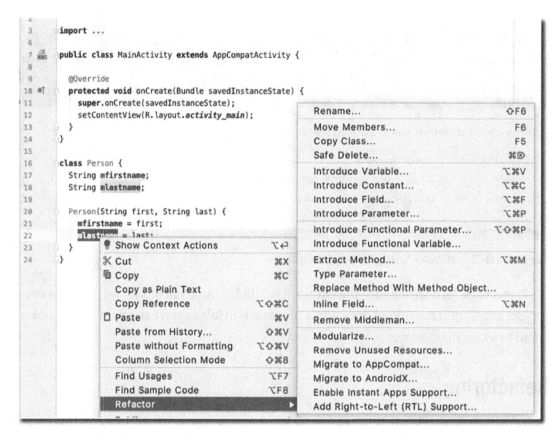

Figure 18-3. *Refactor*

I'm sure you've done refactoring many times before, but let's just jog our memories here.

- **Rename**—This will let you safely rename variables and other identifiers and so on. You should use this instead of Find and Replace. This works across the entire project and not only in the current file.

- **Change Signature**—This will let you change a method, either its name or the parameters. It also works at a class level, for example, you can turn a class into a generic type and manipulate the type parameters.

- **Move**—Moves an element; you can move a method to another class if you want to.

- **Copy**—Lets you copy elements, for example, currently selected class.

- **Safe Delete**—If you need to delete something, Android Studio will verify that what you're deleting isn't in use by anything else in the codebase. If it is in use, you'll be prompted so you can address those things before you actually delete something important.

- **Extract Constant**—Avoid using hard-coded values. Hard coding makes it difficult to modify the program in case you want to change the value later on. The Extract option for refactoring works not only for constants, you can extract fields, methods, superclasses, variables, parameters, and interfaces.

There are plenty more options in the Refactor menu; make sure to check the others out.

Generate

Another time-saving feature of Android Studio is the code generator; it's aptly named because it does exactly what you think it does—it generates code. Let's take an example; Figure 18-4 shows the mouse cursor inside the definition of the Person class. While the cursor is within the class body, launch the Generator action; from the main menu bar, go to **Code ➤ Generate**.

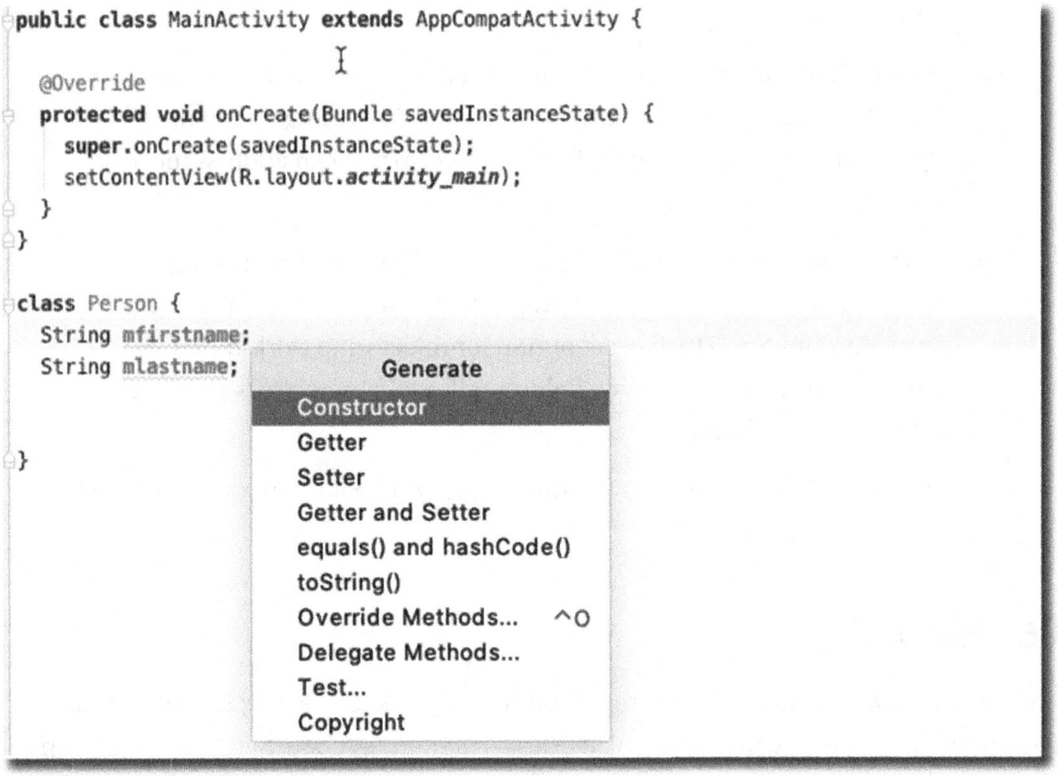

```
public class MainActivity extends AppCompatActivity {
                          I
  @Override
  protected void onCreate(Bundle savedInstanceState) {
    super.onCreate(savedInstanceState);
    setContentView(R.layout.activity_main);
  }
}

class Person {
  String mfirstname;
  String mlastname;
```

Generate
Constructor
Getter
Setter
Getter and Setter
equals() and hashCode()
toString()
Override Methods...   ^O
Delegate Methods...
Test...
Copyright

Figure 18-4. *Generate*

Choose "Constructor" as shown in Figure 18-4. If you have member variables in the class (which I have, in the Person class), Android Studio will offer to initialize these variables. For our example, I chose to initialize both of my member variables, as shown in Figure 18-5.

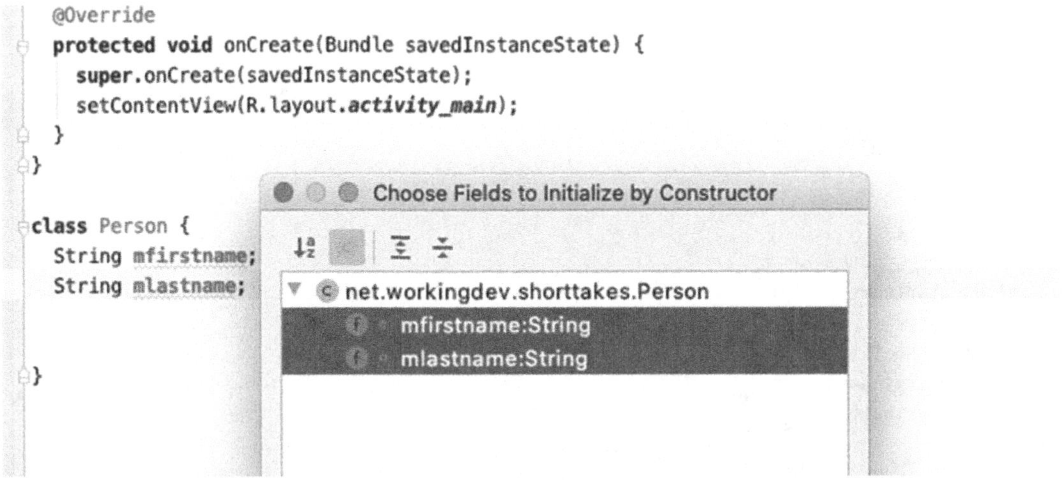

```
    @Override
    protected void onCreate(Bundle savedInstanceState) {
        super.onCreate(savedInstanceState);
        setContentView(R.layout.activity_main);
    }
}

class Person {
    String mfirstname;
    String mlastname;


}
```

Choose Fields to Initialize by Constructor

net.workingdev.shorttakes.Person
    mfirstname:String
    mlastname:String

Figure 18-5.   *Choose fields to initialize*

As you can see, you can generate quite a lot of boilerplate code. When you choose any of the Generate options, Android Studio will generate a generalized stub of code.

Let's generate some more code; this time, let's go with **getter and setter**. Go to the Generate dialog again as we've done before; by the way, you can also get to the Generate dialog using keyboard shortcuts (**Command + N** in macOS or **Alt + Insert** if you're on Linux or Windows). Figure 18-6 shows the Generate dialog again.

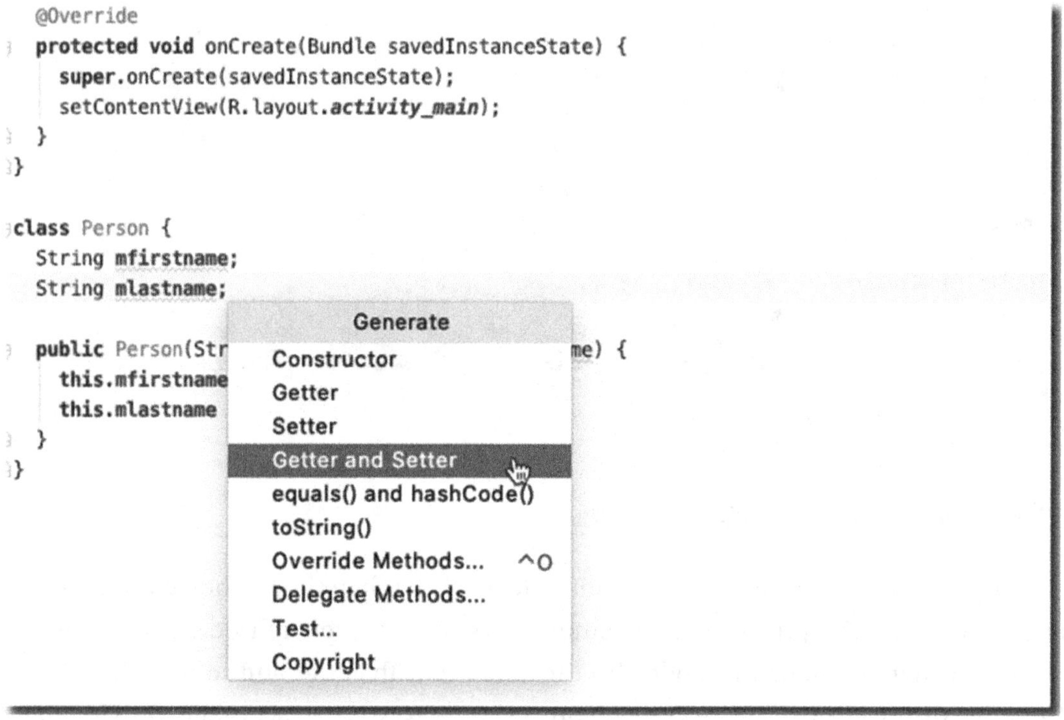

```
  @Override
  protected void onCreate(Bundle savedInstanceState) {
    super.onCreate(savedInstanceState);
    setContentView(R.layout.activity_main);
  }
}

class Person {
  String mfirstname;
  String mlastname;

  public Person(Str                    me) {
    this.mfirstname
    this.mlastname
  }
}
```

Figure 18-6. *Generate getter and setter*

In the following window, choose the fields to generate getters and setters, as shown in Figure 18-7.

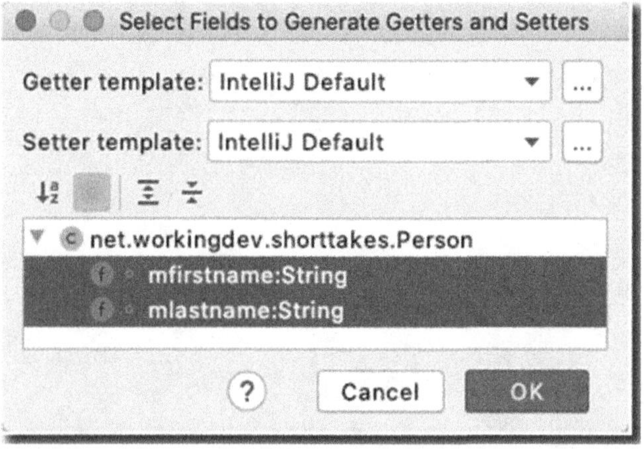

Figure 18-7. *Select fields for getters and setters*

The generator dialog shows all the autodetected fields in the Person class. It shows us the **mFirstname** and **mLastname** member variables; it also lets you do multiple selection. Select both member variables and click OK. Listing 18-1 shows the Person class after code generation.

Listing 18-1. Person class

```
class Person {
  String mfirstname;
  String mlastname;

  public Person(String mfirstname, String mlastname) {
    this.mfirstname = mfirstname;
    this.mlastname = mlastname;
  }

  public String getMfirstname() {
    return mfirstname;
  }

  public void setMfirstname(String mfirstname) {
    this.mfirstname = mfirstname;
  }

  public String getMlastname() {
    return mlastname;
  }

  public void setMlastname(String mlastname) {
    this.mlastname = mlastname;
  }
}
```

This is pretty neat already. Anything that lets us save on keystrokes is a good thing. I'm guessing you probably have just one thing to nitpick on this example; the method naming isn't right. You probably would prefer to call setLastname() rather than setmLastname(), don't you? We'll fix that in the next section.

Coding Styles

If you go to Android Studio's Preferences or Settings, then go to **Editor ➤ Code Style ➤ Java**, you'll find that there's plenty of things you can change about how the editor behaves. Figure 18-8 shows the options for the Code Style, specifically the Java language.

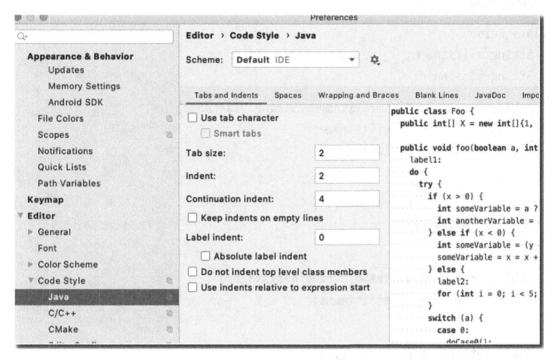

Figure 18-8. *Preferences, Code Style, Java*

If you want to change the number of spaces for tabs and indents, you can do that in the Tabs and Indents area; be sure to check out the other options in this dialog. What I'd like to do is to go to the Code Generation tab (shown in Figure 18-9).

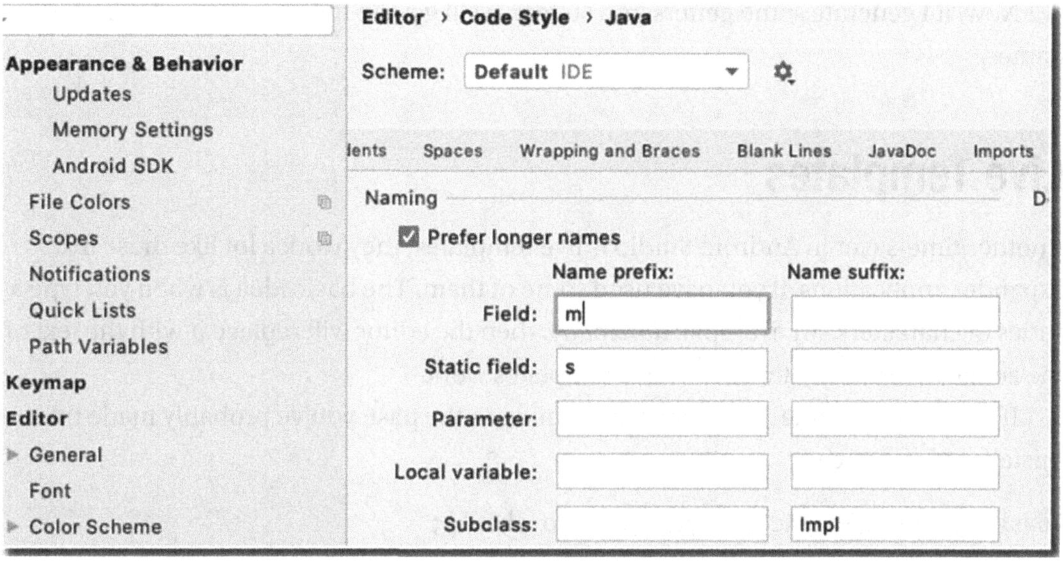

Figure 18-9. *Code Generation*

This is where we can tell Android Studio how we name our variables. If you go back to Listing 18-1, you'll notice that I'd like to prefix my variables with **m**, like **mLastname** and **mFirstname**. Initially, Android Studio didn't know about it; that's why when I generated some getters and setters for the member vars, it gave us setmLastname() instead of just setLastname().

Note   Prefixing a member variable with m comes from AOSP (Android Open Source Project). I used it here because quite a lot of sample codes you will read online use this convention. You can further read about it here: https://bit.ly/styleguideaosp.

To tell Android Studio that I prefix my variables with *m*, I'll put the *m* in **Name prefix** for **Field**, as shown in Figure 18-9. Click OK when you're done.

Now, if I generate some getters and setters, we'll get the more appropriate method names.

Live Templates

Another time-saver in Android Studio is live templates; they work a lot like those text expander applications, if you have used some of them. The basic idea is when you type a series of characters, for example, *datetoday*, then the editor will replace it with the text of the actual date today—that's how live templates work.

If you've done some Android programming in the past, you've probably made this mistake at least once:

```
Toast.makeText(MainActivity.this, "no show");
```

The preceding snippet won't work because (1) the third argument to **makeText()** is missing and (2) you actually have to invoke the show() method for the Toast to appear. This is easy enough to spot, but some other errors may not be as obvious. Anyway, live templates can help you avoid these hassles. Live templates are shortcuts that are displayed as code completion options; for example, try typing **fbc** inside the **onCreate** method as shown in Figure 18-10.

```
public class MainActivity extends AppCompatActivity {

    @Override
    protected void onCreate(Bundle savedInstanceState) {
        super.onCreate(savedInstanceState);
        setContentView(R.layout.activity_main);

        fbd
        fbc                                         findViewById with cast
    Press ↵ to insert, ↹ to replace                              💡  ⋮
    }
```

Figure 18-10. *Live template sample*

You'll see the code completion options; try to press either the ENTER or TAB key to complete the action.

Some of the commonly used built-in templates are listed in Table 18-1.

Table 18-1. *Common live templates*

Abbreviation	Description	Code
fbc	Finds view by ID with cast	`($cast$) findViewById(R.id.$resId$);`
const	Defines an Android style constant	`private static final int $name$ = $value$;`
toast	Creates a new Toast	`Toast.makeText($classname$.this, "$text$").show();`

fori	Creates for-loop	`for(int $INDEX$ = 0;$INDEX$<$LIMIT$;$INDEX++$ ) {`
		`$END$`
		`}`

Make sure you check out the other live templates; go to the Settings or Preferences window. If you're on Windows or Linux, go to the main menu bar, then **File ➤ Settings ➤ Editor ➤ Live Templates**; if you're on macOS, it's **Android Studio ➤ Preferences ➤ Editor ➤ Live Templates**—you can even create your own live templates from there.

Important Keyboard Shortcuts

The Android Developers website maintains a page where you can find the keyboard shortcuts for Android Studio; it's at `http://bit.ly/androidstudiokbshortcuts`. You should really make it a point to read that page; but before we close the chapter, I'd like to leave you with six shortcuts that I find to be very useful for me—it could be useful for you too. Table 18-2 lists these shortcuts.

Table 18-2. *Some useful keyboard shortcuts*

Shortcut	What it does
Press Shift twice	It lets you search for a term everywhere. It searches assets folders, gradle files, image resources, codes, xml configuration files, etc. If you don't know which folder to search, just use this
Ctrl + Space I Command + Space	Android Studio already has code completions and code hinting; this is just a little extra. If you forgot the parameters for a method that uses lots of parameters, you can use this to preview all the variants of the method and the corresponding parameters they expect
Alt + Insert I Command + N	We've used this in the previous section where we generated some code. This is the shortcut for the code generator
Ctrl + O I Command + O	When you want to override methods, use this shortcut
Ctrl + - I Command + -	You can use this to expand or collapse code blocks. It's handy to be able to fold codes when you're working with a large codebase; this shortcut will make your life a bit easier when you fold/unfold blocks
Ctrl + Alt + L I Command + Option + L	Don't manually indent or reindent your code—if you messed up the indentation of a for-loop or nested conditional blocks, just highlight the code block and use this shortcut

Summary

- You can avoid writing boilerplate codes like constructors, getters and setters, and so on by using code generators.

- Android Studio has plenty of refactoring aids; before using the Find/ Replace menu, consider using the refactoring options.

- Live templates are like text expanders; they can save you time and let you avoid common coding mistakes—you should use them.

- You can control how the Android Studio editor behaves; go to Settings or Preferences, then **Editor ➤ Code Style**.

Java Refresher

A Brief History

Java is firstly (and foremost) a programming language; it's also a runtime environment (virtual machine) and has built-in libraries and technology frameworks.

Java began sometime in 1990 while James Gosling was working with (then) Sun Microsystems; he was working on a product that would make Sun an important player in the emerging Internet space. Java wasn't released in 1990—it would take James Gosling five more years to design and create the Java language. In 1996, Java 1.0 was released.

At the time of writing, Java's version is 14; it certainly has gone a long way since the 1.0 release. Table A-1 shows the past Java versions.

***Table A-1.** Java versions*

Java version	Version number	Release date
JDK 1.0 (Oak)	1.0	January 1996
JDK 1.1	1.1	February 1997
J2SE 1.2 (Playground)	1.2	December 1998
J2SE 1.3 (Kestrel)	1.3	May 2000
J2SE 1.4 (Merlin)	1.4	February 2002
J2SE 5.0 (Tiger)	1.5	September 2004
Java SE 6 (Mustang)	1.6	December 2006
Java SE 7 (Dolphin)	1.7	July 2011

(continued)

© Ted Hagos 2020
T. Hagos, *Learn Android Studio 4*, https://doi.org/10.1007/978-1-4842-5937-5

Table A-1. (*continued*)

Java version	Version number	Release date
Java SE 8	1.8	March 2014
Java SE 9	9	September 21, 2017
Java SE 10	10	March 20, 2018
Java SE 11	11	September 25, 2018
Java SE 12	12	March 19, 2019
Java SE 13	13	September 17, 2019
Java SE 14	14	March 17, 2020
Java SE 15	*15*	*Expected in September 2020*

There were some changes in how the Java releases were named. From versions 1.0 to 1.1, it was called JDK (Java Development Kit); some developers still refer to it as such. Versions 1.2 to 1.4 were called J2SE (Java 2 Standard Edition). Starting with version 1.5, Sun Microsystems introduced external and internal versions. The internal version was 1.5, and the external version was 5.0; you need to keep in mind that Java 1.5 and Java 5.0 are the same things, just different version names. From Java 6 onward, the naming changed to Java SE.

Major versions were released after every two years, except Java 7, which took five years after the release of Java 6, and Java 8, three years after Java 7 was released. Since Java 10, the release cadence of Java is every six months.

Editions

You can use Java to build applications for a variety of architectures. Java comes in several editions. The Java SE (Java Standard Edition) can be used to build desktop applications. Java Enterprise Edition (Java EE) can build web applications, web services, high availability back-end processes, and so on. Java Mobile Edition (Java ME) can be used to build apps for mobile or embedded devices; however, in mobile devices like Android phones/tablets, the popular choice is to use the Android SDK.

Setup

The JDK installer is available for Windows, Linux, and macOS. The installer package can be downloaded from the Oracle download page for Java. Currently, the stable version of the JDK is v14.

The URL for the download page changes quite often, but it's easy to use your favorite search engine. Look for "Oracle JDK download" and follow the link. When you get to the Java 14 download page (shown in Figure A-1), click the links for "JDK Download" and (optionally) the "Documentation Download."

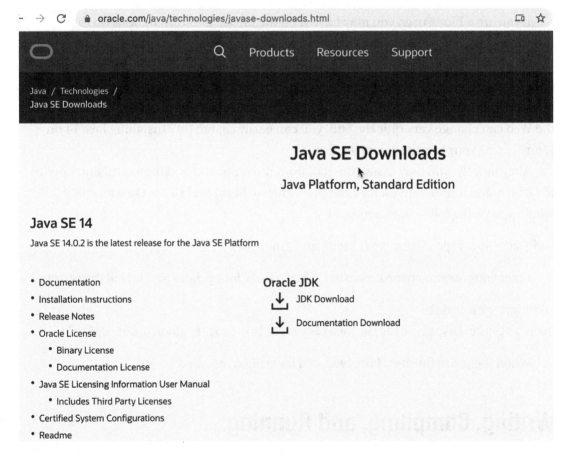

Figure A-1. *Java 14 download page*

The Java documentation can be quite handy if your IDE can take advantage of offline documentation. IDEs like JetBrains' IntelliJ can take you straight to the Java documentation while inspecting your code.

You must agree to the license agreement before you can download the installer.

To install the JDK on macOS, double-click the downloaded DMG file and follow the prompts. The installer takes care of updating the system path, so you don't need to perform any action after the installation

To install the JDK on Windows, double-click the downloaded zipped file and follow the prompts. Unlike in macOS, you must perform extra configuration after the setup. You need to

1.   Include **Java/bin** in your OS system path.

2.   Add a CLASSPATH definition in the **System Path**.

If you are a Linux user, you may have seen the tarball and rpm options on the download; you may use that and install it like installing any other software on your Linux platform. The Oracle page installing Java 14 on Linux can be reached here: `https://docs.oracle.com/en/java/javase/14/install/installation-jdk-linux-platforms.html#GUID-737A84E4-2EFF-4D38-8E60-3E29D1B884B8`. As I mentioned before, links on the Web can change very quickly. Still, you can easily search for "Installing Java 14 on Linux" using your favorite search engine.

Alternatively, you may install the JDK from the repositories. This instruction applies to Debian and its derivatives, for example, Ubuntu, Mint, and so on. On a terminal window, type the following command:

```
sudo add-apt-repository ppa:linuxuprising/java
```

Enter your user password, as usual. Then, check for updates and install the script:

```
sudo apt-get update
sudo apt-get install oracle-java14-installer oracle-java14-set-default
```

When the script finishes, Java 14 would have been installed.

Writing, Compiling, and Running

Java programs are compiled, which means before you can run a Java program, you need to translate the source file (the human-readable version) to an executable file (the machine-readable version). Figure A-2 shows this workflow.

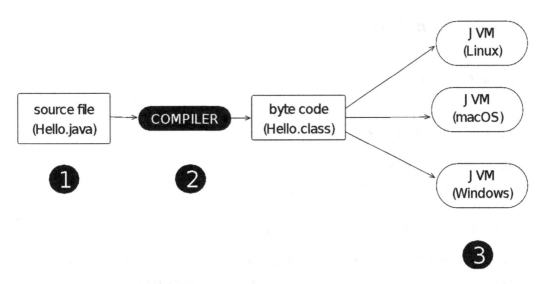

Figure A-2. *Writing, compiling, and running*

❶   A Java source file is something you create, usually with a program editor or an IDE like Vim, Visual Studio Code, Sublime, Android Studio, NetBeans, or Eclipse, to name a few. The source file will have a file extension of *.java*, and it will contain all your program instructions.

❷   To convert the source file into an *executable*, we will compile it with the Java compiler:

`javac Hello.java;`

where "Hello.java" is the source file's name; if the program has no errors, a *byte code* file (an executable) is produced. The executable file will have an extension of *.class*.

❸   You can run the executable file on either Linux, macOS, or Windows. To execute the file, we run the command

`java Hello`

without the *.class* extension.

Syntax

Syntax is "the arrangement of words and phrases to create well-formed sentences in a language"—according to the dictionary. In this section, we'll look at the Java syntax; but instead of words and phrases, it has statements, expressions, blocks, variables, and so on. It's the way we arrange these language elements that makes up a program.

A Typical Java Program

Listing A-1. Hello class

```
package com.workingdev.net.javabook; ❶
import java.lang.Math; ❷

public class Hello { ❸
  public static void main(String args[]) { ❹
    String name = "John"; ❺
    System.out.printf("Hello %s", name);

    double numsqrt = Math.sqrt(8 * 8);  ❻
    System.out.printf("Square root of 8x8 = %f", numsqrt);
  }
}
```

---

❶   This is a **package statement**. A package declaration tells the compiler which folder to
      put the resulting executable file. Think of packages as a way to implement namespaces in
      Java. Not all Java programs will have package declarations (although they should), but if a
      program will have a package statement, it needs to appear as the very first statement in the
      program source file.

❷   This is an **import statement**. It's a way for Java programs to, well, import functionalities
      from other libraries. It's a way of tapping resources from other programs. In this case, we're
      importing the Math library from the built-in libraries of Java. You can create your libraries
      and then import them from one of your programs as well. Like the package statement,
      the import statement is written outside the class declaration. You can have more than one
      import statement, as your program needs dictate.

❸   This is a **class declaration**. Classes are the fundamental building blocks of Java programs.
      It's the smallest unit of code that you can compile. Except for *import* and *package*
      statements, everything must be written inside the class structure; by *everything*, I mean
      methods and statements. There are other constructs in Java, like enums, interfaces, and
      annotation types, written outside the class construct.

❹   This is the **main method**. In some other languages, methods are also called functions. A method is a named collection of Java statements. You can write many statements inside a method, and when you call that method, all the statements inside will be executed. The **main method**, aside from being a named collection of statements, is special; it also acts as an entry point.

❺   This is a Java **statement**; specifically, it's an assignment statement. A statement is a line of (complete) instruction to the compiler. There are a couple of statements in Java; this is an example of an assignment statement. You've seen the *import* and the *package statements* before; they're called *declaration statements*. We'll discuss the other kinds of statements in the upcoming sections.

❻   Java expressions are built by combining operands and operators. The operands could be variables, method calls, literals, constants, and so on—in our example, the expression **8 * 8** comprises two integer literals and the multiplication operator. An expression evaluates to a single value. A critical difference between a statement and an expression is that an expression evaluates to a value, a statement doesn't; but remember that you can convert most expressions to a statement by simply terminating the expression with a semicolon.

If you want to follow this code example, create a file named **Hello.java**, edit it to match the contents of Listing A-1, and then on a command line, compile it using the command:

```
javac Hello.java
```

If there are no errors, the executable file Hello.class would have been produced by the compiler. To run it, type the following command:

```
java Hello
```

If you are using an IDE like IDEA, Eclipse, or NetBeans, there is usually a **Run** or **Execute** button that's prominently displayed on the IDE toolbar; you can use that.

Compilation Unit

Java's compilation unit is a class; that means everything we write has to be inside a class. Classes are declared like this:

```
class Person { /**/ }
```

class is a keyword in Java; it has a special meaning to the compiler. It tells the compiler that the other tokens (the *Person* identifier and the pair of curly braces) are parts of a class definition and, as such, need to conform to certain rules.

Person, in the previous example, is the name of the class. It's something that the programmers (us) would supply. The pair of curly braces marks the boundaries of the class body. Anything we write should be inside the curly braces.

Classes may contain fields and methods—methods, in turn, may contain variables inside them, but we'll get to that later.

Comments

Everything you write in a Java source file will be scrutinized and evaluated by the compiler. Everything. Unless you tell the compiler to ignore certain things, like *comments*. So, if you want the Java compiler to ignore some statements, comment them out, as shown in Listing A-2.

Listing A-2. Comments

```
// this will be ignored ❶
String mfirstname = "John";  // this will also be ignored ❷

/*  ❸
  This comment will span multiple
  lines
*/

public static void main(String args[]) {
}
```

❶   The compiler will ignore anything to the right of the //.

❷   This makes the double slash great for commenting one-liners.

❸   If you need to write a long comment, one that will span multiple lines, use the forward slashes with an asterisk.

Statements

A semicolon terminates statements; much like natural-language statements are terminated by a period, Java statements are punctuated by a semicolon to denote that the statement is finished. If you forget this, the compiler will complain. Here are some examples of statements:

```java
int remainder = 15 % 12;
float quotient = 15.0 / 12.0;
System.out.println(remainder);
```

Keywords

Java has a set of reserved words or keywords. These tokens are special and have meaning to the compiler. These words determine most of the things we can do in a Java program, like defining scopes, directing the flow of program control, defining native types, handling exceptions, and so on. Table A-2 lists all the Java keywords.

Table A-2. *Java keywords*

abstract	continue	for	new	switch
assert***	default	goto*	package	synchronized
boolean	do	if	private	this
break	double	implements	protected	throw
byte	else	import	public	throws
case	enum****	instanceof	return	transient
catch	extends	int	short	try
char	final	interface	static	void
class	finally	long	strictfp**	volatile
const*	float	native	super	while

*	Not used
**	Added in JDK 1.2
***	Added in JDK 1.4
****	Added in JDK 1.5

Identifiers

Identifiers are the names of *variables*, *classes*, *packages*, *interfaces*, and *methods*; these are names that programmers (us) supply, and as such, we have a free hand on how it goes. There are a couple of rules and guidelines to observe, like

- Identifiers have to be made up of letters, numbers, underscore, and the dollar sign ($).

- It has to start with a letter and can't start with a number.

- Although you can use the dollar sign, it's probably best not to, because the Java compiler uses it to name inner classes; so best to stay away from those. This isn't a hard rule at all; this is more a suggestion.

- Identifiers also cannot be the same name as one of the Java keywords.

- It's best to make the identifiers descriptive. Ideally, their meaning and symbology should be closely related to what they hold. Again, this isn't a hard rule, but a suggestion.

I should have mentioned this early on; better late than never, Java is case sensitive. So, the following identifiers are distinct from each other:

- `myVariable`

- `MYVARIABLE`

- `Myvariable`

- `MyVariable`

They may read the same, but they are syntactically different, as far as Java is concerned. So, be careful. This is a very common rookie error—only second to forgetting the semicolon.

Methods

Methods are a handy way of grouping a bunch of statements. Ideally, these statements should work together to achieve only a single goal. The method accomplishes this goal either by producing a side effect or returning a value to the caller.

Methods are always inside classes; there are no stand-alone methods. In Java, you can't write anything outside the class structure, except comments, imports, and package declarations.

Some programmers may know methods by another name, perhaps a function or a subroutine; they wouldn't be wrong, but since we're coding in Java, you need to get used to calling them methods. Listing A-3 shows a sample code for a method.

Listing A-3. Class with a method

```
class Person {
  String name = "John Doe";

  void greet() {
    System.out.println("Hello %s", name);
  }
}
```

In the sample code, *greet* is the name of the method, and it doesn't return anything; that's why its type is void. There is only one statement in the body of the method, but we could have written more.

Note   The *void* type can only be used in methods; you cannot use *void* for variables because it's not a data type; it merely is a return type.

The structure of a typical method is as follows. It has a

- **Return type**—This signifies the type of data the method returns to the caller. It can be a reference type or any of the eight native types. If it doesn't return anything, its type must be written as *void*. When the method's type isn't *void*, it must have a *return* statement somewhere in its body. If the method's type is *void*, it mustn't have a *return* statement.

- **Access modifier**—This determines the method's scope, whether you can call only from within the class (most restrictive), from outside the class but within the same package, or from anywhere (least restrictive). In our previous code example, we didn't write any access modifier for the greet method—it doesn't mean it doesn't have any. Java methods (and classes and variables) have a default scope of *package* access; they are accessible from within the class, and outside the classes provided, the caller is from a class within the same package.

- **Name of the method**—It's the name you give to the method; just make it descriptive and not too long.

- **A pair of parentheses**—This is used to enclose method parameters if you decide to pass any.

- **Method parameters**—Parameters are a useful way to pass data to the methods. You can pass more than one value to the method, and the type of data you can pass can either be of a reference type or primitive type.

- **Body of the method**—A pair of open and close curly braces marks the method's body's boundaries. Within the body, you can write the program statements.

Packages and Imports

A package is used to group related types. Think of it as a folder in a file directory—because that's what it is, at its most basic. If you try to open *rt.jar* (if you can find it somewhere where you installed the JDK) using a ZIP utility, you'll see that it's merely a folder hierarchy of related classes.

Note *rt.jar* contains all the compiled classes (executables) for the core Java runtime environment.

Packages organize the built-in libraries (from the Java API). You can familiarize yourself more by visiting the documentation at https://docs.oracle.com/en/java/javase/14/docs/api/index.html.

You can also use packages to organize your code. By writing a package declaration at the very top of a Java source file, you're giving the compiler an instruction on where to put the compiled codes, like in the code sample shown in Listing A-4.

Listing A-4. Package statement

```
package com.workingdev.javabook;

public class Hello {

}
```

When you compile this code, the resulting directory and file arrangement will look like the one shown in Figure A-3.

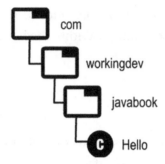

Figure A-3. *Directory structure of the Hello app*

The package statement is optional; it's not a requirement for compilation, but it's a good idea to organize your code via packages because it acts as a namespace. It provides organization and helps to avoid naming conflicts between identically named reference types.

If you don't write a package statement in your source file, the compiler will put the resulting compiled class in the default package, essentially the same directory where the source file is located.

If you provide a package statement, you need to ensure that it's the first statement in the source file; otherwise, the compiler will complain.

Program Entry Point

A program entry point is a location in the program (usually a method) where the first instructions are executed. The program's entry point depends on the kind of program; a Java command-line program's entry point is the **public static void main()** method, as shown in Listing A-5.

Listing A-5. Main method

```
public class Hello {
  public static void main(String args[]) {
    String name = "John";
    System.out.printf("Hello %s", name);

    double numsqrt = Math.sqrt(8 * 8);
    System.out.printf("Square root of 8x8 = %f", numsqrt);
  }
}
```

The main method shown here has a special signature. The keywords static, void, public, and main all need to appear exactly as shown in the preceding sample code; otherwise, it won't be treated by the runtime as an entry point; it will be just another method. Note also that the main method takes a single argument (a String array); this is also part of the signature. This parameter receives command-line arguments that are passed to the program at runtime.

Other types of programs may have different entry points. An Android application will usually have an Activity component as an entry point.

Data Types

Like any other imperative programming language, Java relies on its ability to create, store, and edit values. These values are manipulated and transformed via arithmetic or some other means. We can work with these values by storing them into *variables*, making a *variable* named storage for values or data. Consider the code snippet in the following example:

```
int theNum;
```

In the preceding statement, *theNum* is the variable name, and *int* is what we call a type. The statement is declaring a variable of type *int* (short for integer). A type determines the variable's size in memory, what kinds of operations we can do with it, and what kinds of data we can store. So, since we know that *theNum* is of type int, we can do something like this:

```
theNum = 1;
```

We assigned an integer literal to the variable *theNum*; this assignment operation is permitted because *theNum* is of type *int* and *1* is an integer literal; what would not be okay to do is the following:

```
theNum = "Hello";
theNum = "1";     // even this is not okay
```

The word "Hello" (in double quotes, in the previous code sample) should not be assigned to an integer variable because "Hello" is a String literal; it's of type *String*. Even the second line in the previous sample isn't okay because "1" is not an integer; it is also a *String* literal. Anything that you enclose in double quotes is a *String* literal and, hence, of type *String*—always remember that Java is strongly typed; it won't allow us to do these kinds of things. It should be like for like.

At a high level, Java has two kinds of types: primitive types and reference types. Let's deal with the primitive types first.

Primitive types are built-in to the Java language. It's baked right in, as opposed to a reference type, which is also called a UDT (user-defined type) or a custom type. A reference type is something that the programmer creates to extend the capabilities of the language in terms of complexity in the data structure. There are many other differences between a reference type and a primitive one, but we'll get to that later. For now, let's get to the primitive types first.

Java has eight primitive or native types. They're listed in Table A-3.

Table A-3. *Native types*

Type	Size in bits	Range
byte	8	-128 to 127
short	16	-32,768 to 32,767
int	32	-2,147,483,648 to 2,147,483,647
long	64	-9,223,372,036,854,775,808 to 9,223,372,036,854,807
float	32	1.23e100f, -1.23e-100f, .3f, 3.14F
double	64	1.23456e300d, -1.23456e-300d, 1e1d
char	16	0 - 65535 or \u0000 - \uFFFF
boolean	1	true, false

Byte

The byte is a signed 8-bit 2's complement integer—2's complement is a binary thing; if it's too computer-sciencey for you, don't worry about it, this isn't the main takeaway from all these. I'd like you to take away that its size is 8 bits, and the range of values you can store in it is from –128 to +127. You can calculate the range of value for a given type using the formula $(-1) 2^{n-1}$ (where n is the number of bits) to get the lower bound and $2^{n-1} - 1$ to get the higher bound. So, for the byte, the lower bound is $(-1) 2^7$—we raise 2 to the power of 7 because the number of bits in a byte is 8, remember? 2^{n-1} where n is the number of bits. $(-2)^7 = -128$ and $2^7 - 1 = 127$. This is essentially the formula on how to get the range of values for integer types.

Byte variables are declared like this:

```
byte a = 10;
```

If you declare a byte variable as a member variable (meaning a variable that's not inside a method) without defining it, its default value will be zero.

```
byte a; // default value is 0
```

int

The int is larger than the byte; it's 32 bits. You now know how to get the range of values; you can try calculating that for yourself. Like the byte, if you declare it as a member variable without defining it, its default value will also be zero.

int variables can be declared like this:

```
int num = 20;
int somenum = 32767;
int bignum = 1000000;
```

Starting from Java 7, we can also declare int values like this:

```
int alsobignum = 1_000_000;
```

It's still illegal to put commas as part of an integer literal, but underscores are the next best thing; it reads so much easier, don't you think?

short

The next stop on our list of primitive data types in Java is *short*.

If you want to save memory and *byte* is too small, we can use the type halfway between the int and the byte. Like the int and byte, its default value is also zero when declared (but not defined) as a member variable. Short variables are declared like bytes and ints; no suffixes are needed.

```
short somenum = 32767;
```

long

Our last primitive data type related to integers is *long*; it's the big brother of int. It's stored in 64 bits of memory to hold a significantly larger set of possible values. It also defaults to zero when declared and not defined as a member variable.

float

The integer types byte, short, int, and long are the counting numbers of Java. The float and double are measuring numbers. Measuring numbers have fractional parts. This is a single-precision decimal number. This means if we get past six decimal points, this number becomes less precise and more of an estimate. Its default value is not 0; rather, it's 0.0.

We declare floats like this:

```
float pi = 3.1416f; // float literals have the suffix f or F
```

double

The type is called double because it's a double-precision decimal number. It's stored in 64 bits of memory, which means it can represent a much larger range of possible numbers than float.

We declare doubles like this:

```
double d = 3.13457599923384753929348D; // double literals has the suffix d
or D
```

In the absence of a suffix, the default type of a floating-point literal is double, so you don't have to suffix double literals.

char

A char is a 16-bit integer representing a Unicode-encoded character. Its range is from 0 to 65,535, which in Unicode represents '\u0000' to '\uffff'.

You can declare chars like this:

```
char a = 65;
char b = 'a';
```

boolean

This is probably the simplest; you can only store the literals **true** or **false** with this kind of data.

Overflow

The primitive types, as you have seen on the table, have size limits. When you assign values that are outside the acceptable range, overflow can happen. Consider the following:

```
byte a = 127;
a = a + 1;
System.out.println(a); // prints -128
```

You can probably see by now why Java has six types for the number (byte, short, int, long, float, and double); for the sake of coding expediency, we all could have been okay with using just doubles and longs—why even bother with that distinction, why not just use a single number type for everything? One of the reasons is that not all data requires a 64-bit storage space—what a waste that would have been if we stored everything in a 64-bit space. Java allows us to exercise economy by using the least possible amount of storage for our data. It saves us from being wasteful.

Casting

With primitives, you can assign a value to a variable that has a wider type, for example:

```
int i = 10;
long l = i; // this is okay
```

You cannot do the reverse. A variable or value of a wider type cannot be assigned to a narrower type, like this:

```
long l = 10;
int i = l; // not okay
```

If you need to store a value of a wider type to a narrower type, you need to use the cast operator, like this:

```
long l = 10;
int i = (int) l; // this is okay
```

This is called a narrowing conversion. We store a value of a wider type to a variable of a narrower type. This is usually dangerous because you will lose some precision in the data. Still, if you downcast like in our example, you're essentially telling the compiler that you know what you're doing and that you should be allowed.

You don't need to use the cast operator in a widening conversion.

Strongly and Statically Typed

By now, you're probably noticing a pattern already on how Java declares variables. We write the type first and then we write the name of the variable, like this:

```
int someNumber = 10;
```

Most of the time, you need to tell the compiler what the type of a variable is. The compiler needs to know ahead of time, things about the variable like how much memory to allocate for it or what kind of data is it—so that when it runs its lexical analysis, it can give us warnings or errors if we write some statements that aren't permitted for that type of data. This is how the compiler warns us of things that can go wrong before they even go wrong.

When the compiler scans the source code, it looks for the variable declarations (among other things), and then it scans the rest of the program to see if we're doing something to the variable that we're not supposed to. This is some kind of static analysis because the compiler is analyzing the tokens (parts of the source code) during design time (not runtime). That's why Java is referred to as a statically typed language. We have to declare our types ahead of time; the types of the variables need to be known during design time rather than runtime.

We also need to remember that you can't assign a value of one type to a variable of another type, like this:

```
int i = 10;
i = "10";
```

A variable that's declared as **int** cannot take in a String type. You may have used a language like JavaScript whose typing is a lot more malleable than Java; JavaScript variables don't work the same way as they do in Java.

Reference Types

Native or primitive types are called because they are part of the programming language itself, pretty much like a reserved word or a literal. There is another type of data in Java called reference types; they are not part of the Java language itself, they come from libraries or user-defined types—the types that you create on your own. We'll discuss this some more when we get to the topic of *Classes*. An example statement using a reference type is given in the following snippet:

```
String name = "John Doe";
```

String is a reference type, and it comes from one of the Java libraries. There are many more reference types that we can use, such as ArrayList, Date, System, Object, Map, Queue, Set, and so on. We'll get to some of them in the subsequent sections.

You can already build apps by simply using the primitive types of Java, but you'll soon find out that you need a more sophisticated way to represent data, which you can do by creating classes. Classes in Java are more than just data structures because not only do they have data, they also have a behavior—a class is a collection of data clumped up together with some methods that can act on that data. It's an oversimplification, but you get the point.

When you create an object from a class, the resulting data won't be of primitive type; it will be of reference type. So, reference types are a result of creating objects. Let's build a small class for the purposes of our example; Listing A-6 shows the code.

Listing A-6. class Person

```java
class Person {
  String lastname;
  String firstname;

  public Person(String last, String first) {
    lastname = last;
    firstname = first;
  }

  public String getName() {
    return String.format("%s , %s", lastname, firstname);
  }
}
```

To use this class, we need to create an instance of it, like this:

```
Person john = new Person("Doe","John");
System.out.println(john.getName());
```

Notice the way we created the Person object; we used the **new** keyword for it. This is one of the telltale signs that what you're creating isn't a primitive type but rather an instance of reference type.

There are many reference types built-in in Java, like Date, String, ArrayList, Math, and so on, and you can build so much more on your own. Every new class you create is a new type.

Stack and Heap

Every variable you create will have to be stored somewhere; either it gets stored on the stack or the heap. Another key difference between primitive and reference types is that primitive values are stored on the stack, and reference types are stored on the heap. Let's consider the following example code:

```
int num = 10;
Person john = new Person("Doe", "John");
```

The variable num, since it's a primitive type, will be stored on the stack. This means the location of the variable itself contains the value of the integer literal, as shown in Figure A-4.

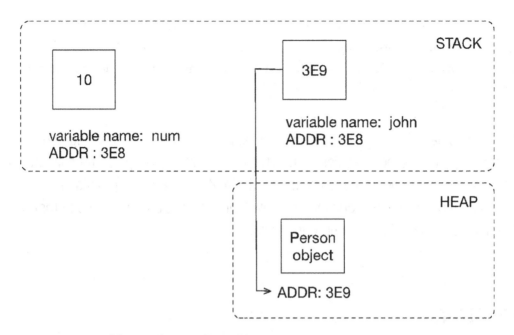

Figure A-4. *Variables in the stack and heap*

The variable john, because it's a reference type, doesn't contain the actual Person object. The Person object is stored somewhere on the heap. What the variable john contains is the address of the actual Person object.

Constants

A constant is similar to a variable; you get to declare it and assign to it. The key difference between a variable and a constant is that once you assign a value to a constant, you can never reassign a value to it later.

A constant in Java is created by using the *final* keyword. The *final* keyword is a special modifier, meaning of which, I think, is immediately apparent. The following snippet creates and declares a constant named PI:

```
final double PI = 3.1416;
PI = 1.0; // This line won't compile. Cannot reassign PI
System.out.printf("Value of PI = %f", PI);
```

If you have experience with other programming languages, you might wonder why Java doesn't have a *const* keyword—well, actually, it does, but it's not used. The *const* keyword is reserved, but Java didn't assign any semantics for it. There is no shortage of discussion on this in development forums; you can look it up if you're inclined. The JCP (Java Community Process) topic for implementing *const correctness* has been closed for a long time now (around 2005); I wouldn't hold my breath waiting for the *const* keyword to appear in Java 14.

Note   The Java Community Process (JCP) is responsible for formalizing and standardizing Java technologies. Interested parties like developers and companies cooperate in this process to evolve the platform. If there are any proposed enhancements or the introduction of a new language feature, these are introduced through JSRs (Java Specification Requests).

Operators

A program is mostly made up of statements and expressions. What we commonly do in programs is create and transform data values; to do these things, we need to learn how to use Java's operators.

Assignment

The assignment operator is the equal sign, for example:

```
int firstNumber = 10;
```

10 is the integer literal that we're assigning to the variable *firstNumber*. In an assignment operation, the RHS (right-hand side of the operator) is assigned to the LHS (left-hand side of the operator). Here are some more examples of assignment operations:

```
int secondNumber = firstNumber;  // variables may appear on the RHS
int thirdNumber = someFunction(); // methods may also appear on the RHS
```

Arithmetic

Arithmetic operators are straightforward; they do what you expect them to do. They're the same Math operators we've learned in elementary school.

Addition, **multiplication**, **subtraction**, and **division** (+ * - and /) work for the number types *byte*, *short*, *int*, *long*, *double*, and *float*, like in the following examples:

```
int a = 1 + 2;
int b = a * 10;
System.out.println(b); // prints 30
```

It works as expected, no surprises here.

```
int c = b / 4;
System.out.println(c); // prints 7
```

You probably expected to see the value 7.5 printed out, but both operands (*b and 4*) are of type *int*, and we stored the result in variable *c*, which is also of type *int*; perhaps if we stored the results in a *double* type, we'd get the correct result. Let's see:

```
double d = b / 4;
System.out.println(c); // prints 7.0
```

Well, it printed 7.0; it's got a decimal portion now, but it's still not what we expected. The principle we need to remember here is that when you perform an arithmetic operation between two *ints*, the result will be of type *int*. If we want to get a result with the decimal portion, we need the operands to be of type *double* or *float*. Let's see the next example:

```
double e = b / 4.0;
System.out.println(e); // now it prints 7.5
```

We didn't have to convert variable *b* to *double* or *float*; we simply divided *b* with *4.0* (a double literal). This changed the expression result's type to double. We only needed to change one of the operands' types to double, which got the job done.

Please keep the following rules in mind when constructing arithmetic expressions. When one of the operands

- Is a *long*, the expression results in a *long* type

- Is a *float*, the expression results in a *float* type

- Is a *double*, the expression results in a *double* type

Just remember that if none of the operands is *long*, *float*, or *double*, the result of the operation will be of type *int*.

Modulo (%) also works on the number types. It's similar to the division operator, but instead of getting us the quotient, it gets us the remainder, like this example:

```
int rem = 15 % 12;
System.out.println(rem); // prints 3
```

Unary

Unary operators work on a single operand. When used, it changes either the sign or the value of the operand.

The plus sign (+) signifies that the number is positive—which is the default, however, so you don't have to use this operator to indicate a positive number; that is already the default. For example, instead of writing

```
int i = +10;
```

we simply write

```
int i = 10;
```

The unary minus (-) negates an expression. It changes whatever sign the operand has. See this example:

```
int a = 5; // a is 5
int b = -a; // b is -5
int c = -b; // c is +5
```

The unary minus doesn't automatically change the operand's sign to negative; it simply reverses it. Going back to unary plus, it doesn't do anything. Consider this example:

```
int a = -5; // a is -5
int b = +a; // b is -5
a = 5; // a is now 5
int c = +a; // c is 5
```

See, it didn't do anything. The variable **b** is negative in value; even after applying the unary +, the value remained negative. One can only surmise that Java added this operator out of a need for balance, but that's just me, feel free to search for other interpretations.

The increment operator (++) increases the value of a variable by 1.

```
int counter = 0; // counter ==> 0
System.out.println(counter++); // prints 0
System.out.println(counter++); // prints 1
System.out.println(++counter); // prints 3
```

Note that it matters where you put the increment operator. If you put it to the operand's right, the result of the expression is still the original value of the operand. The increment was performed after the expression has been evaluated, not before. Contrast that when we put the increment operator to the left of the operand, the effect is more immediate.

The decrement operator (--), in contrast to the ++ operator, decreases the operand by 1.

```
int counter = 100;
System.out.println(--counter); // prints 99
```

Equality and Relational

The double equals (==) operator is used to determine equality of two operands, like in this example:

```
int a = 1;
int b = 1;

if(a == b) {
  // true path
}
```

There were three statements in the previous code snippet; the first two were assignment statements, and the other one was *if* statement, a branching structure. We haven't discussed control structures yet, but you can probably follow what was going on in that code. Don't worry too much about the details of the structure. If you could get the meaning that "*if a is equal to b*, then execute the statements in the true path," you got it right. That's precisely what it means.

Take care not to confuse single equals with double equals; the former is used to assign a value to a variable, and the latter is used to test for equality. The equality operator works on all the primitive types (byte, short, int, long, double, float, char, and boolean). You should only use the double equals operator for primitive types, never for reference types (like String). To determine equality among reference types, the `.equals()` method must be used. We haven't gotten far enough on reference types, but we will, in the following sections. For now, just don't use double equals on reference types.

The not equal (!=) operator is the opposite of the double equals. Instead of testing for equality, this operator returns true if the operands aren't equal. See the following example:

```
int a = 1;
int b = 1;
if(a != b) {
  // this will be the false path
}
else {
  // this is the true path
}
```

The other relational operators are the following:

>	Greater than
<	Less than
>=	Greater than or equal to
<=	Less than or equal to

They behave exactly as you think they do. They're the same relational operators we learned in our basic mathematics.

Logical Operators

Java has four operators for performing logical operations, the **AND** and **OR** operators and their short-circuit counterparts.

&	Conditional AND
&&	Conditional AND, short circuit
|	Conditional OR
||	Conditional OR, short circuit

Here's an example on how to use them:

```java
if ((a > 10) & (a < 100)) {
  System.out.println("a is between 11 to 99");
}
```

You use logical operators to join conditional operations, as demonstrated in the preceding code. A couple of things to remember about logical operators are as follows:

- The logical **AND** will return true only if all operands evaluate to true. In our example, it will only return true if the variable **a** is both more than 10 and less than 100.

- The logical **OR** will return false only if all operands are false; if one of the operands evaluates to true, the whole operation evaluates to true.

- The **&&** and **||** operators perform *Conditional AND* and *Conditional OR* operations on two boolean expressions. These operators exhibit "short-circuiting" behavior, which means that the second operand is evaluated only if needed.

Be careful of short-circuit operators; you need to remember that short-circuiting may cause some of your program path to be ignored. Consider the sample code in Listing A-7.

Listing A-7. testOne and testTwo methods

```java
private boolean testOne() {
  System.out.println("testOne");
  return false;
}
private boolean testTwo() {
  System.out.println("testTwo");
  return true;
}

if (testOne() && testTwo()) {} // prints testOne
```

The methods **testOne()** and **testTwo()** both return boolean values, and they both cause some side effects as well (printing on the console). In the example, we only see the side effect of **testOne()** because **testTwo()** was no longer evaluated; it was skipped—short-circuited, to be more precise. The short-circuit **AND** (&&) returned false because one of the operands is false. It didn't bother to evaluate testTwo() any longer.

Loops and Branches

Java statements, by default, are executed sequentially, one statement after another, until there are no more statements to execute; by then, the program stops. Java also comes with statements that change the program flow. Some statements can cause the flow to branch or fork, and some statements can cause the flow to go round in circles, like in a loop. That's what this section is about.

If and Switch Statements

The *if* and *switch* statements cause the program flow to fork or change directions. It does this using a test condition. If the test evaluates to *true*, then the program goes one way; if it's *false*, it goes another way. These statements have some similarities, but they differ in form.

The if statement looks like this:

```
if (<expression>) {
  // statement
  // statement
}
```

The *expression* in the previous code snippet is required. You cannot have an *if* statement with a missing expression. The expression must also resolve to either *true* or *false*—it must be a *boolean expression*; you can imagine that you'll use the equality and relational operators in here, quite a lot. Here's an example of how to use the *if* statement:

```
import static java.lang.System.out;

public class Hello {
  public static void main(String[] args) {
    int a = 1;
    double b = 1.0;

    if (a == b) {
      out.printf("%d == %f", a, b); // prints 1 == 1.000000
    }
  }
}
```

The expression will evaluate to true so that you will see the printout "1 == 1.000000". You can compare an *int* value with a *double* value, and it will behave as you expect it to. Note that a double value is wider than an int value; in this case, Java performs some type coercion and converts the narrower type (the *int*, in this case) to the wider type (the *double*, in this case) before it performed the comparison. This widening conversion, or *upcasting*, is performed automatically by Java.

If you need to account for multiple pathways, you can use the *else if* and *else* clause. Let's see that in an example.

```java
import static java.lang.System.out;
import java.util.*;

class Hello {
  public static void main(String[] args) {

    Calendar c = Calendar.getInstance();
    Date d = new Date();
    c.setTime(d);
    int dayOfWeek = c.get(Calendar.DAY_OF_WEEK);

    if      (dayOfWeek == 1) { out.println("Sunday");}
    else if (dayOfWeek == 2) { out.println("Monday");}
    else if (dayOfWeek == 3) { out.println("Tuesday"); }
    else if (dayOfWeek == 4) { out.println("Wednesday"); }
    else if (dayOfWeek == 5) { out.println("Thursday"); }
    else if (dayOfWeek == 6) { out.println("Friday"); }
    else if (dayOfWeek == 7) { out.println("Saturday"); }
    else { out.println("Unknown"); } // we will never get here
  }
}
```

The *else if*, like the *if*, also takes on a boolean expression as an argument. When the expression is *true*, the block immediately following the else if is executed.

The *else* clause, which you need to write last, is a catch-all block. When none of *if* and *else ifs* evaluates to true, the block of the *else* clause is executed.

Switch Statement

The *switch* statement is another branching structure that we can use. You'll find that this structure is a bit more convenient to use than *if-then-else* when you need to deal with multiple pathways; its basic form is as follows:

```java
switch(<expression>) {
    case value:
        // statement
        break;
```

```
    case value:
        // statement
        break;
    default:
        // statement
}
```

where *expression* is either of type *byte, short, char, int, String,* or *enum.* Let's see how to use it.

```java
import static java.lang.System.out;
import java.util.Calendar;
import java.util.Date;

class Hello {
  public static void main(String[] args) {

    Calendar c = Calendar.getInstance();
    Date d = new Date();
    c.setTime(d);
    int dayOfWeek = c.get(Calendar.DAY_OF_WEEK);
    String day = "";

    switch(dayOfWeek) {
      case 1:
        day = "Sunday";
        break;
      case 2:
        day = "Monday";
        break;
      case 3:
        day = "Tuesday";
        break;
      case 4:
        day = "Wednesday";
        break;
```

```
    case 5:
      day = "Thursday";
      break;
    case 6:
      day = "Friday";
      break;
    case 7:
      day = "Saturday";
      break;
    default:
      day = "Dunno";
  }
  out.printf("Today is %s", day);
 }
 // when break is encountered, program control
 // goes here
}
```

When you use the switch statement, remember the following:

- **First match wins**. How you write the *case* statements' order matters. Java will try to match the first case statement, then the second, then the third, until it reaches the structure's end. When one of these cases matches, the statements inside that particular block will be executed.

- **Always put a break** statement on every *case* block. When a matching case is found, all the statements in that case's block will run; but after that, Java will also run the statements in the remaining blocks (*case* blocks). That's why you have to use the *break* statement; *break* simply instructs the runtime to get out or break out of the current control structure. That means program control will jump to the statement immediately after the *switch* structure.

While Loop

The while loop lets you run statements repeatedly—in a loop. Its structure looks like this:

```
while(<condition>)  {
  // statements
}
```

where *condition* is a boolean expression. As long as that condition remains true, all the statements in the block will be run. So, be careful in using this. Make sure that somewhere in the while block, you have an instruction that will make the condition false at some point; otherwise, you will have a loop that doesn't end—that's not what you want usually. Let's see some sample codes.

```
import static java.lang.System.out;

class Hello {
  public static void main(String[] args) {
    int count = 0;
    while (count < 11) {   ❶
      out.println(count);
      count++;              ❷
    }
  }
}
```

❶   The runtime evaluates the *condition*; if it's true, we enter the loop's body and run all the block statements. If the condition turns out to be *false*, we skip the whole *while* block and run the first statement immediately after it.

❷   Let's increment the *counter* to make sure that, at some point in time, it will be either equal or greater than *11*, which will make the condition *false*.

A close relative of the while loop is the do-while loop; they're very similar in format and function, but their key difference is the placement of the condition. Let's see an example of the do-while loop.

```java
import static java.lang.System.out;

class Hello {
  public static void main(String[] args) {
    int i = 0;
    do {
      out.println(i++);
    } while (i < 0);
  }
}
```

The preceding code will still run the *println* statement inside the block even if it turns out to be false. Unlike in the while loop, the statements in a *do-while* loop are guaranteed to run at least once.

For-Loop

The for statement is another structure we can use for looping constructs. Its basic form is as follows:

```java
for (<initial value>;<condition>;<increment/decrement>) {
  // statements
}
```

That looks like a handful; let's break down its components:

- The *initial value* is a statement. It sets or defines the initial value of a counter.

- The *condition* gets evaluated every time the loop completes or circles back. As long as this condition evaluates to true, all the statements in the loop block get to run.

- The increment or decrement is a statement that increases or decreases the value of the counter.

These three components, the *initial value, condition,* and *increment/decrement,* are separated by a semicolon. Let's see how it looks like in code.

```
import static java.lang.System.out;

class Hello {
  public static void main(String[] args) {
    for(int count = 0; count < 11; count++) {
      out.println(count);
    }
  }
}
```

Simple Application of Control Structures

Let's build a fizzbuzz code. This is a popular exercise for beginners. You may see some variations of this problem in various places on the Internet, but the basic idea is to use looping and branching constructions. You need to route program logic when a number is either odd or even. Our version of this problem is broken down as follows:

1. Count from 1 to 100, and as you count, assign the value to a *counter* variable.

2. Check for the counter's current value; if it's exactly divisible by 3, print "fizz."

3. If the present value of *counter* is exactly divisible by 5, print "buzz."

4. If the counter's current value is exactly divisible by both 3 and 5, print "fizzbuzz."

It looks like this in code:

```
import static java.lang.System.out;

class FizzBuzz {
  public static void main(String[] args) {
    for (int i = 1; i <= 100 ; i++ ) {
      if ( i % 15 == 0) {
        out.printf("FizzBuzz %d\n", i);
      }
```

```
    else if (i % 5 == 0) {
      out.printf("Buzz %d\n", i);
    }
    else if (i % 3 == 0) {
      out.printf("Fizz %d\n", i);
    }
    }
  }
}
```

Counting from 1 to 100 can be managed by using a **for-loop**. It's got a built-in counter which we can increment.

The three possible branches (fizz, buzz, or fizzbuzz) can be managed using an **if-else if** construction.

In the first branch, we tested if (i == 15), which means the number is divisible by both 3 and 5 (3 * 5 is 15); then, we print "fizzbuzz."

In the second branch, if the number isn't divisible by 3*5, is it divisible by 5 then? If yes, we print "buzz."

If it's not divisible by 3*5 and not divisible by 5, is it divisible by 3? If so, then we print "fizz."

We didn't put an else clause because we're merely interested in numbers divisible by 3, 5, or 3 and 5; we'll simply ignore the rest.

The next code sample shows how to print a 5x5 multiplication table. Here's the code:

```
class Multiplication {

  public static void main(String[] args) {
    int columns = 5;
    int rows = 5;
    for (int i = 1; i <= columns; i++) {
      for (int j = 1; j <= rows; j++) {
        System.out.printf("%d\t", i * j);
      }
      System.out.println();
    }
  }
}
```

The code doesn't need a lot of commentaries—one loop to generate the columns and the other loop to walk through the rows.

Arrays

An array is a named collection of data. Like a regular variable, it contains data. It has a type, but unlike a regular variable, it can hold more than just one value; it's nonscalar, while a regular variable is scalar.

The term scalar comes from mathematics, specifically linear algebra, where the term is used to differentiate a number from a vector or matrix. The way we're using scalar here is similar. A regular variable has a one-to-one correspondence with the data it holds. A statement like this

```
int numRooms = 10;
```

means the variable **numRooms** contains only one data point, and it's the integer value 10; numRooms is a scalar variable. Could a variable refer to more than one data point? Yes. That's precisely the case of the array. An array variable refers to multiple data points.

Think of an array as a container of data—because that's what it is. It stores a sequence of values of the same type. It can hold different values, but they all need to be of the same type:

```
int numbers[] = {1, 2, 3};
```

An array of ints, such as the one shown in the preceding snippet, is okay. An array of Strings like this following example:

```
String fruits[] = {"Apples", "Oranges", "Peaches", "Bananas"};
```

is also okay. It's not okay to mix data types in an array declaration, like in the following code sample:

```
String mixed[] = {"John", "Doe", 5}; // mixed data type is not okay
```

Array Creation

To create an array, we need to declare a variable that points to the array; in this declaration, we need to specify the type of array, whether it's an array of ints, bytes, Strings, and so on. The declaration looks like the following:

```
int myNumbers[];
```

You'll notice that the array variable has a pair of square brackets; that's how we distinguish them from regular variables. By the way, square brackets don't need to always be in the right side of the variable name; it can also be written on the left side of the variable name, like this:

```
int []myNumbers;
```

But the convention of many programmers is to write the brackets to the right of the variable name. This is a matter for coding convention, and I'm sure you will adopt one for yourself sooner or later, but in our examples, I'll write the brackets to the right side.

Now that we know how to declare array variables, we can now define the array itself. Arrays can be defined in two ways. We can use array literals, which you've seen in earlier examples, or use the *new* keyword. Let's take a closer look at array literals.

We can construct an array literal by using a pair of curly braces, then declaring the array contents inside the curly braces separating them with commas, like this:

```
int arrNum[] = {35, 60, 79};
```

The **arrNum** variable now points to an array of three integers. By the way, you may have noticed that in that previous code snippet, I declared and defined the array in the same line. You can do that in arrays, just like with regular variables.

Another way to declare the same integer array is to use the **new** keyword, like this:

```
int arrnum[] = new int[3];
```

The new keyword is followed by the type of the array, **int**, in this case, then immediately followed by the bracket notation. In this example, **new int[3]** means we are creating an array with three elements—elements are what we call each component of the array, and these elements are arranged in sequence, like this:

```
arrNum[0]
arrNum[1]
arrNum[2]
```

Array elements don't start with 1; instead, they start at 0. You need to get used to this kind of numbering when working with Java arrays because this is one of the sources of programming mistakes committed by newbies. To refer to the first element of the array, you need to address its 0th element.

But our task is not done yet; we've simply initialized the array, but we haven't populated it with our data yet. The array has three elements that have all been initialized to 0—this is the default value that Java used to populate the array because this is the default value for an *int* type. To populate the array with our data, we need to refer to the array's individual elements.

To refer to a specific element in the array, we use the name of the array and its index, like this:

```
arrNum[2] = 79;
```

where **arrNum** is the name of the array, and [2] is the index number. The index number is always the **length of the array – 1** because it starts at 0, not 1. In this case, index number 2 is the third (and last) element of our array.

To populate our array, we can do something like the following:

```
arrNum[0] = 35;
arrNum[1] = 60;
arrNum[2] = 79;
```

The preceding example code is functionally equivalent to the following code:

```
int arrNum[] = {35, 60, 79};
```

Both codes declared an array of ints with three elements and populated the elements with the integer values 35, 60, and 79, respectively.

Managing Arrays

What if we want to add another element to **arrNum**, how should we do that? The answer is, we cannot. An array has a fixed size; once declared, we cannot add or remove elements from it without creating another array. We can change the values of the existing elements, but we can't reduce or increase its size; it's one of those types in Java called *immutable*—once created, they cannot be modified anymore. If you need a data structure that can change its size dynamically, I'd advise you to consider the more robust classes in Java Collections, for example, *ArrayList*; but that is not part of our current discussion.

A data structure, like an array, has many advantages over using simple variables. Imagine for a moment that we are managing a motel system, and we need to keep track of the occupancies for each room. If we were using regular variables, how would you represent five rooms in code? Some will probably do something like the following:

```java
int room1 = 0;
int room2 = 3;
int room3 = 2;
int room4 = 0;
int room5 = 5;
```

The values for each room are arbitrary; I just made them up for the purposes of this example. Our five-room motel has some occupants; room 1 and room 4 are not occupied, though. If we wanted to find the total number of occupants, you could do it like this:

```java
int totalOccupants = room1 + room2 + room3 + room4 + room5;
System.out.printf("Total occupants is %d", totalOccupants);
```

This might work for a five-room motel, but what if we had 100 rooms? What then? Do we declare 100 variables? Surely, we can do better, and we can, with arrays. Let's see how that solution works.

```java
/*
* let's declare the array using a literal.
* in a real application, the values of the array might come
* from an interactive input system
*/

int rooms[] = {0, 3, 2, 0, 5};

int totalOccupants = 0;
for(int i = 0; i < rooms.length; i++) {
  totalOccupants += rooms[i];
}

System.out.printf("Total occupants is %d", totalOccupants);
```

The array version of our solution may not seem shorter than the other solution, where we used five variables to compute the total, but lines of code aren't the point here. If we were managing 100 rooms, computing for the total would require the creation and management of 100 variables; but if we used arrays, our for-loop wouldn't change much—the array solution scales, whether for 5 rooms or 100 or 1000.

Our for-loop solution is very straightforward; it's textbook for-loop, but a couple of items deserve a closer look and discussion. The expression **rooms.length** is aptly named because it does what you think it does. It gives you the length of the rooms array; **length** is a property of the array (any array for that matter) and returns an int type. The expression

```
totalOccupants += rooms[i];
```

gets the value of whatever is in **rooms[i]** and then accumulates that value in the variable *totalOccupants*.

The use of arrays over simple variables gives your code orders of magnitude in sophistication because of our ability to refer to an array element using an expression. This makes it a perfect fit for the loop constructs of Java.

The astute reader must have caught our use of the **new** keyword earlier. We use the new keyword for creating arrays because like other reference types, for example, String, the array is also a reference type; it's an object. See it for yourself, if you run the following code:

```
int arrNum[] = {35, 60, 79};
int fruits[] = {"Apple", "Orange"};
System.out.println(arrNum.getClass().getName());
System.out.println(fruits.getClass().getName());
```

The **getClass().getName()** calls are a dead giveaway that *arrNum* and *fruits* are reference types.

Using the Enhanced for-loop

Looping through arrays seems like a natural fit for for-loops; surely, you can also use the while loop, but most developers gravitate toward for-loops for array processing. You need to be mindful, though, of the array's index system. Remember that it's zero-based; I know that I must have mentioned this a couple of times here already, but I can't stress it enough. Consider the following code:

```java
int rooms[] = {0, 3, 2, 0, 5};

int totalOccupants = 0;
for(int i = 0; i <= rooms.length; i++) {
  totalOccupants += rooms[i];
}

System.out.printf("Total occupants is %d", totalOccupants);
```

It's almost the same code that we did earlier, but can you spot the difference? That's right, the second expression of the for-loop is different; now it reads **i <= rooms.length** instead of **i < rooms.length**. Why is this important? It's because the latter expression is correct, and the former will result in an *ArrayIndexOutOfBoundsException*. Arrays are zero-based, so we start counting from zero, not one. If you try to access an element of the array that doesn't exist, you'll get an out of bounds exception.

Lucky for us, Java has an enhanced for-loop that keeps us away from out of bounds error. In Java 1.5 (Tiger), a new type of for-loop was introduced, designed to simplify arrays (and Collections) processing. When used with an array, the enhanced for-loop has the following usage:

```java
for (type identifier : arrayName) {
  // statements
}
```

The **type** identifies the type of the array, pretty much like when we declared an array. The **identifier** becomes a placeholder for each of the array elements as we iterate through the array. The **arrayName** is the name of the array we want to process. So, rewriting our motel rooms example will look like this:

```java
int rooms[] = {0, 3, 2, 0, 5};
int totalOccupants = 0;

for (int room : rooms) {
  totalOccupants += room;
}
System.out.printf("Total occupants is %d", totalOccupants);
```

More on Arrays

Any nontrivial program will require things beyond what we've done here. To be sure, our ability to create arrays, populate them, walk through them, and get the sum is already awesome; but, real-world problems will require you to do more than these. Very quickly in your coding journey, you will encounter some use cases where you compare one array with another array and see if they are equivalent lexicographically; you may need to sort the array or find a value within the array. You can write your code to meet these functionalities, but it will not be easy, nor will they be trivial. Fortunately, Java comes with built-in libraries, so we don't have to whip up our own. The **Arrays** class in the **java.util** package is part of the Java Collection Framework that makes working with arrays much more manageable. You can learn more about **java.util.Arrays** at **https://docs.oracle.com/en/java/javase/14/**; just search for the Arrays class. Alternatively, if you have a locally installed JDK in your workstation and you've set up your PATH variable correctly to include the JDK, you can open a command line and type

```
javap java.util.Arrays
```

This command will print the method headers of the Arrays class. You won't be able to read the full documentation, but you'll see an API signature for the class. Let's explore some usage scenarios for the Arrays class.

If you want to print an array's contents to the screen, you might be tempted to write a code like this:

```
String fruits[] = {"Apples","Bananas","Oranges"};
System.out.print(fruits); // prints [Ljava.lang.String;@31b7dea0
```

That won't work because all it prints is the address of the array. You can quickly whip up a short for-loop that walks through the array and then print the content one by one, like this:

```
for(String fruit: fruits)
  System.out.println(fruit);
```

That wasn't so bad, and it won't take us long to do it too; alternatively, you can just use the Arrays class like this:

```
import java.util.Arrays;

public class ArraySample {
  public static void main(String args[]) {
    String fruits[] = {"Apples","Bananas","Oranges"};
    System.out.println(Arrays.toString(fruits));
  }
}
```

Just make sure to import the Arrays class before you use it.

We can sort arrays like this:

```
int nums[] = {0, 3, 2, 0, 5};
Arrays.sort(nums);
System.out.println(Arrays.toString(nums)); // prints [0,0,2,3,5]
```

If you need to compare arrays, we can do it like this:

```
int nums[] = {0, 3, 2, 0, 5};
int numsToo[] = {3, 2, 0, 0, 5};

Arrays.sort(nums);
Arrays.sort(numsToo);

Arrays.compare(nums, numsToo);
```

The **compare** method returns an int value. It may return either 0, a negative number, or a positive number. Here's what the result means:

- 0 is returned if the two arrays (num and numsToo) are equal and contain the same elements in the same order—this is why I sorted both arrays first.

- A negative number will be returned if the first array (nums) is lexicographically less than the second array (numsToo).

- A positive number will be returned if the second array (numsToo) is lexicographically less than the first array.

Reference Types

We already know Java has eight primitive types: the byte, short, int, long, char, float, double, and boolean. You can already accomplish quite a lot by using just these types, but you'll accomplish so much more when you start to understand and unlock Java's custom types. A custom type is a type that you can create on your own; they're built using native types, like this:

```
class Point {
  double x = 10.0;
  double y = 0.0;
}
```

In the preceding sample code, we created a new type called Point by combining two *double* types, which we aptly named *x* and *y*; you'll remember from trigonometry that a point needs two coordinates, the *x-coordinate* and the *y-coordinate*. By the way, to create a custom type, you need to create a class—we'll discuss classes a bit more in the following sections. To use the custom type, we need to create an instance of a class, like this:

```
Point objPoint = new Point();
```

Let's slow down a bit and examine what "creating an instance of a class" means. Remember, in the introduction, when I said that Java is an object-oriented language, well, what it means is that Java uses objects as a primary way to organize data and functionality.

Some programs use functions, modules, or subroutines to organize data and enable us to decompose a problem into manageable chunks—Java uses objects. You can think of objects as a data structure; that won't be wrong, but it will be incomplete. Apart from clumping up simple types to form more complex types (like what we did in the Point example earlier), an object also clumps up methods (you'll remember that methods in Java are called functions in other languages). So, an object is more than just a data structure; it's an organizing entity where both data and methods are contained.

Containing both data and methods in a single entity is a big deal because it promotes cohesion. Before object-oriented programming (OOP), the data and operations (functions) were disjointed. The operations don't know anything about the data unless you pass that same data to the operation as an argument (or God forbid, your function acted on global data). When OOP came, it became possible for both data and usage semantics (operations) to be enclosed in the same structure. Let's see another example:

```java
class Account {
  String accountName = "John Doe";
  double balance = 1000.00;

  void deposit(double amount) {
    // statements
  }

  void withdraw(double amount) {
    // statements
  }
}
```

The preceding code shows a custom type which models a rudimentary bank account object. It defines two data points, an *accountName* and a *balance*—as you can see, it's made up not only of native types (balance, which is a *double*) but also of another reference type (accountName, which is a *String*, which is a reference type).

The usage semantics (operations) of our Account type are deposit() and withdraw(); both methods expect that you pass an argument when you use them. Sample usage of this custom type could be as follows:

```java
Account acct = new Account(); // create the object

acct.deposit(100.00);
acct.withdraw(15.00);
```

We passed an argument to the method *withdraw* to tell the *Account* object how much we're withdrawing. The amount to withdraw is not intrinsic to the Account object, so there's no way it can know how much we want to withdraw unless we tell it. The same reasoning applies to the deposit method.

To use a custom type, we first need to instantiate it using the **new** keyword, like this:

```java
Account acct = new Account();
```

The new keyword will create a unique instance of the Account class and return the location of that instance to our **acct** variable. Once you reference the Account object, you can call its methods, like this:

```
acct.deposit(100.00);
acct.withdraw(15.00);
```

Classes

By now, you probably have a good idea of how to write classes. We've been using them for a couple of examples already. To create a class, you need to use the **class** keyword, and you need to provide a body for it, like this:

```
class Car {
}
```

where **Car** is the name of the class, and the pair of curly braces encloses its body. The class' name doesn't need to be in proper case (capitalized first letter), but that's just a common way of writing class names. At a minimum, this is what you need to define a class. A class definition may also include other keywords that can affect its scope. For example, you may see some class definitions like this:

```
public class Car {
}
```

The **public** keyword is an example of an access modifier; there are three of them. The other two are protected and private, but you can't use either protected or private in our example. For top-level classes, either you put a public keyword for an access modifier or don't put anything at all—which implies that the class has package access.

Inheritance

Java is an object-oriented language, and as such, it supports inheritance. Inheritance is a mechanism of reuse. When a class inherits from another class, a parent-child relationship is established. The child class inherits everything that the parent class has, except for variables or methods declared private by the parent class. Listing A-8 shows a basic example of inheritance.

Listing A-8. Inheritance example

```
public class Employee {
  void work() {
    System.out.println("Working");
  }
}

class Programmer extends Employee { }

class Test {
  public static void main(String[] args) {
    new Programmer().work(); // prints Working
  }
}
```

The class **Employee** has one method named **work()**. The class Programmer inherited the Employee class, and it did so using the **extends** keyword.

Notice that the definition of class Programmer doesn't have any methods of its own; however, when we created an instance of Programmer and invoked its **work()** method, it printed "Working." This is possible because the Programmer class inherited the **work()** method from its parent class (Employee).

You may have noticed that our previous examples didn't use the **extended** keyword; our Hello class from earlier examples didn't have an extended keyword. Does that mean it doesn't have a parent? Of course not. Every class you will create in Java has a parent, which means that if a class doesn't have an extended keyword, it will automatically extend **java.lang.Object**.

The **java.lang.Object** is the top-level class or the root class in the Java library. Every class in the Java library extends from Object. So, at the time of compilation, our Hello class became like this:

```
class Hello extends java.lang.Object {
}
```

For brevity, it can also be written like this:

```
class Hello extends Object {
}
```

We don't have to write the fully qualified name of Object because the package java. lang is automatically imported in every source code. We can simply use the short name, which is Object; and because all classes in Java implicitly inherit from Object, we don't have to write the **extends Object** explicitly; we can simply write like this:

```
class Hello {
}
```

Going back to the sample code in Listing A-8 (class Programmer and Employee), we can now say the following:

- The class Employee implicitly extended **java.lang.Object**; we don't have to write the extends keyword anymore.

- The class Programmer explicitly extended class Employee, which means it now inherits Employee. Programmer only inherits from Object indirectly—Programmer ➤ Employee ➤ Object.

You might be wondering if class Programmer can inherit from both Object and Employee directly, instead of through an inheritance hierarchy. The answer is NO. The following code snippet is illegal in Java:

```
class Programmer extends Employee, Object { }
```

Java has a rule on single-rooted class inheritance; that is, a class can only extend, at most, one parent class.

Constructors

A constructor looks a lot like a method but slightly different. A constructor (**ctor**, for short) is a piece of code that's responsible for creating instances of a class. It's the one that creates the objects. Listing A-9 shows an example of an Employee class with a ctor that takes a String argument.

Listing A-9. Employee class

```java
public class Employee {
  String name;

  Employee(String mname) {
    name = mname;
  }

  void work() {
    System.out.println("Working");
  }
}
```

Employee(String mname) is the ctor in this example. Notice how it looks like a method; it takes on a parameter, and it has a body, just like a method. However, unlike a method, it doesn't have a return type, it doesn't have a **return** statement, and its name is the same as that of the class.

To create an Employee object with this kind of constructor, you need to pass a String argument to the constructor, like this:

```java
Employee emp = new Employee("John Doe");
```

When you create a new class, constructors are optional. If you don't write a ctor, the compiler will insert a default no-arg (no argument) ctor for your class. A no-arg ctor looks like the one in Listing A-10.

Listing A-10. Employee with the no-arg constructor

```java
public class Employee {
  String name;

  Employee() {}

  void work() {
    System.out.println("Working");
  }
}
```

A no-arg constructor will be provided by default; that's why you don't have to write it explicitly. However, you need to remember that the freebie ctor from the compiler will no longer be given when you write your constructors. So, if you need the no-arg ctor on top of your other constructors, you need to provide it explicitly already, as shown in Listing A-11.

Listing A-11. class Employee with constructors

```java
public class Employee {
  String name;

  Employee(String mname) {
    name = mname;
  }

  Employee () {
  }

  void work() {
    System.out.println("Working");
  }
}

class Programmer extends Employee {}

class Test {
  public static void main(String[] args) {
    new Programmer().work();
  }
}
```

In this example, we wrote an Employee ctor that takes a String argument and another ctor that takes no argument. You can write as many constructors as you need in a class.

Overloading

As you can see in Listing A-11, the Employee class has more than one constructor. A constructor (or a method) may appear more than once in a class definition. This is known as overloading. When constructors or methods are overloaded, they still need to be unique, and that uniqueness is determined by the constructor's or the method's signature. The uniqueness of a signature is determined by the number and type of parameters that a method accepts.

The constructors in our Employee class (Listing A-11) are distinguishable because one accepts a String argument, and the other doesn't accept any argument at all. You can add more constructors to the Employee class as long as it can be parametrically unique.

Overriding

Continuing with our Employee-Programmer example, Programmer is already inheriting from Employee; whatever Employee has, Programmer also has. The **work()** method of Programmer is precisely the same behavior as the **work()** method in Employee, and for good reasons, we simply inherited it. We didn't change anything in the implementation of work in the Programmer class. But what if we have to change some aspects of the work in the Programmer class? Well, we can, by overriding the **work()** implementation in Programmer. Listing A-12 shows the code.

Listing A-12. Overriding work()

```java
public class Employee {
  String name;

  Employee(String mname) {
    name = mname;
  }

  Employee () {
  }

  void work() {
    System.out.println("Working");
  }
}
```

```
class Programmer extends Employee {
  @Override
  void work() {
    System.out.println("Writing codes");
  }
}

class Test {
  public static void main(String[] args) {
    new Programmer().work(); //  prints "Writing codes"
  }
}
```

When we invoke **new Programmer().work()**, instead of printing "Working" (which was inherited from Employee), it will now print "Writing codes." The programmer object will no longer use the **work()** method from its parent because it already has its implementation of the method now.

If you want to use still the behavior of **work()** from the Employee class, then add some more behavior, you need to invoke the **work()** method of Employee from the overridden **work()** method of Programmer, as shown in Listing A-13.

Listing A-13. Overriding work, with super

```
class Programmer extends Employee {
  @Override
  void work() {
    super.work();
    System.out.println("Writing codes");
  }
}
```

The **super** keyword refers to an instance of the parent class. When you invoke the Programmer's **work()** method, you will now get the behavior of the parent class plus whatever you added in the override.

Strings

Whenever you enclose a series of characters in double quotes, like "this," you are effectively using the **java.lang.String** class. You don't pay attention to this type much; I bet because it seems so natural and simple to use, but there lie some problems that trip up beginning programmers when it comes to the subject of the String—it's deceptively simple that programmers sometimes forget that String isn't a primitive; it's a reference type.

String Creation

The most natural way to create a String is probably like this:

```
String name = "John Doe";
```

It can't be any simpler than that. Just enclose a bunch of characters in double quotes, and you should be done. However, since this is some sort of a deep dive into the String class, we'll look at the other ways you can work with String objects.

The String constructor is overloaded; there are plenty of ways to create a String.

```
String name = new String();
```

The preceding code creates a new String object whose length is zero. If you want to find out for yourself, you can test the following code (either in a proper source file or in a JShell):

```
String s = new String();
System.out.printf("length of String is %d", s.length());
// prints "length of String is 0"
```

The easier way to create a zero-length String is of course like this:

```
String s = "";
```

Another way to create a String is to pass a String literal to its constructor, like this:

```
String name = new String("John Doe");
```

You can create a String object by passing a character array into its constructor, like this:

```java
char nameArray[] = {'J','o','h','n',' ','D','o','e'};
String name = new String(nameArray);
System.out.printf("nameArray reads %s", name);
```

I don't think you'll encounter a situation where you actually create a String like the sample I showed here, but there might be an occasion in your coding life where you have to read from a network I/O or a file (or an API) where what you have is an array of character, and you need to convert it to a String. If you ever are in that situation, you now know how to build Strings from character arrays.

You can also create a String from a byte array, like this:

```java
byte byteArray[] = {65,66,67,68,69,70};
String nameToo = new String(byteArray);
System.out.printf("nameToo reads %s", nameToo);
```

Again, when will you use this? If you find yourself in a situation where you are given a byte array—very common when working with Java I/O APIs—this is how you create a String from that.

Strings Are Immutable

Immutable objects are objects that once you create, you can no longer modify its contents. Strings are like that. Once you create a String, you won't be able to change its contents anymore.

You might wonder, if Strings are truly immutable, then why can I do things like this:

```java
String fruit = "Apple";
fruit = "Orange";
```

Surely, if I can change the value of the String variable **fruit**, then I am able to modify the original "Apple" String object. Isn't that so? Well, no. What Java did, in this case, was to create a completely different String object ("Orange") and assigned it to the variable

fruit. Every time you try to change the content of a String, the Java runtime will create a completely new String. Consider the following code:

```
String empName = "John";   // (1)
empName += " ";            // (2)
empName += "Doe";          // (3)
```

(1) Created a new String from the literal "John."

(2) Copied the contents of the empName variable (currently contains "John"), then appended a space and created a second String object, the content of which is "John" (with empty space); then this new object was assigned to **empName**, and now the **empName** variable points to "John " (length = 5) and no longer to "John" (length = 4).

(3) At this point, we take the content of empName ("John ", length = 5) and append "Doe". Same thing as number 2, the runtime copies "John ", adds "Doe", and reassigns it to variable **empName**. Now, **empName** points to "John Doe". The previous String objects "John" and "John " are now orphan objects, which makes them a candidate for garbage collection.

This is a very common operation. Accumulating String by using the addition operator is a very common technique among developers, and there's nothing wrong with this concatenation if you won't be creating too many objects. Be extra careful with String concatenation when you're inside loops, because things can go very wrong (and very fast) inside loops. Consider the following snippet which reads values from a database table and then concatenates the results to a String variable:

```
Statement stmt=con.createStatement();
ResultSet rs=stmt.executeQuery("select * from emp");

String result = "";
while(rs.next()){
  result += rs.getString(1) + " " + rs.getString(2);
}
System.out.println(result);
con.close();
```

If the table has tens of thousands of rows, this code will be a source of performance problems. It can drag your app to a screeching halt as you run it. Remember that Strings are immutable, and every time you do a concatenation, Java will create a new String object. If the table has 100K rows, the code will easily create 200K String objects by the time the while loop has exited. These will be 200K orphaned objects waiting for the garbage collector (GC). The garbage collector's schedule cannot be predicted, and by the time the GC sweeps the heap, there might not be enough memory left for your app.

If you really need to concatenate Strings inside loops, it will be better to use either the StringBuilder or the StringBuffer class. These classes are mutable, unlike the String class. Let's rewrite our database code using the StringBuffer.

```
String result = "";
StringBuffer sb = new StringBuffer();
while(rs.next()){
  sb.append(rs.getString(1));
  sb.append(" ");
  sb.append(rs.getString(2));
}
result = new String(sb);
System.out.println(result);
con.close();
```

The **append()** method of StringBuffer lets you add new String objects to the buffer; but unlike the String object, the StringBuffer does not create another StringBuffer object, it modifies its internal structure to accommodate the new content. Later on, you can convert the StringBuffer to a String object by passing the StringBuffer to the String's constructor, like this:

```
result = new String(sb);
```

Why Can't We Modify Strings

If you peek at the source code of **java.lang.String**, you'll find the following declarations:

```
public final class String
    implements java.io.Serializable, Comparable<String>, CharSequence,
             Constable, ConstantDesc {

    private final char[] value;

    // LOTS of other statements
}
```

It implements a couple of interfaces, which are interesting, but not part of our current discussion, so we won't get distracted by that. Notice that the class is final, which means you cannot subclass or extend it. What's more important to notice is the member variable named **value**. It's an array, and it's declared as final. This array is used to store the characters of the String value. Arrays are fixed; once you create them, you can no longer add any more elements. Arrays cannot grow in size after they have been defined. This is the main reason why you cannot modify the contents of a String without creating a copy of the original.

Comparing Strings

Strings are reference types, which means they are stored on the heap; so, when comparing them with one another, you generally cannot use the equality operator ==. To compare Strings, you should use the **.equals()** method, like this:

```
String str1 = "Hello";
String str2 = "Hello";

if(str1.equals(str2)) {
  System.out.println("str1 is equal to str2");
}
```

However, you may see some programmers use the == to compare Strings like this:

```
String str1 = "Hello";
String str2 = "Hello";

if(str1 == str2) {
  System.out.println("str1 is equal to str2");
}
```

And it actually works. So, what's going on? This is a special case for the String object. The rule you should follow when comparing Strings for lexical equivalence is to always use the **.equals()** method. The == operator is what you use for comparing primitive values, not object types, but why is it working in the previous code example? The answer is because of the String constant pool (other programmers call it String literal pool or simply String pool; these terms may be used interchangeably).

The String constant pool is a special area in the heap memory that the runtime uses to create String literals, and once a String literal is created in this area, it can be reused so as to avoid duplicate copies of the same literal. Let's see that in code.

```
String str1 = "Good morning";  // (1)
String str2 = "Good morning";  // (2)

if (str1 == str2) {
  System.out.println("str1 == str2");
}
```

(1) The runtime creates a new String object and places it in the String constant pool.

(2) When str2 is declared and defined, the runtime will search the String constant pool if this literal has been created already; and it is, so Java won't create another "Good morning" String object; instead, the address of the existing "Good morning" String will be assigned to the str2 variable. Now, str1 and str2 point to exactly the same address. This is why when you test them using double equals, the expression returns true.

An important point to remember about the String constant pool is that String literals end up in the String constant pool only when String literals are plainly assigned to a variable, like this:

```
String str2 = "Good morning";
```

When you create String objects using constructors (with the **new** keyword), the String objects don't end up in the constant pool. Let's consider the following code:

```
String str1 = "Good morning";            // (1)
String str2 = new String("Good morning"); // (2)

if (str1 == str2) {                       // (3)
  System.out.println("str1 == str2");
}
```

(1) This gets stored on the String constant pool; str1 points to "Good morning" in the constant pool.

(2) This gets stored on the heap like all other objects; str2 points to "Good morning" in the regular heap, not in the constant pool.

(3) str1 contains the address of an object in the constant pool; str2 contains the address of a completely different object in the heap memory. This happened because we used the new keyword in creating the String object. Whenever you use the **new** keyword, it creates a new object in the heap.

If you want to compare Strings without care or regard for case sensitivity, you can use the **.equalsIgnoreCase()** method, like this:

```
String str1 = "Hello";
String str2 = "hello";

if(str1.equalsIgnoreCase(str2)) {
  System.out.println("str1 is equal to str2");
}
```

Common Usage

charAt(int indexPosition)

You can use this method to retrieve a character at a specified index of the String. Take note that ordinal positions of characters in a String start at zero, not one. Remember that a char array is used within the internal mechanism of the String class; and Java arrays are zero-based. Let's look at an example:

```
String name = new String("Paul");
System.out.println(name.charAt(0));  // prints P
System.out.println(name.charAt(2));  // prints u
```

indexOf(String arg)

The **indexOf()** method takes either a character or String arguments and searches the String for any match. When a match is found, the ordinal position of the argument in the String is returned, for example:

```
String letters = "ABCAB";
System.out.println(letters.indexOf('B'));   // prints 1
System.out.println(letters.indexOf("S"));   // prints -1
System.out.println(letters.indexOf("CA"));  // prints 2
```

When a match is not found, -1 is returned.

substring(int position)

The **substring()** method takes an integer argument, which it uses to mark the beginning position from where to extract the substring. If you don't pass a second argument to this method, then it will return all the strings from the beginning position (marked by the argument) up to the last character of the String, for example:

```
String exam = "Oracle";
String sub = exam.substring(1);
System.out.println(sub);          // racle
```

You can also specify the ending position of the substring to extract by passing the second integer argument, like this:

```
String exam = "Oracle";
String result = exam.substring(2, 4);
System.out.println(result);       // prints ac
```

trim()

The **trim()** method returns a new String object, but all the whitespaces (leading or trailing) are removed.

```
String withSpaces = " AB CB ";
String trimmed = withSpaces.trim(); // returns "AB CB"
```

Note that the space in between AB and CB has not been trimmed. The trim function only removes leading and trailing whitespaces; it doesn't remove the ones in between.

length()

This method returns the number of characters in a String. Please don't confuse the String's **length()** method with the array's **length** property.

```
String withSpaces = " AB CB ";
System.out.printf("Length of %s is %d", withSpaces, withSpaces.length());
// prints 7
```

startsWith() and endsWith()

Both these methods take an argument, and they match those arguments against the series of characters in the String. In the case of startsWith(), if the argument passed to is a match to the characters in the String beginning at position 0, then the method returns true. See this example:

```
String letters = "ABCAB";
boolean a  = letters.startsWith("AB")); // true
boolean b = letters.startsWith("a"));   // false
```

```
boolean c = letters.endsWith("CAB")     // true
boolean d = letters.endsWith("B")       // true
boolean e = letters.endsWith("b")       // false
```

replace()

This method takes two arguments:

- The first argument is the pattern to match. The method tries to find all the occurrences of this pattern within the String.

- The second argument is the replacement String; if the method finds a match for the first argument, all matching string will be replaced by the second argument. Think of it as a find-and-replace functionality in your editor.

```
String letters = "ABCAB";
String result letters.replace('B', 'b'); // returns AbCAb
You can also use Strings as arguments, like this:
```

```
String letters = "ABCAB";
String result = letters.replace("CA", "12"); // returns AB12B
```

Exceptions

Despite our best efforts to get the program right and behave as predictably as possible, they can still fail because of various reasons. When programs fail because of abnormal conditions in their environment, the Java runtime throws an exception. When an exception is thrown, the normal flow of the program is disrupted, and if the exception is not properly handled, it may cause the program to terminate in an ungraceful manner. There are two ways to handle exceptions, either we handle it using a try-catch structure, or we rethrow it and let it be somebody else's problem. In this section, we will look at how to handle exceptions using the try-catch block.

The general form of the try-catch is as follows:

```
try {
  // statement that can throw exceptions
}
catch(ExceptionType1 obje) {
  // error handling statement;
}
```

```
catch(ExceptionType2 obje) {
  // error handling statement;
}
catch(ExceptionTypen obje) {
  // error handling statement;
}
```

The try-catch, like the if-else, routes the program flow. It branches program control when some conditions become true. When an exception is raised inside the body of the try block, the program flow automatically jumps out of that block. The catch blocks will be inspected one by one until a type of exception thrown is properly matched to any of the catch blocks. When a match is found, the error handling statements on the matching catch block are executed. Let's see how that looks on real code.

```
String filename = "something.txt";
try {
  java.io.FileReader reader = new java.io.FileReader(filename);
}
catch(FileNotFoundException e) {
  // ask the user to input another filename
}
```

In the preceding example, we only have one catch block; that's because the statement inside the try block can only throw a "FileNotFoundException" and nothing else. If we had other statements in the try block that can throw other kinds of exceptions, then we should write the corresponding catch blocks for those. You might ask, "how do we know if an exception is going to be thrown by a method call?". The answer to that question is "by reading the documentation." If you read the Java language API reference for the FileReader class, you will learn the details of how it is used and what kinds of exceptions some of its methods may throw, among other things. Another way you may find out the kinds of exceptions that can be thrown by the FileReader (or any other method/constructor call) is to simply write it like a regular statement, that is, without any error handling structure, like so.

```
java.io.FileReader reader = new java.io.FileReader(filename);
```

As soon as you try to compile the source program where this line is written, you will find out that the FileReader constructor may throw a "FileNotFoundException" because the Java compiler will complain loudly.

The try-catch structure is used for many situations, but if you want to be thorough in handling the error, you may use the more complete **try-catch-finally** structure. The general form of try-catch-finally is

```
try {
  // statement that can throw exceptions
}
catch(ExceptionType obje) {
  // error handling statement;
}
finally {
  // this code will execute
  // with or without encountering
  // an error
}
```

In a try-catch structure, if an exception happens, the program control will jump out of the try block, leaving the remaining statements inside the try block unexecuted. If one of those unexecuted statements is critical to the program, for example, closing a file or database connection, that may introduce another problem. This is the kind of situation where you need to use the "finally" clause. The codes written inside a finally clause are guaranteed to execute whether or not an exception happens. Let's see the file reading code sample again, but this time, with a finally clause.

```
String filename = "something.txt";
try {
  java.io.FileReader reader = new java.io.FileReader(filename);
}
catch(FileNotFoundException e) {
  // ask the user to input another filename
}
finally {
  // close any connections you may have
  // opened e.g. "reader"
}
```

Index

A

Activity
    AppCompatActivity class, 60
    component, 55
    layout file (*see* Layout file)
    MainActivity.java, 60
addNumber() method, 73
Android
    activities, 51, 52
    app, 47–50
    application entry point, 50, 51
    history, 1–3
    intents, 53, 54
    OS, 3, 4
Android Developer Tools (ADT), 7
Android package (APK), 59
Android Runtime (ART), 59
Android Studio (AS)
    configuring, 10, 12, 14
    create AVD, 22, 23, 25–29
    create project, 17, 19–21
    hardware acceleration, 14, 15
    setup, 7–10
Android Virtual Device (AVD), 14
append() method, 311
App, releasing, 225
    account, 233
    APK, 228
    asset, 226
    build release-ready, 227, 228
    configuration, 226, 227
    Google Play, 232
    Google Play Console, 236, 237
    JKS, 229
    launch Play Console, 235
    prepare material, 226
    signed APK, 232
    signed Bundle, 231
    website, 234
Arithmetic operator, 276–278
Array
    creation, 292, 293
    definition, 291
    for-loops, 295, 297
    java.until, 297, 298
    managing, 293, 295
    scalar, 291
Assignment operator, 276

B

Broadcast, 193
    adb program, 201
    Android SDK, 201
    context registration, 198
    custom, 194
    MainActivity class, 199
    manifest registration, 195
    register, 194
    system, 194
BroadcastReceiver class, 194

C

Cache directory, 182
Casting, 271
Classes
    constructors, 303, 305
    creation, 301
    definition, 301
    inheritance, 301–303
    overloading, 305
    overriding, 306, 307
Code generator, 243–247
Compatibility testing, 158
Compliance/conformance testing, 158
Components, navigation
    Android Architecture, 114
    Jetpack, 114, 116
    UI, 115
Composite view, 58, 74
Context registration, 198
Control structures, 289, 290
createNumber() method, 210
currVal variable, 73

D

databaseBuilder() method, 222
Data types
    assignment operation, 267
    casting, 271
    constant, 275
    overflow, 271
    primitive/native, 268–270
    reference, 273
    stack/heap, 274
    strongly/statically, 272
Debugger
    breakpoints, 153
    single stepping, 154, 155

    window, 153, 154
Declarative event handling, 75
Developer testing, 159
Device Explorer, 190, 191

E

Equality operator, 279, 280
.equals() method, 312
.equalsIgnoreCase() method, 314
Event handling
    activity_main.xml file, 78
    button view, 79
    listener objects, 76, 77
    listener objects, 75
    MainActivity.java, 79, 80
    model, 76
    onClick() method, 76
    onLongClick() method, 76
    project details, 78
    registration, 77
    setOnClickListener, 78
    toast message, 80, 81
    user interacts, 75
External storage,
        pros/cons, 181, 182

F

Fragments
    activity_main.xml, 107
    app, 110
    BookTitle class, 105
    composition unit, 101
    creation, 102
    fragplaceholder, 108
    high-resolution displays, 101
    layout resource file, 103

MainActivity, 106, 109

new Java class, 104

TextView object, 104

transactions, 109

XML file, 101

Functional testing, 157

G

getNumber()
      method, 208, 210

H

Hello World, activity

annotated
      activity_main, 63, 64

attributes panel, 69, 70

button view, 67

design editor, 71

design view, 65

drag and drop controls, 66

emulator, 74

infer constraints, 69

MainActivity.java, 72, 73

project information, 61, 62

TextView, 68

I

IDE

editing layout files, 35, 37

main editor, 34

opening dialog, 31, 33, 34

Project tool window, 41, 43

screen space, 39, 41

settings/preferences, 43, 44

TODO items, 38

if/switch statements, 282, 284

Implicit intents

Android's package manager, 96

browser/navigate, 95

camera-specific code, 95

MainActivity, 97

overriding, 98

project, 99

web page, 95

indexOf() method, 314

Instrumented testing

activity_main.xml, 171

espresso, 170

espresso actions, 179, 180

matchers, 178, 179

onClick() method, 172, 173, 175

recording espresso
      test, 175–177

sample test, 170

Integer.parseInt() method, 73

Intents

activity, 90

activity_main.xml, 92, 93

component activation, 89

empty activity, 91

getApplicationContext(), 94

logical representation, 90

operation, 89

startActivity() method, 94

Internal storage, 181

components, 186

load data, 189

pros/cons, 182

reading file, 184, 185

resume, 190

save data, 183, 188

working, 183

writing files, 183

J

Java
    definition, 253
    editions, 254
    exceptions, 316–318
    reference types, 299, 300
    setup, 255, 256
    typical program, 257, 259
    versions, 253, 254
    writing/compiling/running, 256, 257
Java 2 Standard Edition (J2SE), 254
Java Community Process (JCP), 276
Java Development Kit (JDK), 254
Java Enterprise Edition (Java EE), 254
Java Keystore (JKS), 229
java.lang.String class, 308, 311
Java Mobile Edition (Java ME), 254
Java Standard Edition (Java SE), 254
Java syntax
    comments, 260, 261
    compilation, 260
    identifiers, 262, 263
    keywords, 261, 262
    methods, 263–265
    packages/imports, 265, 266
    program entry point, 266, 267
    statements, 261
    typical program, 258, 259
Jetpack navigation
    actions, 121
    Android fragment, 122, 123
    build.gradle file, 117, 118
    connect one to two, 126, 127
    destination, 122
    editor, 124
    empty project, 117
    graph, 121, 125
    modified fragment, 128
    NavHost, 125
    new resource file, 119, 120
    onCreateView() method, 128, 129

K

Keyboard shortcuts, 251

L

Layout file
    activity_main, 56
    container, 59
    parts, 57
    text mode, 56
    view objects, 57
    XML file, 55
Lifecycle aware components, 203
Lifecycle observer, 204
Lifecycle owner, 204
Linux kernel, 4
LiveData
    MainActivity, 215
    RandomNumber, 214
    use, 217
    ViewModel, 214
Live templates, 250, 251
Localization testing, 159
Logcat tool window, 152
Logical operator, 281, 282
Logic errors, 150–152
Long-click events
    build.gradle file, 84
    displaying Snackbar, 85
    emulator, 86, 87
    id property, 82
    MainActivity.java, 85, 86

onCreate method, 81
    toast message, 82
for-loop statement, 288

M

MainActivityObserver, 205
makeText() function, 80

N

Narrowing conversion, 272
Navigation
    activity, 111, 112
    Android development, 111
    baggage, 112
    component (*see* Components,
        navigation)
    component snippet, 114
    pass data, 112
    screen management, 112
    snippet, 113

O

onCreate() method, 61, 209
onLongClick method, 85
onPause() method, 199
onReceive() method, 195
onResume() method, 199
openFileOutput() method, 149
Operators
    arithmetic, 276–278
    assignment, 276
    equality, 279, 280
    logical, 281, 282
    relational, 280
    unary, 278, 279
@Override annotation, 60

P, Q

Penetration/Security testing, 159
Performance testing, 158
Primitive/native data types, 268
    boolean, 270
    byte, 268, 269
    char, 270
    double, 270
    float, 270
    int, 269
    long, 269
    short, 269
Productivity
    code generator, 243–246
    coding styles, 248, 249
    getters/setters, 246
    importing samples, 239–241
    person class, 247
    refactoring, 241, 242
Publish-subscribe pattern, 193

R

RandomNumber class, 208
Recovery testing, 159
Refactoring, 241, 242
registerReceiver() method, 200
Relational operator, 280
Room
    advantages, 218
    components, 218
    dependencies, 219
    Java source file, 219
    MainActivity, 222, 224
Runnables
    activity_main.xml, 140
    AndroidManifest file, 141

Runnables (*cont.*)
    app's layout, 139
    binding class, 142
    build.gradle, 142
    class worker, 136
    fetchUserInfo, 137, 138
    interface, 137
    java.lang.Thread class, 136
    MainActivity, 143, 144
    object, 137
    RunBackground class, 144–146
runOnUiThread() method, 146
Runtime error, 148–150

S

setContentView method, 61
setText() method, 73
Soak testing/endurance testing, 158
Sound testing, 159
Spike testing/scalability testing, 158
Strings
    comparing, 312–314
    constant pool, 313
    creation, 308, 309
    immutable, 309, 310
    usage, 314–316
substring() method, 314
Switch statements, 284, 286
Syntax, (*see* Java syntax)
Syntax errors, 147, 148
System broadcast, 194

T

TextView, 57, 58
Try-catch structure, 149

U

UI thread, 132
    blocked state, 132
    GCF calculation, 133
    GitHub info, 134
    nested calls, 134
    resource-intensive
        operation, 135
    setText()/setHint(), 132
    technique, 135
Unary operator, 278, 279
Unit testing
    assertEquals methods, 167
    Factorial.java, 161–164
    functional, 159
    implementation, 165
    JUnit, 160
    JVM vs. instrumented
        test, 160, 161
    running, 167, 168
    successful test, 169
    tearDown() methods, 167
User-defined type
    (UDT), 268

V

ViewGroup, 57, 58
ViewModel, 210
    MainActivity, 211
    RandomNumber, 211
Volume testing, 158

W, X, Y, Z

While loop statement, 287, 288

Printed in the United States
By Bookmasters